THE GIFT OF HEALING

A Thesis of Knowledge and Insights where Biblical Prophecy is explained in Nature

DR. REV. DIANA B. ST. CLAIR

authorHOUSE®

AuthorHouse™
1663 Liberty Drive
Bloomington, IN 47403
www.authorhouse.com
Phone: 1 (800) 839-8640

Published by AuthorHouse 12/21/2016

ISBN: 978-1-5246-5590-7 (sc)
ISBN: 978-1-5246-5588-4 (hc)
ISBN: 978-1-5246-5589-1 (e)

Library of Congress Control Number: 2016921030

Print information available on the last page.

Any people depicted in stock imagery provided by Thinkstock are models, and such images are being used for illustrative purposes only. Certain stock imagery © Thinkstock.

This book is printed on acid-free paper.

Contents

Acknowledgements

It is a pleasure to thank those who made this thesis possible. My grandfather, Reverend John Allen Brumfield, who gave me the vision to follow my dreams. The Alliance of Divine Love Ministerial program staff members who suggested this program to me. I offer my regards and blessings to all who enabled me to develop an understanding of the gift of healing. My gratitude to advisor professors Dr. Linda Marie Nelson D.D., Ph.D. and Dr. Nancy Ash D.D., Ph.D. for their support.

This work is presented in thesis form in fulfillment of the requirements for the Ph.D. in Religious studies from Metropolitan Interspiritual University.

Introduction

In this dissertation I shall defend the thesis that the Gift of Healing exists from our Creator in many forms. By the time you finish reading this paper you will learn the history of healing and ways to restore and keep healthy. Looking into the past I have found the Holy Bible to be a connection to God from the prophets of long ago, where prayer released the Divine Love of our Creator and meditation is revealed to be listening to the Spirit of God and allowing our bodies and minds to receive healing. The many techniques of healing given to us by the Creator of the Universe will be discussed in this paper. Parallels exist between ancient healing practices, Christianity, and modern medicine. The methodologies used include research from the Christian Holy Bible, Native American herbs and plants, religious experiences, gem stones in healing, Jesus the Healer, Pastoral Counseling and other healing techniques. The ancient prophets of long ago provided us with a history of many scriptures on healing from the Christian Holy Bible. The first example of organic healing begins in the book of Genesis of the Holy Bible. Chapter 1:29-30 is a quote of God stating, "Then God said, 'I give you every seed-bearing plant on the face of the whole earth and every tree that has fruit with seed in it. They will be yours for food. And to all the beasts of the earth and all of the birds of the air and all the creatures that move on the ground, everything that has breathe of life in it, I give every green plant for food. And it was so." The Lord God sent rains so his garden would grow, the streams and rivers formed and this process of gardening for food has not changed to this very day. This was a growth process given to man and woman, entrusted to be taught to all future generations. Our bodies need to be fed good food and herbs to get well and stay well. The Bible clearly is a divine guide to moral consciousness of the basic needs that humans have to avoid sickness and disease. (1)

Our ancestral past contains many insights to the condition of humanity and the state of the earth at this present time. God's grace placed the first man and woman in a newly created environment that had been designed to be comfortable as a home. This home was not modern but an old fashioned medicine chest of many plants. When my ancestors came from France to America this country was like a Garden of Eden that would take time to learn and navigate. My grandfather would come to marry a Native American as many Americans carry Native American bloodlines. Europeans came so far from the days of the Garden of Eden that the Indians were considered an indigenous people that must be colonized and taught the ways of the people of Europe. An open mind to all worldviews of healing would be needed to survive life here on this planet, called earth. Walking together and accepting other viewpoints can bring healing to the world of which, I am a small part. Mother- nature has always been a good judge of what will keep us healthy and safe over the long term of years we spend here establishing our lives and families.

"The Lord said, "I have indeed seen the misery of my people in Egypt. I have heard them crying out because of their slave drivers, and I am concerned about their sufferings. So I have come down to rescue them from the hand of the Egyptians and bring them up out of that land into a good and spacious land, a land flowing with milk and honey, the home of the Canaanites, Hittites, Amorites, Perizzites, Hivities and Jebusites, and now the cry of the Israelites has reached me, and I have seen the way the Egyptians are oppressing them." Exodus 3:7-9. For example, many people fled to America to get away from oppression of government and Christian church rules. (2)

America is a spacious land of many diverse cultures with many resources said to be of Milk and Honey. The history of America lies in a vision from an ancient time and place of Native American people that freely traveled on feet, by canoe or on horse- back. The land was filled with Indians, Mountains, and Gold. Apache Mountain Spirit dancers would impersonate the sacred spirits who drive away sickness and evil to bring good fortune. They would wear black buckskin hoods with fake eyes of abalone or turquoise, attached wooden headdresses painted with symbols of strength to challenge the forces of evil. This ceremony is combined with a young girl's puberty rite. The Apache had sacred buckskin prayer charts with closely guarded secrets by the medicine men as to the interpretation. The Apache were expert basket makers and all homes held a burden basket. (3)

Native American dance ceremonies are performed for the majority of curing disease and restoration of universal harmony when it has been disturbed. This is called the Blessing Way through group rituals and singing, which has psycho-therapeutic benefits to the patient and all who participate. The Yeiblchei dance is of the Navajo tribe of which they are also the most skilled weavers of blankets still highly sought after as an important handicraft. This skill was also copied from the Pueblos and later developed into vertical rug looms with complex design. The Navajos were great horse-people and also owned herds of sheep. The Mohave Native Americans were a more, simple tribe of the deserts whose lives focused on gathering plants, hunting, and fishing in the Colorado River. The tribe was physically superior to many other tribes probably due to the environment which they lived. Cactus fruit and saguaro fruit played a big part in their diet. (4)

The Indians of Southern Arizona and Mexico grew crops of corn, beans, and squash which needed irrigated water. These tribes also depended on wild foods and hunting. God was called the Great Mystery as prayers were offered holding the skull of a buffalo to represent the spirit of the animal that provided food, shelter and clothing. Except for the cultivation of tobacco, the Crow People were true nomadic Plains people, dependent on horses for hunting Bison, gathering roots and berries for food. The crow people made winter camps in the thick forests along the banks of rivers. Before smallpox and reservations came the Blackfoot Indians were the most powerful tribe of the northern plains. Their territory once spread from the North Saskatchewan River, Canada, to the headwater of the Missouri River in Montana, including the foothills of the Rocky Mountains. The Native Americans moved to reservations as the Europeans fled to this country and a new nation was built. Hidden in mystic are still many of the Native American prayers, religion, healthy diets, and medicines of plants. Native Americans were known as gifted hunters, tool-makers, and warriors. Because of the view of Indians as savages much is hidden about their practices of healing and the mind-body connection. Alternative healing methods and the use of prayer to heal leads us back to the Native Americans. The methods of herbs, visualization, meditation, and more to strengthened the body as well as the mind and emotions. Antibiotics kill bacteria that is making you sick, as the body is exposed to billions of bacteria every day. Antibiotics are vital for fighting some infections for a temporary defense. They do not strengthen the body to fight future infections. In 1650, the Dutch explorer Adrian Vander Donick wrote about the many cures Native Americans performed with roots, leaves and other things. Later in 1714, John Lawson wrote about the history of North Carolina and wondered why no one had cataloged the illnesses that the Native Americans had cured. These wilderness people had discovered many of the properties of medicines that we know today. (5)

Chapter **1**

NATIVE AMERICAN HEALING

Native American Herbs

Our friends the Native American people held a knowledge of plants used for medicine that has held true to this day. The Native Americans used more than 500 healing herbs thought to be healing secrets that are used in many modern day drugs. Native American healers regarded plants as relatives with the same energy, elements, minerals, and living compounds that are found in the natural world. Researchers in laboratories estimate that 25 percent of the drugs in use have actual ingredients either derived from or chemically similar to those in plants. Some of the drugs that have their roots in nature are the cancer drug tamoxifen, the heart drug digitalis, and painkillers morphine and aspirin. The powers of observation and the passing on of this knowledge to future generations is a great discovery. One of the most popular herbs is the Aloe Vera plant first used in Florida and southwestern United States. The Aloe is used for skin conditions, the healing of burns and wounds. Other uses are as a treatment for insect bites, fungal infections, frost bite, eczema, dry skin, and poison Ivy. Researches have shown that Aloe helps skin cells to regenerate, also effective for treating gum disease, acne, colitis, and ulcers. Many people use it as a liniment to help the inflammation of arthritis, or take it internally to ease constipation. The Aloe plant resembles a cactus and prefers a warm climate. (6)

The peace pipe was often smoked with more than tobacco present.

A pinch of Bearberry was added for a mild sedative effect during tribal council meetings. Bearberry was also used as a potent diuretic and antiseptic, to treat kidney stones as well as urinary tract infections. Teas made from bearberry are used to treat enlargement of the prostate gland. Women used the herb during heavy menstrual periods or vaginal infections. Some forms of diabetes are treated with this herb because it increases the body's output of insulin. Bearberry can also be used as a douche, mouthwash, and antiseptic. The herb Black Cohosh is so effective in relieving women's menopausal problems that some doctors find it as an acceptable alternative to conventional hormone replacement therapy. Black Cohosh has been shown to reduce hot flashes, sweating, headaches, vertigo, heart palpitations, and tinnitus. The Native Americans used it in difficult childbirth to relax the muscles of the uterine walls. Other uses for this herb were to relieve arthritis pain, scarlet fever, smallpox, and whooping cough. One of the best features of Black Cohosh is to repel insects. A plant called Black Haw was uses to relieve menstrual cramps and has been proven to work as a uterine antispasmodic or relaxant. Dr. John Brickwell, an 18th-century medical authority used the plant to heal wounds. Dr. James A Duke, PH.D found that the plant contains four substances that help to relax the uterus. Native Americans chewed the plant and used the leaves as a paste to reduce the swelling of sprains. Black Haw grows as a bushy shrub 10 to 25 feet tall. The plant produces dark blue berries that are very sweet to eat. One of the greatest contributions Native Americans made to the modern world was the introduction of corn. Corn has also been used for its healing powers. Native Americans would drink a beverage made from corn to treat problems with the Kidneys and Bladder. A corn beverage was also used to treat dysentery and indigestion and to increase milk production in nursing mothers. Corn was used to make poultices for skin ulcers, burns, swelling and corn oil to ease eczema and dry skin. Corn cobs were burned to help relieve itching caused by insect bites and poison ivy. The silk of corn has diuretic properties also used to treat high blood pressure. Cornstarch that is used as a powder today helps to relieve eczema. (7)

The Native Americans had so many uses for the plant Dandelion that it is hard to list them all. Dandelion was used for infections. Dandelion is very rich in calcium helping to prevent osteoporosis. Boron and silicon are trace minerals found in this important plant that may also be helpful in preventing bone diseases. Studies have shown dandelion contains lecithin and choline which might prevent Alzheimer's disease. Dandelion roots can be used as a topical antiseptic for wounds, sores, and inflammation of the mouth. A tea brewed from the leaves can be used as a mild laxative and digestive aid. In today's world the tea would be used as a tea can help to relieve pneumonia, bronchitis, and act as a diuretic to reduce swelling caused by sprains internal cleanse to the kidneys, bladder, liver, and spleen. The dandelion plant can be eaten raw, juiced, or boiled supplying the body with iron, potassium, phosphorus, and vitamins A, B, C, and D. The dandelion flower is eatable for the lecithin to help treat problems of the liver. The milky sap is often used to remove corns and warts. The Pennsylvania Dutch used the dandelion leaves for salad greens with cider vinegar and sugar as a dressing. Native Americans knew to use Echinacea to kill a cold virus or upper respiratory infection. The founder of Platonic Academy of Herbal Studies Paul Lee, lists Echinacea as a leading immune-stimulant. This means that Echinacea can strengthen the immune system so the body can resist sickness and disease. This herb supports the body when a person has laryngitis, tonsillitis, and inflammation of the nose and sinuses. As a mouthwash Echinacea is helpful in treating diseases of the gums. Fennel is an herb that was used for bad breath and relieving intestinal gas. It can also be of use to calm coughs or indigestion. It has also been used as a compress to relieve conjunctivitis of the eyelid, or as a poultice to treat muscle pain. Fennel tea is used to increase breast milk in nursing mothers. The seeds are used to season fish, soups, stews, salads, and breads. The fennel bulb can be used as a vegetable. Native Americans used Garlic to treat snakebites and wounds. The medical community discovered that garlic could cure scurvy. Garlic is rich in vitamin C, when crushed it releases a substance called (allicin), which has antiviral and antibacterial properties. It has been shown to help combat infections caused by fungi and yeast. The Native Americans also used it to fight intestinal parasites. (8)

Life for the Native Americans was not easy, the people learned to observe their world closely and discover how to put it to use. Native American healers guided people to use the body's inborn ability to heal itself. Good health is a never ending cycle of discovery, faith, and gratitude. The power for achieving good health was through the strength of Mother Nature. Each tribe had healers that had their own methods of preparing herbs, as some were smoked through special ceremonial pipes, or burned so that the fumes could be inhaled. Mixtures with alcohol as tinctures, or combined with animal fats to make salves were methods often used. Chewing on herbs to release the oils, then applying it to the body was a primitive method. There were also healing ceremonies that called for the patient to be burned with smoldering branches. The Shamans of yesterday still prepare herbs as many herbalists do today, such as teas. Herbal poultices were used externally for problems such as wounds, sores, skin irritations, or swelling. Native Americans were different from Europeans in that they took baths more often using herbs and fragrances, ate healthful diets and had good dental hygiene from the land. When chewed fennel or cardamom freshens ones breathe by killing bacteria. Native Americans were deeply attracted to nature's mysteries as shamans also discovered the health giving benefits of massage. They observed that birds, deer, and other animals ate certain plants when they were sick. This knowledge was passed on to succeeding generations. Scientists today would call these case studies as they gained the knowledge to keep people healthy. Herbal remedies have lasted because nature's cures have been shown to be safe and effective with fewer side effects than modern drugs. (9)

Hanna Kroeger a natural herbalist is called the "Grandmother of Health" due to her contributions and awards of the understanding of healing herbs. She was a mother and a nurse who moved to the United States in the 1950's from Germany. She opened the first Herb shop in Boulder, Colorado. Hanna studied nursing at the University of Freiburg and Natural Healing at a hospital in Dresden. The Kroeger's migrated to the U.S after surviving World War II to start a new life. Hanna took over the Imperial Tea and Coffee Company on Broadway Blvd. She renamed it the Imperial Tea and Health Food Store introducing whole grains, nuts, and herbal teas. The store moved to 1115 Pearl Street, where she baked whole wheat and German breads and started carrying vitamin supplements in the back of the store. Hanna started teaching nutrition classes to help people restore their health. Hanna and her husband built a house and incorporated a European style spa and retreat. The property had a lake and a garden where visitors could relax and find a moment of peace in their lives. She established a natural foods restaurant in her store to give back to the community. For years Hanna filled capsules and mixed teas by hand until she and her husband founded a company called Kroeger Herb Products Company. The response for her herbal formulas had become over-whelming. Hanna was summoned to court and had to defend her rights to heal ourselves naturally standing up for the cause of all people. Hanna Kroeger passed away May 7th, after publishing more than 22 books, on healing, herbs, and nourishment. She was later named by "New Life magazine" as one of the top 6 healers for the 20th century, and is considered a master healer. (10)

Many of Hanna's discoveries were from intuition as well as studying and experimenting. In her early years Hanna made here own herbal combinations at the kitchen table and soon became known for her formulas of using two or more herbs to improve the whole system of the body. In today's world Hanna would be called a medical intuitive with a sensitivity to energies of people even before physical symptoms manifested. She was one of the foremost dowsers or pendulum users in the country. She did not claim to have any special gifts only a higher source. She studied healing techniques from around the world, including massage, energy work, homeopathy and nutrition, also working with Native American healers. She used diet, herbs, homeopathies, vitamins, minerals, physical alignment, massage, acupressure, and aura balancing. Hanna taught classes on natural and vibrational healing at her home in Boulder, Colorado. She explored ideas such as the seven physical and spiritual causes of ill health and interpreting auric energy for healing, clearing, and rebuilding programs. (11)

Hanna new that Americans are the do-it-yourself type building farms, chapels, greenhouses, raising chickens and vegetables. They will attempt to fix a leaky roof or faucet, bake and cook. The knowledge had to be presented to take care of their own health. Herbs work on your spiritual body to harmonize and balance. Herbs heal the aura and heal subtle, vital energies of the physical body. They go beyond what the physician prescribes by healing the spirit of man and strengthening the bio-life power. Our spiritual bodies reflect the physical needs of the body. All herbs have iron but some have more and give off the vibration of iron more readily. When one works with herbs you are working with the vibrations of mother earth. The plant gives up the vibration to heal us and herbs that are in your vicinity are more powerful to you such as Malva leaves and dandelion in your backyard. The vibration is closer to you than an herb from India and China. The Chaparrel bush is unique to the desert shiny and green all year long and is the most beneficial for healing to the Native Americans. When a person comes to America from a foreign place they must first get use to our soil, sun and food before using our herbs. Chaparrel is a cleanser and detoxifier that takes a fever away in a short time used as a tea to drink. (12)

Calcium herbs may be helpful in bone and teeth conditions, poor blood, and asthma, overweight and nervous conditions. These herbs include Caraway seeds, Chamomile, Chives, Cleavers, Coltsfoot, Dandelion, Dill, Horsetail, Pimpernel, and Tormentil Root. Chlorine herbs may be helpful in sinus trouble, Bright's disease, magnetism, pyorrhea, bloated abdomen, blood purifier, cleaning arteries, and the lymphatic system. Copper herbs may be helpful in overcoming chronic gastric indigestion, gallbladder, insufficient bile secretion, insufficient thymus secretion, low blood sugar, spleen problems and water retention. Fluorine herbs may help to overcome poor eyesight, old age problems, skin disorders, repair broken bones and curvature of spine, prevent pyorrhea and help resist disease. Iodine herbs are often helpful in goiter problems, retaining natural color in hair, obesity, nerves and protecting body and brain from body toxins. Iron herbs are helpful with anemia, weakness in old age, shortness of breath, fever of all kinds, helping the body to be resistant to all contagious diseases, increasing physical power, mental power and strengthening the liver. Magnesium herbs are helpful in tooth decay, irritability, poor circulation, tired blood, nervous prostration, backward children, dull adults, excessive acidity, insomnia, and to remove toxins from the body. They include Broom Tops, Carrot leaves, Devils Bits, Meadowsweet, Mullein Leaves, Nettle, Primrose, and Walnut Leaves. Manganese herbs may be helpful in neurites, mental instability, mental alertness, sorrow, emotional shock, poor joints. These herbs include Burdock, Kelp, Sheep sorrel, Strawberry leaves, Wintergreen, and Yellow Dock. Nickel herbs may be helpful in disorders of the pancreas, weak lining of the intestines and assimilating nutrients. Algae, Kelp, Bladder wrack and Liverwort are the Nickel herbs. Potassium herbs are often helpful in diseases of the lung and chest, liver, spleen, constipation, Brain, nerves, stomach acid, heart muscles, skin eruptions, and the problem of sores healing. Phosphorus herbs are helpful in the development of the sixth sense, body poise, and electromagnetic efficiency, nervous disorders of the heart and stomach, neuritis, nourishing the brain, and preventing fatigue. People who work indoors are in need of these herbs. Silicon herbs may help in preventing infections, retard cancerous growth, sort teeth and bones, nervous exhaustion, ridged nails and bad complexion. These herbs are Chickweed, Corn silk, Flax Seed, Horsetail, Lamb's-quarters, Oat Straw, Red Raspberry Leaves, and Sunflower Seeds. Sodium herbs may help in hardening of the arteries, diabetes, gallstones, arthritis, bladder stones, and the retarding of old age. Sulfur herbs may be helpful in dissolving the acids in the body system, warming the body and feet, give energy, strengthen the tissues, help with impure blood, leukemia, hemorrhoids, and septicemia. These herbs are Coltsfoot, Eyebright, Fennel, Meadowsweet, Mullein, Pimpernel, Plantain leaves, Scouring Rush, Shepherd's Purse, Stinging Nettle, and Watercress. Zinc herbs may be helpful when a person has weak pancreas as in Diabetics, failing eyesight due to insulin, flatulence due to weak pancreas, prostrate troubles and tumors. The Zinc herbs are Horsetail, Paprika, and Shepherd's Purse. (13).

Dian Dincin Buchman has a Ph.D. in Health Sciences and an interest in holistic and botanical medicine to help people get well and stay well. Self-defense medicine can be practiced with the use of foods, herbs and traditional cooking spices. Plants have continued to be the mainstay of country medicine passed down from family to family and within communities. Tribes, clans, villages, towns, sometimes entire countries have similar styles in healing. The information on discoveries of how to use plants is just passed along such as Chamomile is used as a digestive aid throughout the world. Pharmaceutical firms comb the most primitive places on earth to bring back and explore nature folk medicine to duplicate specimens of plants. Some plants cannot be duplicated and only fresh fruit or bark can be used for the healing effects. Willow bark which has been used for thousands of years by Native Americans for an anti-inflammatory. Consistent use of the bark affected the digestive tract and a German scientist used the Spirea plant family resulting in what we now call aspirin. European people were saved from dysentery by what is called Ipecac. Quinine was used to control malaria. Digitalis was discovered from the plant Foxglove and is still used today as a heart-saving medicine. Plants can help to rebalance the body so it can rebalance itself. A combination of water, plants and good nutrition is often effective. Not all herbal applications work for every person as each person is different in needs. Whole dried blackberries can be crushed into a powder and then used as a resource against diarrhea. The bark, leaves, and root can also be used. When a dash of blackberry powder is added to chamomile or peppermint tea you have an organic cleanse to rid the body of impurities. Blackberries also help with a sore throat as apple cider vinegar will also work. Red Raspberry can be used in many of the same ways as the blackberry for a sore throat, body cold or flu and red raspberry vinegar will bring down a fever. Vinegar can be added to blackberry or raspberry jelly to dissolve the tarter on your teeth. The mouth must be rinsed quickly as the mixture has high amounts of sugar content. Mid-wives use raspberry leaf tea to reduce bleeding during childbirth. Where there is too-profuse menstrual flow. Red raspberry leaf tea may slowly decrease the flow. (14)

Echinacea is also known as the purple coneflower and is an herb that strengthens the body's ability to resist infection. This herb was used by over a dozen Native American Tribes such as the Pawnee tribe who would chew on the root all during the day. Echinacea stimulates the immune system and increases one's ability to eliminate invading bacteria. It is useful with colds, bronchitis, sore throats, abscesses, and yeast infections. Rosemary was once regarded as one of the great cure-all herbs. It was mentioned by Pliny, by Dioscordes, Galen and early Arab physicians for its medical and cosmetic powers. Today it is known as an antiseptic, a gentle stimulant to the whole body and a headache aid. Superstitions handed down by the gypsies hold that a sprig of rosemary under a pillow could prevent children's nightmares and use of rosemary could prevent miscarriage. Added to shampoos the herb can prevent dandruff and strengthen hair. Hungarian Queen Elizabeth used a recipe of Hungary Water with Rosemary on her limbs and was cured of paralysis. The water was sold all over Europe in 1235 in European apothecaries and also sold by European gypsies as a face beautifier and cure-all. The original water was made from more than a pound of the flowers in a gallon of white wine and then distilled. (15)

Man-kinds first sweet was honey made from honey bees. The Honey bee extracts nectar from flowers and the color, taste and the aroma are derived from the type of flower they were feeding on. Because honey is produced from flowers it is sometimes used as an antihistamine. Honey was used by primitive people in New Guinea, Africa, South America, and New Zealand. Ancient Hebrews and Egyptians used honey as a medicine in the form of a salve. It is considered an anti-fatigue as many cultures of people were long-lived. Honey cannot be used uncooked or unpasteurized for newborn infants as it will cause diarrhea. Eruptions around the mouth can be quickly healed with honey. About 500 known Egyptian medical formulas are based on honey. Early Olympic athletes used honey in water before the games, as do long-distance swimmers, runners, and mountain climbers. The RAF pilots working long missions during the battle of Britain in World War II were given enormous quantities to increase their capacity to work. Honey can be used as a cosmetic on the face as it acts like a moisturizer. (16)

The Holy Bible speaks about honey in a number of places such as, Matthew 3:4, "John's clothes were made of camel's hair, and he had a leather belt around his waist. His food was locusts and wild honey." Psalm 19:10, "They are more precious than gold, than much pure gold: they are sweeter than honey, than honey from the comb." Psalm: 119:103, "How sweet are your words to my taste sweeter than honey to my mouth." The Holy Bible is full of knowledge of human traditions and honey to sustain the body if we only read the wonderful words of the faithful prophets who loved us enough to leave their thoughts and experiences. The book of 1ˢᵗ Samuel in the old- testament Chapter 14:24-30 speaks of Jonathan eating honey as a food. "Now the men of Israel were in distress that day, because Saul had bound the people under an oath." Saying, "Cursed be any man who eats food before evening comes, before I have avenged myself on my enemies." "So none of the troops tasted food. The entire army entered the woods, and there was honey on the ground. When they went into the woods, they saw the honey oozing out, yet no one put his hand to his mouth because they feared the oath. But Jonathan had not heard that his father had bound the people with the oath, so he reached out the end of his staff that was in his hand and dipped it into the honeycomb. He raised his hand to his mouth, and his eyes brightened. Then one of the soldiers told him." "Your father bound the army under strict oath saying." 'Cursed be any man who eats food today.' "That is why the men are faint." Jonathan said "My father has made trouble for the country. See how my eyes brightened when I tasted a little of this honey." The victory was in the nourishment from this gift of nature and the Bees. (17)

Native American Worship

The Native Americans worshipped at certain locations such as mountain tops, dense forests, springs, lakes, and waterfalls. They performed religious ceremonies for spiritual guidance or to seek help in healing. These were natural power spots where the senses peaked and consciousness was raised. The site of Slide Rock State park in Oak Creek, Arizona is a powerful site used for purification by the Hopi Indians. The site was used to restore balance and drive out negative influences. Native Americans continue to make yearly pilgrimages to bathe in Oak Creeks sacred waters. Shamans used the Great Basin at Grimes Point, Nevada for ceremonies that would ensure a successful buffalo hunt. By capturing the collective Soul of the herd this would bring buffalo's to retrieve their Souls. Indian Hot Springs in Hudspeth Courts, Texas has twenty-two artesian wells used as healing springs. One of the springs is a Lithium spring and another is similar to an Epsom Salt Bath. Mud from the springs was used to cure rashes as the skin is also considered to be an organ and needs to have special care. The springs were used so often that the paths have worn into the earth and have formed permanent hiking trails. Eureka Springs, Arkansas holds a legend that the blind daughter of a Sioux Chief had her sight miraculously restored by the waters at the spring. Assateague Island was also used as a healing site by multiple tribes because this site was considered to be a portal for souls to enter and exit this world. Point Conception in California was the counterpart to enter and exit the earth plane. Fakahatchee Strand, Florida is considered to be the home of God. The Seminole legend is that the healing forces intertwined with the body at this sacred place. Lost Sea Cave, Sweetwater, Tennessee contains the largest underground lake in the world. This site is considered sacred by the Cherokee people. The cave is the home of an ancient spirit who heals the body, mind and spirit of people who bathe in the lake. A chapel in Chimayo, New Mexico built in 1816 attracts people on Good Friday each year for healing miracles. Mt. Shasta in California has been used by tribes for thousands of years. Sweat lodge, vision quest, and purification ceremonies were designed to heal the body and mind. A tribe known as the Esalens thought Big Sun California was a magical healing area. Shamans used the springs to wash disease residue off after a healing. Where a spring tumbled into the ocean were openings into the underworld and Shamans could retrieve souls that needed to be healed. Ku-Ku-Haele and Wai-Manu, Hawaii are the sites for healing for the Kahunas and tribal leaders of the Hawaiian Island. (18)

The Native Americans agree that there is a great power that created all. This is such a great mystery that no one can describe the mystery and it is not worth arguing over. The answers lie in the higher spirit world where our spirits travel. The Indians do not accept that one person or religion has the only key to the spirit world and beyond and that key can only explain the Great Mystery, such as beliefs in hell-fire and damnation. This is regarded as ignorance and the line must be drawn as to projecting your visions on others. The positive Americans have awakened to the realization that spiritual and philosophical knowledge outside of one's own culture can be rewarding. Native Americans maintain that open-mindedness and meeting together without age-old religious narrow-mindedness will result in harmony for all. Sharing and generosity were values common to the North American tribes and formed the basis for their closeness to mother earth. When a different way proved to be spiritually enhancing, they adopted the custom as an improvement to their religious concepts. The Native Americans were not held back by an organized hierarchy of religious leaders. (19)

The sweat lodge was an example of a simple beautiful temple that did not need building plans or funding drives. The Sioux tribe is a reflection of the North American Indian tribes with ceremonies in the sweat lodge, vision quest ceremonies, the sun dance, and spirit-calling ceremonies. Most tribes had annual thanksgivings to the Great Spirit such as the corn harvest or wild rice harvest. The key ingredient toward fulfillment of inner peace was to be thankful to the higher powers. The spirit-calling ceremonies were calls to the ancestors called Yuwipi, Kiva, shaking tent, or longhouse. Before the migration from the Carolinas the Sioux had medicine pipes mostly made of clay. The Native American Black Elk as a boy had a vision of a red peace pipe from a Spirit called the Buffalo Calf Woman. She introduced the power of the pipe in ceremonies under the Great Spirit. In the vision the six forces were introduced consisting of the four directions, or four winds, Mother Earth, and Father Sky. The red peace pipe and the six forces were also thought of as spiritual symbols. Black Elk's vision was of trying times for the Native Americans, but these nature-based wisdom would be very helpful in later times for all people. Black Elk's prophecies included a flowering tree and a rainbow which were symbols to the future of harmoniously spiritual people to evolve and respect the environment. The rainbow is the symbol of the Great Spirit and the many races unifying. This is referred to as the new Rainbow Tribe. The Peace Pipe has long been used by the Native Americans. It is considered a portable Alter used for a simple ritual. The pipe is loaded with tobacco or bark of the red willow. The true Native American way finds the Great Spirit through fasting, knowledge and observance of God's creation, and the Sun Dance, Vision Quest, and Sweat Lodge ceremonies. The pipe ceremony acknowledges the four directions, Mother Earth, and Father Sky. The final offering is to the Great Spirit. The pipe is held firmly with stem pointed straight forward, out into the center of the universe. The pipe holder begins with the east direction because the sun rises in the east and is the beginning of a new day for all people. A pinch of tobacco is sprinkled on the ground to acknowledge that we must always give back to Mother Earth. This also shows the spirit world that a portion of tobacco is given for the powers from the east. A prayer is offered in each direction to acknowledge the powers of each and for spirit protection. (20)

The Native Americans follow the motto of do no harm to one another or interfere with one another's spiritual visions. A crystal can serve the same purposes as a peace pipe. Hold it up and you can see a rainbow in the crystal. Take the crystal and beseech the four directions, Mother Earth, Father Sky, and Wakan Tanka (The Great Spirit.) The Native American people believe that everyone should have a relationship with all living things. In the old days the Sweat Lodge Ceremony was to get them ready for a higher, deeper plane or dimension. Sweat lodges are constructed with saplings bent together and tied to form a half sphere. A pit is dug with heated racks in the center. Tarps, or blankets cover the frame and then this is a church. Sage, flat cedar, flowers, grass, or reeds are placed all over the floor. The average sweat lodge is 8 by 12 feet and is a culmination of spiritual, mystical, and psychic expression. The Sweat Lodge Ceremony is a way to bond to the Earth and find a spiritual link to God's creation. Nature and the environment lead back to the elements of fire, water, air and earth. Water is the lifeblood and as you sweat your mist is carried to the four corners of the world. The visible breathe symbolizes truth. The Great Mystery Creator's ultimate truth is found through Ceremonies. (21)

A Vision Quest is done for self-improvement of the person, for right living, or better health. It is something that involves an individual ceremony. The Sun Sioux Dance is a tribal gathering and expression of thanksgiving. The ceremony lasts four days and was held after the summer buffalo hunts. The people cut a tree for the ceremony and dance to the sun. The Native Americans feel this will help their people live. On the fourth day of the ceremony the pledged dancers are pierced. This is done while lying down on a bed of sage and then the person rises and dances attached to a rope. This is the Native way to remove the hurts of life. A sage wreath is placed on the head with eagle feathers. The drums are beating in the background of the ceremony. When the dancers have ended their connection to the tree of life in the center the Sun Dance Chief ends the ceremony. The Yuwipi or Spirit-calling ceremony involves a holy man who conducts the ceremony and acts as a medium to call in the spirit man. Songs are sung out by the beat of a drum. This ceremony is usually held for an individual and predictions come forth, or healing, and sometimes to find a missing person. This ceremony is always done by a holy person who has lived a virtuous life. The holy person must live a life of sacrifices and no drinking of alcohol. The person has their power by Vision Quests and fasting. Ceremonies are not a secret because the knowledge can help to heal the earth and the people. Indian people take signs from what they observe and hold that flying animals and the elements are all in contact with each other and with creation. The spirits who enter the ceremony are animals that confer information. Although Spirits can come in many forms when information is needed. They come from a higher realm that is freer from the constraints of time and space, so they can be of help to us. Many of the Native American people avoided dwelling on bad spirits and concentrated on the Great Spirit as having created only good. There is no such thing as a bad waterfall, a bad stream, a bad rain, a bad owl, or a bad eagle, wolf, buffalo, or tree. Only good is created in nature as the man can make something to be used for bad. Preparation for any ceremony means coming with a clean mind. People that are not in tune or have disbelief are asked to leave the ceremony. When the Indians were moved to reservations many of the old ceremonies and rites had to be hidden. The Cavalry had come with missionaries who had their own ideas. America was a continent of land with unlimited resources and the industrial age was upon the land the Native Americans loved so much. (22)

John 3:16-18 "For God so loved the world that he gave his one and only Son, that who- ever believes in him shall not perish but have eternal life. For God did not send his Son into the world to condemn the world, but to save the world through him, but whoever does not believe stands condemned already because he has not believed in the name of God's one and only Son." (23)

The Moravian missionaries had arrived in the New World to open the doors to a new spiritual power and cultural conversion. As the Mohican Natives were baptized and given Christian names hoping to save their ancestral lands. The Moravian Christian Rituals of Jesus death by wounds and blood appealed to the Indians. The blood and wine of communion service was a strong message of a Savior who was a powerful warrior. The Moravians placed special emphasis on Christ's gruesome death, describing it in detail such as the spear wounds, the blood that ran like sweat, and his death upon the cross. Jesus was now invoked as a spirit helper who could assist the hunters. The Savior was the keeper of the forest and would keep the Indians from danger as they hunted. The Mohicans were sure that the consumption of Christ's flesh in the form of bread at the communion ritual had transformative powers to all who participated. The Indians began to hunger and thirst after the body and blood of the Savior. The rituals of war were second nature to the Indians as people captured were tortured as a ritual to gain spiritual power. This was to quench the crying blood of lost relatives. The whole village would gather and participate in the ritualized torture of victims. These people were trying to make sense of their lives in a great upheaval. As communities were formed and churches built the Savior was the protection and healing force that helped to restore the Native American people in the hope of a future. (24)

Chapter *2*

EXAMINATION OF RELIGIOUS EXPERIENCE

John 3: 19-21 "This is the verdict: Light has come into the world, but men loved darkness instead of light because their deeds were evil. Everyone who does evil hates the light, and will not come into the light for fear that his deeds will be exposed. But whoever lives by the truth comes into the light, so that it may be seen plainly that what he has done has been done through God." (25)

Max Freedom Long moved to the Hawaiian Islands in 1917 and began studying what the Native Hawaiians practiced as a religion. The ancient "Huna" system. The words of wisdom from old sages can be found scattered in the Bible as well as in the Koran. The Polynesian Kahunas ere known as "Keepers of the Secret." When a disciple reached the stage of spiritual perfection, he would be able to create a world with God and know precisely how it is done, as God gives us understanding according to our faith and needs. The Intelligence behind and in all material things moving about is what we call the "law." All things visible and invisible progress under definite laws that never change as they move within time and space. The whole of creation and its laws when meditated upon create a picture of God and his creation. We depend on God and his laws to be unchangeable, more powerful, and more loving, as a foundation of faith is built on the stability and order of the Universal laws. When our faith does not reflect the light of inner or intuitional knowing, then we are walking a path of darkness. People must have a clear idea of God and how he works through his universe. We must clear our minds of unproven ideas handed down to us by men. Every religion has its dogmas and as children we are taught to accept certain religious ideas and teachings as given under divine authority. As we grow into adults theories need to be re-evaluated to fit the realities of life. Our progression as human beings will be with good time and bad, going forward and slipping back, but with the law of God's universe we will eventually learn the lessons needed and prayers. Part of faith is being able to trust God completely. Man has free will and can fail us in our trust. (26)

The Huna's were convinced that man had a threefold constitution, a low self, called the subconscious, a middle self which is the conscious mind and a high self that is also called the superconscious or God within. God is the air I breathe, the sun that lights the earth and water upon the earth. Without God there is no existence. Within God there is life, order, goodness, joy, growth and a tomorrow. Knowing God is in all things such as our bodies and mind, we still do not sense him with the five senses. The senses make us aware if we are hot or cold, happy or sad, not the internal things that make up the "I." We still have an overpowering sense of the individual being or own self. The "I" is independent of the body as it is ingrained faith. As individuals we have faith that we do exist, as we must have faith that God and his creation exists. Our reasoning process must develop an inner feeling that tells us God is near and real. This is similar to a sixth sense or an intuition that allows us to know without physically feeling. Our middle self must realize God as our lower self learns to feel God through all living things. We are entering into God where he is more than pure Spirit. The "I-ness" is often called the River of Life by ancient sages. We stop reasoning about God and try to feel God through the sixth sense of faith that comes from the low self. When you find God you will know he is inside of you. Many people who meditate and let go of all thought begin to see a white light. God in us is intelligence as well as force and substance. I am that I am. The spirit of man cannot be taken into a laboratory and examined by scientists. This is called the First Mystery that of the High Self as it cannot be observed. The goal of man is the full union of the three selves to form a complete man or woman. The law and middle selves are often divided by their own purposes and drives. Religion comes into play to work on perfecting the lower and middle selves. The Kahunas taught that man had been given endless joys as well as some sorrows. Life is good and beautiful when normally lived and growth is necessary. To live a healthy life a person needed to unite all three selves under the guidance of the high self. Part of normal living and happiness was the union of a marital partner. Any man who tried to improve on God's way of living in an abnormal way was far from the understanding of God and his creation. Idols were a way to try and bring God closer and make him more approachable. The ancient Kahuna seers new the prayers to go through the High-Self and call on God. The High-Self Father- Mother is part of ourselves. It is the highest of the three selves of man, the Guardian Angel, Father within, the personal savior. All prayers, no matter to whom addressed, what gods, or idols, can only go to the High-Self. This is considered the greatest secret of all time, the High-Self is within us as a god and a representative of Universal God. The High-Self is where we address our prayers, with its superior wisdom we can depend upon it to pass on any prayer request or prayer force to higher beings in the ascending side of growth and evolution. Once we recognize the High-Self it is ready to guide us and help us. Because of Universal Law and free will the High-Self must be asked. When we invite the Higher-Selves to be part of us they can use their superior wisdom and power to guide us into paths that will make happy and normal living. This is opening a door to let God into our lives. This takes training for the middle (or conscious) self to training the low (subconscious) self. Affirmations, meditations, and periods of visualization are tools in training the low self. (27)

The initiate teacher Jesus taught in veiled language: "To contact the High-Self you must get the low self, which is child- like, to carry your message." His actual words were: "Whosoever shall not receive the kingdom of God as a little child, he shall not enter therein." The ancient prayer used to accomplish this is to first take eight breathes, then: "I Diana St Clair command Beverly (my middle name High-Self) to accumulate Mana –Mana- Loa, the Holy Breathe of God, and send it to my Higher –Self and to Heaven; I love you Father/Mother God,

I praise your Holy Name, I ask you for this request? Bless this prayer with Mana- Mana- Loa and send it back down through my Higher-Self Beverly to manifest in this world, Amana." This prayer is very effective in the shower or standing in water, as water grounds the person. This ancient prayer is a method to put your request straight into the Light of God. In the animal world we see Mother-Nature as the God instinct, furnishing the guiding of higher intelligence under which all animals live. The animals lack reason and high knowledge. (28)

The second of the three great mysteries concerns vital force, or mana. God is in all life, and that is a living force. It is the sunshine and stores in the plants we use for food. The worship of the Sun was the worship of God and of the High-Self. This life force extracted from sunshine, air, and foods by the low self was symbolized by clear water (mana). In the ancient writings this was known as "the water of life." The middle self is that of twice powerful water called (mana mana). The High-Self is given the title of "Lord," which means the one who supervises the division of the waters. When the vital force is used by it the Kahuna's say it is magically strong to bring the answers to prayer and called, "the strongest life force" (Mana -Loa). The High-Self and the mana are what brings about changes to the physical plane. This process is how healing takes place on the earth plane. The Hawaiian Kahunas knew that this vital power was an act of worship. In the Lord's Prayer, "Thine be the power, and the glory…" is a hidden prayer which is recorded in the Holy Bible. This prayer was taught by Jesus to the people he initiated. In ancient writings ladder of words is often mentioned and is the Third Mystery. It is the ectoplasmic invisible cord along with the telepathic prayer and the mana travels sent by the low self of the High. The Ladder is also the "beam" or "ladder" along which the High-Self sends a return flow of the purified mana to help the two lower selves. The Hindus call it the Goddess Kundalini and have their yoga form of the ladder which opens the chakra centers. So this whole process is the Huna method of prayer. In the early days of Christianity the High-Self was called the white light or "illumination." Later the word "baptism" was substituted for "illumination." Our search for God is a search for ourselves as he is within us. Intuition is a flash of knowing as if God has spoken to us and given us a final word of truth. (29)

The early version of the Christian Bible states: "And when the Pharisees demanded when the kingdom of God should come, he answered them and said, the kingdom of God cometh not that it may be observed: Neither shall they say, lo here! Or, lo there! For behold, the kingdom of God is within you." Luke 17:20-21. Man is three just as God is the Father, Son, and Holy Spirit. We can never be sure about ourselves until the truth of the intuitional knowing has been added. (30)

Thinking Philosophically St. Thomas of Aquinas championed the theory of Natural Law Ethics based on the view that Universal Moral values can be discovered in nature by using the faculty of reason. People can discover Natural Law Ethics by using their rational, intellectual and emotional capabilities. People that believe in God assume that these moral values are part of God's nature, as God is good and created us. The divine spark of God in us is the gift of reason. By people using the gift of reason they can discover morally good and right without God commanding it. From culture to culture and age to age natural law exists. This is universal and binding of all people. The constitution and the Declaration of Independence reflect these truths that the Creator endowed us with certain rights. Many people turn to religion to develop the highest enlightened values. Humans are designed in God's image and follow a path of religion and our natural moral intuition to reach both moral and spiritual enlightenment. Thomas Aquinas thought we are able to discover God's ethic encoded in our human nature, as we are able to discover the mysteries of the physical universe through the study of science. Our critical thinking abilities reveal the essential nature of people. The abilities guide us to informed moral choices and personal development. Thomas Aquinas was a significant Christian thinker in the development of natural law theory. He was influential in the development of ethical theory in the Catholic Church. The Summa Theologica is one of his works in which he tries to integrate key elements of Aristotle's thinking with Christian Theology. His hierarchy of laws include, eternal law, the uncreated reason of God that guides the universe, Divine Law, the law that directs humans to a vision of God and eternal blessedness,

Natural Law, moral laws derived from Divine Law that humans can discover through reason. (31)

People become virtuous by acting virtuous, which is why education and proper laws are necessary to help people develop good habits. Human languages are responsible for creating virtuous laws that reflect natural law, which reflects divine law. Aquinas world was dominated by the Catholic Church and the rulers of his time. Kings were seen as representatives of God on Earth. The supernatural-metaphysical dimensions of a religion are intertwined with how we humans should conduct ourselves during this life on the earth plane. Whether to achieve salvation, nirvana, eternal life, or a relationship with the divine, with the goal of certain principles and values. (32)

There is a branch of philosophy called Metaphysics. This philosophy studies the characteristics of reality or existence, meaning of life, freewill, the nature of mind, fundamental principles of the universe, and life beyond death. Many students explore this philosophy as the path to intellectual enlightenment. Most people do not see reality, they see images created by others that shape their minds and manipulate their thinking. Today most information is filtered through the media. This information is passively accepted and forms or manipulates their attitudes. Philosophy teaches people to critically evaluate the information and beliefs that we use to guide our choices in life. Metaphysics looks at what is the place of humans in the universe and does each life have a purpose. Humans also question whether we can increase our freedom by eliminating internal and external constraints. Do I have the power to create alternatives and to think of new possibilities to improve my situation? Sometimes we find ourselves in limiting situations and need to create new situations by making different choices. Philosophy is about critical thinking to find alternative choices, as to use your imagination to create new ways of viewing your current reality and future possibilities. Sometimes bad habits and how we react to situations hold us back from fulfilling our own unique potential. Metaphysics inquires as to whether people have souls and what is a mind? How the mind and body influence each other is of importance to this search of bettering one's life. This also opens up our minds to see that there is more than one side or a story or how events are perceived. Knowledge is constructed from information and the distinction of appearances and reality are often different from person to person. This also leads to the question of how we increase our wisdom. (33)

The Book "The Secret" contains wisdom from people through the centuries who have found it to eradicate disease, acquire massive wealth, overcome obstacles and achieve impossible feats. The greatest people in history knew the secret such as, Plato, Shakespeare, Newton, Hugo, Beethoven, Lincoln, Emmerson, Edison, and Einstein. All ages, all races, and all nationalities can experience the joy of the secret. The great secret of life is the law of attraction. Your thoughts are magnetic, and thoughts have a frequency. As a person thinks thoughts they go out into the universe and they magnetically attract all things that are on the same frequency. Everything you send out returns to you. You change the frequency by changing your thoughts. What you think about the most will appear in your life. The law of attraction is a law of nature. The things we complain about we have attracted into our life. Once you have accepted this your life can be transformed. Persistent thoughts bring experiences into your life. Fear that you have no control over circumstances or that you can be at the wrong place at the wrong time cannot come into your experience without constant thought. Unwanted things come into your life from a lack of awareness of the creative power of our thoughts. We would have a hard time monitoring our thoughts every moment. Our feelings let us know what we are thinking. Your feelings are your greatest tool to help you create your life, always remembering your thoughts are the cause of everything. Your feelings are a signal for you to know what you are thinking. People have two sets of feelings one good and one bad. When you start asking yourself often during the day you will become aware of how you are feeling. Whatever your feeling tells you what frequency you are on. If you are feeling bad you will draw more bad things into your life. You can be blocking your own good from coming to you because you are on a negative frequency. By adding feeling you can transmit an even more powerful frequency. (34)

Learn to elevate your feelings with the intention to lift yourself. The universe will respond to the way you feel. Your thoughts and feelings will always create your life just like the law of gravity, the law of attraction is always at work. If something came to you it was with prolonged thought. So a shift in your thoughts and awareness can undo your present situation. You have the power to change anything in your life. Keep a list of Secret Shifters to change your mood, such as music, or beautiful memories. Love is the greatest emotion that can bring goodness into your life. The combination of thought and love is what forms the force of the law of attraction. The feeling of love is the highest frequency you can emit. This is the power that will transform your life. This is also the fundamental principle in every system of Philosophy, Religion and Science. The greater you are able to love, the greater power you are harnessing. Once you begin to understand and master your thoughts and feelings you will create your own reality. This is also where your freedom comes as you are no longer trapped in old situations. This is the magic of life to create whatever you want in your life, and remember it is your birthright. Learn to make a command to the universe and let it know what you want. Believe in faith that what you want is already yours. You do not need to know how it is going to happen as the Universe will rearrange itself. Be happy and receive, as many of us do not feel that we deserve happiness, health, a mate, decent housing or wealth. Be grateful for what you have every day. This is the recipe to heal your body, by first healing the thoughts that go through your mind. (35)

Swami Sriyukteswar was born in India in 1855 and extolled the ancient science of Kriya Yoga Meditation as the most effective means of attaining the God-realization. There are many schools all-over America which teach this Science. He attained spiritual illumination that was not a result of intellectual studies but of direct perception of reality. The virtue of love is the heart's natural love that is the principal requisite to attain a holy life. This love is a heavenly gift of nature that removes all cause of excitation from the system and cools it down to a perfectly normal state. This in turn ignites the vital powers and expels all foreign matter such as the germs of diseases in a natural way usually perspiration. This in-turn makes man healthy in body and mind so he understands the guidance of nature. When love becomes developed in man he is able to understand the real position of his own self as well as understanding those around him. The developed love is said to help man gain the God-like company of divine beings and he is saved forever. Without developed love man is not able to live in natural ways. He often becomes excited and takes foreign matters into his own system through mistakes in understanding nature and suffers in body and mind. Man can never find any peace and his life becomes a burden. So the culture of this love which is a heavenly gift is the principle requisite for the attainment of holy salvation. It is impossible for man to advance without love. The people that remove our troubles, dispel our doubts, and bestow peace are the true teachers. This is a God-like work in the Universe to help our fellow man. Out of this creation the object that relieves our miseries, doubts, and administers peace is due our respect. The people of India accept this object whether animate or inanimate as the savior. People are at different stages of evolution and choose objects that they can comprehend as their savior. In general people think of illness as a calamity and water is to remove the illness. Some men choose water itself as their divinity. (36)

Philosophers able to comprehend the internal electrical light that shines within them find their hearts to flow towards this light. This light relieves them of all causes of excitement, cools down their system to a normal state, igniting the vital force and makes them healthy, both in mind and body. This light is accepted as their divinity and savior. The adepts feel they have control over the whole material world and find their Divinity or Savior in the Self, not in the outside world. The people of India find that a firmness of moral courage can be attained by the culture. The religious forbearances of abstention from cruelty, dishonesty, covetousness, unnatural living, and unnecessary possessions must be followed. Religious observances of purity in body and mind and cleaning the body externally and internally from all foreign matter will prevent diseases to the system. The mind must also be cleared of all prejudices and dogmas. (37)

Ecclesiastes 1:7, "All streams flow into the sea, yet the sea is never full. To the place the streams come from, there they shall return again." (38)

The Planet Earth is distinguished from other planets by water. The earth was created by it and is sustained by water. Seventy percent of the earth is covered by water. Man is born from it and all life depends on it. We are made of 75% water as it is the essence of life. Newborn humans are 97% water, Adults are about75% water, the human brain is 75%, Bones are 2.2% water, and tooth enamel is 2% water. Our life and health and the health of the planet depend on water. It carries all of present life and the seeds of the future. Water is the mediator between health and sickness. Because it is so universal water has lost its magic to people and is taken for granted. People are used to turning on the tap and have forgotten the crystal clear natural springs, the mountain pools and the deep water of ancient wells. If handled incorrectly water can itself become diseased and spread that disease to all other organisms. When we put mistreated water into our bodies, our metabolism becomes unnatural and both chemically and energetically unbalanced. This would confuse the messages to our brains, and cause our emotions to be out of balance. Water is itself a source of power and can empower us. Even though water is a colorless liquid it enables people to see the colors of the rainbow. We are all attracted to water in some way. It speaks to us on a deep subconscious or spiritual level. The Sun and the moon work together to create the ebb and flow of tides, as the Earth's gravity pulls water towards the oceans. Because of the Moon and the Sun water is always on the move. Our blood and fluid in our bodies respond to the same cosmic forces. Babies are happy in water for the first year of their life as it is similar to being in the womb. Ancient wisdom holds that in the cycles of nature wind turns to rain, rain to earth, earth to sea and back to clouds again. The constant element of water is what changes. People use to live near flowing streams, waterfalls and praised God for rains. They accepted and treasured the powers of water. (39)

Earlier cultures understood pure water as the Chinese saved the water from glaciers in jade vases, Incas and Aztecs put water in jars of obsidian, witch doctors in Africa used quartz crystals. The minerals in these containers affected the water and prevented it from becoming polluted. These cultures knew that water collects, stores, and transfers physical and vibrational information and energy and must always be kept moving. Today we are seeing that water's role as a channel for vibrational information is a new discovery. This is associated with the phenomena of resonance and magnetic fields. Water is one of the best cure-alls. In

Chinese tradition water is the key to the fire elements of wood being created from water, that encourages the growth of plant matter, fire is brought about by wood, the earth comes out of fire, metal comes from earth, and water arises out of metal. Water also links the five levels of human existence, physical, vital energy, emotional, mental, and spiritual. Water allows the vital fluid that allows vital energy to flow affecting as physically, mentally, and emotionally. Humans cannot be healthy without healthy water. The ancient Greeks thought of water as a medium and the possibility for all elemental change. In the systems of magic and alchemy water was crucial as the principal elements were fire and water. Fire was seen as something subtle like electricity. Water is represented in physical form by rivers, streams, and oceans, but in alchemy water is magnetism. Water has a role in transmitting electromagnetism. In Northern Europe thousands of people flock to Lourdes in France each year believing in the healing powers of its waters. Rituals with water are practiced all over the world. Water is like a mysterious living creature which nurtures all life. (40)

The prophet Elisha demonstrated intercession by God for people through the healing of a town's water. 2 Kings 2: 19-22 "The men of the city said to Elisha, Look, our lord, this town is well situated, as you can see, but the water is bad and the land is unproductive. Bring me a new bowl, he said, and put salt in it. So they brought it to him. Then he went out to the spring, and threw salt into it, saying, this is water. Never again will it cause death or make the land unproductive. And the water has remained wholesome to this day, according to the word Elisha had spoken." (41)

The Cherokee Indians see water as the Earth's lifeblood, the rivers and streams that flow down the mountains are the arteries and veins that allow blood to go through the body. Water is part of the Native American consciousness. Walking by the ocean or a stream of water makes us feel good. Water is also the most refreshing drink when we are thirsty. People travel the world to see the spectacular sight of Niagara Falls. Western society changes in the 16th and 17th century known as the Age of Rationality and demanding that religion and science be separated. Before that time people understood the world in a different way. They knew that the heavens and Earth were connected, as religion and spiritual beliefs were a combined part of life. Deities and the elements were respected and a practice of intuitive understanding containing the mysteries were a part of life. Separating rationality and spirituality may be one of the major contributions to stress. Throughout history water has been used as a symbol of life and carried a mystery to it. In the ancient Tantric manuscripts water is prana the vital breath which brings life. Myths appear from Native American tribes that the creator sent animals down to the bottom of the sea to bring up mud and this was how Earth was created. Plains Indians give credit to an Old Man appearing on a raft and willed Earth into the existence out of the water. The Pima Indians of New Mexico have a story that Mother Earth was impregnated by a drop of water that fell from a cloud. There is a connection between fertility and water due to the inconvenience of traveling or making outdoor plans when it is raining. Water begins in the underground and after the rain falls returns to the ground so it is thought to be what transforms death to allow life to begin as a seed cannot grow without water. Flood waters have often been looked upon as sacred for their cleansing abilities. Water is also a powerful symbol in death as the process of laying out and cleaning a dead person's body which can be a ritualistic washing away of sins or a symbol of the purification of the soul before it enters the next world. North American Indian tribes place a bowl of water near the dying person so that their spirit may leave the temporal body and enter the water. The Spirit will then be reborn by this universal element of water. Holy Water is thought to be healing water symbolically and physically. People are baptized in Holy Water as a symbol of purification and regeneration. Baptism started in Egypt by the Great White Brotherhood in Rites and ceremonies. An Avatar had learned in meditation that water would purify man spiritually and physically. The Baptism of Jesus by John prepared him to accept his mission on Earth as the son of God. The contact of water was like magic. (42)

When a child was baptized salt was placed on the child's lips as a ritual to drive out the powers of darkness. People often attend a church because they want their children to be baptized or christened by a priest. This relates back to the ancient ritual of Blessing mind and body. The blessing of the water will confer on the child some kind of protection against evil forces. There would seem to be something in all of us that needs to have a spiritual nature. People have held onto the idea of sacred water in every culture and society. There is a search for healing waters, springs and wells that never ceases throughout history. Springs, wells, pools and fountains have often been blessed by people with the gift of prophecy. In Celtic Europe water cults were very popular, even though the Christian church did not approve. The time invested on water deities took away from the Christian message and was suppressed by the church. Churches were built around wells with the intention of the sacred waters belonging to the church. People still make pilgrimages to wells for healing as water cults have never died out. Sacrifice of animals were used in earlier times to appease the water Gods and spirits. Leaving offerings such as flowers was a custom as people asked to be cured. Ireland is a land of many small springs and wells where people leave plants with ribbons tied to them. The hope is that what we give we give to water it will give back to us. Stones were offered to wells that could influence the weather. Two Italian scientists measured the electrical fields of water at different healing wells in Europe discovering significant results that were different among wells due to minerals. The level of minerals such as germanium which maintains high oxygen levels in the water. People project loving thoughts into water in hopes that this will affect the water. Water flows through every level of existence from heaven too deep in the Earth. When we treat water with reverence we will recognize it has many powers, to inspire, heal, relax, give- life and to take it away. Water acts out on a subconscious and conscious level, as well as on our physical body and emotions. It is a treasure that can nourish us. When people realize how important water is and that we rely on it they will be more careful. The Chinese art of Feng Shui states that water is a powerful force as it absorbs and stores energy. It is a key to spiritual, emotional, and physical well-being. The key to health and longevity is water. (43)

The Hunza people in the Karakorom mountains in north of Pakistan, and another area is a mountain in Ecuador. The Hunza people use ice-melt from ancient glaciers which is one of the purest forms of water. The people age slowly and live well over 100 years. The Hunzas water does not contain mineral salts as many mountain springs have. Scientist have discovered 36 different types of water with very different combinations of hydrogen and oxygen. The more crystalline the structure the healthier the water. Water expands when it freezes which is helpful in preserving life. A sheet of ice protects the lower waters of a lake so fish are able to thrive underneath. Water is called the universal solvent as it dissolves almost everything it meets to some degree. Every object and substance, natural or manufactured has its own vibrational pattern. Every living thing has a specific frequency due to energy vibrating. In understanding the principle of resonance we can understand that all living things communicate via vibrations. Water is a powerful channel for conducting resonance. Physicists have determined that as electromagnetic waves of particular atoms come apart at certain frequencies as the electromagnetic energy disrupts them. Our bodies are a complex system of harmonic frequencies and any change in the harmony can cause pain, discomfort, and disease. (44)

Homeopathy is a safe and gentle form of healing because water is able to extract and store types of subtle energies. The remedies work on the energy frequencies within the body. Flowers are the crown of any plant and contain a high concentration of life force or energy. Bach flower remedies are the energy of sunlight to transfer the essence of a flower onto water. Energetic and vibrational information from the Sun and the plant are transferred to the water. Sunlight transfers an electrical charge from the plant to the water. A traditional Native American healing method was to walk through the grass barefoot in the morning with the Sun and the dew. Edward Bach an English doctor was a homeopath in the 1920's. He thought the link between illness and personality was a result of disharmony between the personality and the Higher Self or Soul. This could create a dysfunctional energy pattern. Flowers were placed in a bowl of spring water in the sunlight for a few hours. Then the flowers were removed and the water was mixed with alcohol to stabilize the essence. These remedies are called vibrational remedies. Flowers treat emotional disorders and temperaments. This causes changes in the chakras and meridians of the body. (45)

Our molecules in the body form the tissues of our bodies and are charged electrical entities. Any deviation from the norm of the structure of these molecules can cause disease. All of the organs and tissues have their own individual sound pattern. In healthy organs the molecules work together to form a harmonious relationship. Cymatic therapy is one vibrational field of medicine that aims to restore physical harmony for the body to resonate at an appropriate frequency. This is accomplished by sound waves with water as the medium to transfer sound vibrations to the patient. The technique of Aquasonics was developed by Peter Guy Manners in Worcestershire, England. Aqua sonics emits specific frequencies into a bath or pool of pure mineralized spring water. An electrochemical process traps the frequencies in the water energy. The vibrations energize the water for up to twelve weeks. The plants, animals, and minerals all have an aura or bio-electromagnetic field. The aura oscillates at a specific frequency and is affected by all it comes into contact with. This is how cells and crystals communicate with each other and become part of an energy system. Crystals have been used for thousands of years to heal environments and people. The ancient Egyptians built pyramids to harness earthly and cosmic energy. They would also crush gems and mix them with liquids, drinking them for healing. Crystal healing also works on the theory of resonance or vibrations. Healthy water sources are important to a healthy body and long life. (46)

Spirituality is our way of responding to God and our style of living in relation to God. It is our pattern of acting in a world with our values. Part of spiritual growth is becoming conscious of our values by what motivates our choices and action. Humans are continually in a growth process physically, psychologically, spiritually, socially, and culturally. Growth can be adding something new to our life or letting go of something no longer useful. Spiritual growth calls us to consciously work toward wholeness. God inspires us to become whole and holy. The Old Testament times is a place of exploration of dreams and spiritual life. This takes us back to the Judeo-Christian religion and the dreams of the Hebrew prophets, leaders and people. Consciousness is an awareness that is followed by an action. This may be grasped by the outer senses, the mind's reasoning, or an inner realization, but this is not consciousness. To be conscious one needs to act, or take the energy of awareness and actualize it into the world. Our dreams call us to a state of consciousness which is awareness and action. We are given insight into situations in our dreams. The knowledge can make a difference in figuring out a challenging situation. Dreams and dream work can guide us to our destiny, or life purpose. We need to know how to impact other people's lives and find peace and happiness in our own life. It may take years to find our destiny but keeping a journal of our dreams may help the process. (47)

The Book of Matthew Ch. 1:18-23 tells us of a dream Joseph had in marrying Mary. "But after he had considered this, an angel of the Lord appeared to him in a dream and said, "Joseph son of David, do not be afraid to take Mary as your wife, because what is conceived in her is from the Holy Spirit. She will give birth to a son, and you are to give him the name Jesus, because he will save his people from their sins." There is a lot of information in this dream. We learn of the Holy Child to come, that Angels are messengers of God, that the Holy Spirit is the way Mary conceived and that the child was to be named Jesus. This dream also brings the news that Jesus will save his people from a life of sin. This also confirms God's power over the Laws of the Universe to bring about miracles. (48)

We think of our Soul as that dimension most directly connected to God. The Soul carries the destiny information and guides us by our dreams. Dreams are the voice of the Soul at work. In the traditions of the Christian movement the Soul is the unique existence of the individual. This is the personal expression of life, vitality and energy of the person. The Soul is also called the Spark of God in us. The will, intellect, imagination and memory are conscious, although the Soul can also operate on the sub-conscious levels. God is seen as having both conscious and subconscious aspects. The unconscious is often referred to as the Force. This is where the mystery of dreams take place. Our destiny gives us a sense of a journey and a guiding force beyond our choosing that influence our thoughts, actions, and calls us to a greater wholeness and holiness. (49)

Mother Teresa of Calcutta had a dream in her life that all people know that they are loved before they die. She devoted her life to this mission. She was quoted as saying "How wonderful to see a person die in love." "With the joy of love, the perfect peace of Christ on his face." Mother Teresa and the members of her order began picking up the dying in the streets of Calcutta in 1952. Mother Teresa was born Agnes Boyaxhul in Skopje, Yugoslavia in 1910. She became a member of the Loreito nuns in Ireland in 1928. She was sent to India to do her novitiate and to begin teaching at St. Mary's High School in Calcutta. She taught for nearly 20 years until 1946. Mother Teresa heard the call of God to give up all and follow the Lord into the slums and serve the poor. She left the order but still worked under the Archbishop of Calcutta. Mother Teresa learned some basic medicine from the American Medical Mission Sisters and she began to go into the homes of the sick to heal them. She turned a temple dedicated to the Hindu Goddess Kali as a home for the sick known as Kalighat. She expanded her work to minister to every kind of suffering she encountered. This includes finding shelters, and homes for orphans, feeding the hungry, clothing the naked, family planning clinics and mobile dispensaries, and caring for the lepers. Mother Teresa founded the Missionaries of Charity working in 52 countries, dedicated to carrying out the missionary vows of poverty, chastity, obedience and free service to the poor. She lives a very simple life and often sleeps on the floor with the other sisters, eats lightly, and uses cold water from a pump. Wearing only two white cotton saris and washes her own laundry and dishes. The sisters use only the electricity that is absolutely needed. When people ask her where they can help she urges them to start in their homes and neighbor-hoods. To say a word of kindness to your children, spouse, or to God. Mother Teresa loved Jesus and lived the joy of the resurrection in her life and work. She taught that Jesus is the bread of life, our hope, joy, peace, and love. She truly believed by helping the poorest of the poor she was showing her love for Jesus. This is the basis of her spirituality and what makes her spiritual commitment to God. Mother Teresa was an angel of comfort to people who were overlooked in society. There are times when God reveals himself in a particular person and his powerful message of love is revealed. Mother Teresa stands for what many people admire in Christianity. A spiritual vision and the love in her heart to see it through. (50)

Whether you participate in organized religion or wish to have a more joyful individualized spirituality in your daily life learning about the ten laws of healing. Elizabeth Lesser is the cofounder and senior advisor of the Omega Institute in Rhinebeck, New York. She has professional training in Holistic Health, psychology and religion. Without your conscious awareness, your body continues to perform the miracle of healing in an invisible way. Spiritual healing is a way of aligning our consciousness and will with the human body's innate ability to mend and regenerate. Spiritual healing is an investigation into the workings of the body in health and disease. People need to look deeper than curing a symptom and investigate healing the whole body. The First Law of healing is: We want to care for the things we love. It would be difficult to heal something you don't like. Without respect and reverence for your body you will not nurture it. You take care of a pet or child because you love it. A person must learn to love their own body and listen to what it needs. An intuitive understanding of the body makes this more successful. The Second Law: The body remembers. Your body remembers your personal history. Storing memories of childhood, shame, trauma, and abuse. People are often teased as a child for being uncoordinated, or fat, skinny, short or tall. People often build up physical defenses against childhood wounding. Meditation, bodywork, with psychotherapy are often helpful. Practicing forgiveness, gratitude, and love are needed on the path to healing. The Third Law: Separate body image from body reality. People often have an unobtainable image of the "perfect body." Instead of focusing on diets, face lifts, workout programs, learn to appreciate what is working inside of our bodies. Showing appreciation and gratitude for your body is a healthy choice. The Fourth Law: Come into animal presence. The interconnectedness of all life celebrates connection through the pleasure of touch, like the sharing of food, the nourishing of relationships, the protection of life. Part of this is somatic perception where each person has the capacity to know what is best for our own body. Somatic perception is the ownership of healing that we take away from an expert and give it back to our body. Our inner wisdom tells us what to eat and how much, how much to exercise, when to heal and how to heal. Healing is instinctual when we stop trying to fix or control the body. Shamanic cultures say we enter into dreams when we slow down, rest or retreat with nature. Our body can't tell us what we need when we skip sleep, use stimulants and relaxants to make it through the day. The body loves good food, good medicine, exercise, and the body loves to rest, sleep, and dream. The Fifth Law: Listen to the body. Develop a trust with listening to your body and its inner wisdom. When a person fears illness and tries to prevent it or rush to cure it, you are not listening to the body. The body wants to be healthy, but it can be overwhelmed by too much outside treatment. The Sixth Law: Understand the mind/body connection. Sixty to ninety percent of all visits to the doctor are stress related conditions and are poorly treated by conventional medicine. Transcendental meditation and prayer meditation that uses repetition to quiet the thinking process are measurable in causing changes such as lower blood pressure, respiration and brain-wave activity. The Seventh Law: Let energy flow. This law of healing is based on the idea that illness is caused when the body's vital energy system is impeded. This is true of most of the world's healing systems. Chinese medicine calls vital energy Qi and the ancient Indian system of yoga and Ayurveda is called Prana. In the Western world life energy is called the Breathe of life, the Universal life energy, and the electromagnetic field. Our life energy circulates through the body, warming us, protecting us against illness, and giving us vitality. Finding where the body is out of balance and where the energy has stopped flowing is the path to correcting the system. Yoga is helpful and evidence proves this system has been around for at least 3000 years. Other systems are Polarity therapy, Reiki, Therapeutic Touch and Massage Techniques. (51)

The Eighth Law: Be a skeptical explorer. To bring the body back to a healthy spiritual state we run the risk of irrational healing practices. This can be a waste of time, and harmful. So the eighth law says trust in God but do your research. Investigate all forms of healing practical, scientific, and natural ways of healing. The Ninth Law: Get support. The healing power of human support and intimacy has proved to be a major force in healing the patient. Groups, friends and love relationships have a powerful effect on our bodies. It is important to make your primary love relationship as consciously healing as you possible can. Attempt an atmosphere of openness, compassion, acceptance, and commitment.

Stress and loneliness create a harmful life to promote healing. Hostility in the family and a spiteful marriage and an ugly divorce wear on the nerves and body. The Tenth Law: Take responsibility but give up control: People need to set boundaries for energy to flow and for their own personal protection. Take responsibility for your health but you cannot control all of the twists and turns in life. Sometimes we have to surrender the outcome to a higher power. Healing is a complex process of needing doctors, medicine, exercise, food, pleasure, friends, values, and time. People can learn new skills of self-healing abilities at any age. (52)

There are ways to nourish our Soul such as setting time aside each day for meditation. Let go of our social identity that we have created and be open to new ideas. Integrate the aspects of our being through meditation with spiritual study. This is helpful in discovering your unique strengths and weaknesses. Learn to fall in love with the Soul that is inside of your human body. Jog your spiritual memory each day that you are a Soul. When we create rituals they are often a comfort to us such as blessings at meal-time, giving thanks for all we have, honoring your ancestors. Slow down and take time to rest and sleep more. The Soul is sensed more when we are relaxed in peaceful pleasures. Grudges block the energy and sometimes we must pray for God to help us forgive the people who have hurt us. Faith often helps us to remove the barriers in our life and go on to a brighter future. Leaning on God and know he has a plan for your life. The obstacles you are faced with are sometimes being used by God to produce an incredible blessing. With the leading of the Holy Spirit, through the release of the healing blessing, God can come into your present circumstances. A movement of the Holy Spirit can be directed toward your healing needs. Pain is discomfort created by disorder in your body, in your relationships, your finances or anywhere in your life. God allows us to feel, in the spirit, some of the things that are of burden. The Holy Spirit is there to say: do not accept your present situation as your permanent situation. Adversity always affects you. It slows you down physically and drains you mentally and emotionally. The simplest things become major ordeals. Your biggest weakness is the Father's greatest opportunity to reveal his love and power to you. The present storm can pass as God opens doors for you, to fulfill his purpose in your life. Personal matters, which presently oppress you, can be transformed, through your faith in God, into your blessing of fulfillment and spiritual growth. Never run from a battle, because the next event God has planned may be your crown of victory. Look up from the storm and let faith change you from a prisoner of your circumstances into a creator of your circumstances. When you honor God's word you can release special blessing power in your life. (53)

John 3, Ch. 1:2. "Dear Friend, I pray that you may enjoy good health and that all may go well with you. Even as your soul is getting along well." (54)

Edgar Cayce was known throughout America as the Sleeping Prophet. He had an ability to put himself into a self-induced sleep state and place his mind with all time and space. He was a devoted Sunday-School teacher, gardener, and medical clairvoyant. People would ask him questions and he gave answers which are documented as readings. He provided help on subjects such as how to maintain a well- balanced diet, improve human relationships, how to overcome life-threatening illnesses and experience a closer walk with God. Many of these readings were taken down by a stenographer and are on file at the Association for Research and Enlightenment, Inc. (A.R.E.) in Virginia Beach, Virginia. This is the most massive collection of psychic information ever obtained from one source. The organization makes available a large collection of Edgar Cayce Books, New Age Books, Self-Help books and Metaphysical Books. The Cayce readings have also given insights into Judaism which have been verified after his death. (55)

Dr. Herbert Puryear received his Ph.D. from the University of North Carolina and his B.A. from Stanford University. He is an acknowledged authority on Cayce's work and is Director of Research Services for the Association for Research and Enlightenment in Virginia Beach, Virginia. Dr. Puryear was given a great opportunity to study the work of Edgar Cayce and has knowledge of scientific study of parapsychology and comparative studies of religions at Stanford University. (56)

Everyday people make decisions with our families and others. This is with our mental and spiritual attitudes. Man searches for knowledge and turn's to many authorities such as Aristotle's Divine Interpretation, the Bible, personal experience and the physical senses, by reason and findings of scientific research. Our civilization is deeply influenced by philosophies that maintain all knowledge is originated in the outer world and comes through the senses, as this is scientific knowledge. Edgar Cayce was an exceptional individual who presented solid evidence that any kind of information may be obtained from within. Since we are all Souls we each have the psychic ability to go within and find the answers and solutions to our problems. When Edgar Cayce speaks of his work as being psychic or of the soul, he is referring to all peoples being children of God with a spiritual nature. (57)

Psalms 82:6 "Ye are Gods: and all of you are the children of the Most High." (58)

Edgar Cayce was able to connect to his subconscious mind and go up to the Superconscious or Divine Mind in a consistent manner almost at will. He talked about religion as forms and structures such as organizations, belief systems, dogmas, constructs, rituals and procedures. Spirituality refers to the one energy of God, the life force, and the motivational qualities of the individual who gives expression to this force. This one force of the Spirit is a force of life, light, and love. The force quickens us as individual humans to relate to our motivations, our ideals, purposes, intentions and desires. If the spirit of love is flowing through us we will manifest in our attitudes and actions love to ourselves and others. Religions all over the world have their own religious structures and various denominations. These groups work in different ways such as television preaching, community ministries, publications, rituals, creeds, dogmas, doctrines and belief systems. Being religious and being spiritual are not the same. Religion can sometimes cut off the flow of spirit through us. Many people also think they can be spiritual without the limiting forms of religions. This can also cut them off from the spirit of God. Both form and spirit are needed in a proper relationship to one another. In Cayce's readings: "The spirit is the life, mind is the builder, and the physical is the result." He described our earth experience as three-dimensional. One of the dimensions is space with manifestations described as form, materiality, projection, and structure. Cayce states that when spirit and force manifest on the earth plane. It will always be in some form of patterning. (59)

So we need form for Spirit to manifest on earth. Spirit and form are both necessary for our spiritual growth on the earth plane. When we inflate form with concept's, ideas, belief systems, ideas, dogmas, doctrines, organizations, ritual techniques, procedures, policies and traditions. We may become too rigid in our religions that we cut ourselves off from the Spirit that gives life to the religion. We then fail to make an attunement to spirit and fail in service to others. We don't want to cut ourselves off from organizations or churches, as we do not want to become fanatical forcing our beliefs on others. When we cut ourselves off from certain religious structures or have been discouraged by them. We may cut ourselves off from spiritual heritages that house great souls on this plane and beyond. We must look at the long term growth in our communities and make friends with others that have similar ideas to our own. Our children learn in Sunday -School classes and share in activities with their peers. People come to see there is truth in all teachings and we are able to learn from offering viewpoints. Mankind often seeks to belong to the special organization or church that will guarantee salvation. People also seek results in the best meditation techniques or teachers, and we engage in rituals that will make us right with God. We also look for the secret or mantra that will give us what we want. This behavior has continued for thousands of years. (60)

Edgar Cayce made a strong distinction between ideas and ideals. We cannot all have the same ideas but we need to have the same ideals. One day all souls in our solar system will need to have the same ideals. Problems arise when people foster narrowness, exclusiveness, and holier than thou attitudes towards others. We cannot require others to have our beliefs, or hold a judgmental attitude toward others when they are different. If mankind is ever to love his neighbor it will be by sharing the same ideals not the same ideas. Every person is unique and God works through imperfect channels. With this in mind we need to view our religious organizations as opportunities to serve and build love. We must remember just because a person is a great spiritual leader and maybe nationally effective does not mean he has been approved by God.

Just as there are many ministers and not everyone is ordained by God to be a minister. This is also where spirituality leads us to the great commandment as an ideal for all to love your neighbor as ourselves, and God. The Spirit of God is a force of love, life and law. (61)

The Holy Scripture tells us: Psalm 107: 20-21 "He sent forth his word and healed them; he rescued them from the grave." "Let them give thanks to the Lord for his comforting love and his wonderful deeds of men." Each time you are alone in the presence of God, inward fear will diminish, and divinely ordered courage will grow. This divine courage makes you different from the people that are unaware of God's amazing power that works through your faith. The Bible is a connection to God through his word, it makes no difference what version is used the Holy Spirit can interpret the meaning into your life. What is important is that you are not alone, when God gets involved miracles happen, and dreams come true. Your reaction to Gods message is documented in Heaven. Your respect and honor to your Heavenly Father's words open his heart and draws favor to his people. (62)

Edgar Cayce is most characterized by his contribution to holistic healing. Healing wasn't just becoming symptom free it is a process of wholeness of at-one-ment, or becoming attuned where the physical and mental are one with the spiritual. The natural state of the soul is to be one with God. This also means one with the Universe, our neighbors, and within ourselves. All of us need healing and to be in accord with which each person was created. We are God's children and we were created out of his desire for companionship. We were also meant to be co-creators with him. For us to be whole we need to be companionable with him. We were meant to truly be channels for his spirit. This is a creative expression of being whole and well. Unless we are actively manifesting these functions we are not being our true selves. Our blood vessels must be healthy and carry blood as our muscles must be strong and our joints moving. Our bodies are made for wondrous functioning in attunement with God. The Edgar Cayce readings tell us that all illness comes from sin, whether we like it or not. Then we must understand what real sin involves. Sin is simple disobedience or irrelevant moralism. There are Universal laws that by our free will and actions we place ourselves in harmony with these laws. When we are working out of harmony with the whole, we move into sin. That disharmony is built into our own being, physically, mentally, spiritually, and manifests in illness. Our healing begins when our desires and choices, are in the harmony with the whole. Cayce revealed that holistic healing results from balances, integrated, and properly, times physical, mental, and spiritual applications toward wholeness. This is not a routine of therapeutic modalities, or treatments. Cayce would instruct people to do a certain application for a period of time. When it was completed to start a new application. This was a holistic approach that considers time and sequence. This is the same principle as do not give a plant all the water that it will need at one time. Spiritual healing is a path that acknowledges God as the source of all healing and that healing comes through the Spirit from within our own being. We attune to the Spirit within and consider our purpose, intent, desire, motivation, and ideas. Edgar Cayce would ask people why they wanted to be healed and would they change their lifestyles to stay well. To be healed people needed to desire to change the patterns that led to the illness. Our desire to be healed should also be that we want to serve God with all of our hearts. Spiritual healing can then happen as we change our desires, purposes, and ideals wanting to draw to God and act as a channel for the flow of the Holy Spirit. Cayce also states that spiritual healing is characterized as an imbalance of the rotary forces of the atoms of our bodies. Healing involves taking away or adding to the forces about the atoms. The system that brings about the most changes in the body in the endocrine system. When quickened, attuned, and aligned and working with the higher centers such as the pituitary glands they may send out hormonal messages to the cells of the body, awakening and instructing them as to their proper functioning. Cells also respond to the molecules and atoms within each cell. Transformations in our bodies take place at the subatomic level, within the atom. (63)

This entering energy brings the vibratory forces into proper balance. This is where creation takes place according to Cayce. The glands of the endocrine system are termed spiritual centers, or sensors and are attuned to energies of other dimensions. A pattern exists such as the Law written within that we may enter into the very presence of the Creative Forces within ourselves. This is the source of healing for ourselves and others. When this pattern is raised as a channel to heal others, the channel becomes a magnet to attune or raise the attunement of the person who is seeking healing. Healing can come from prayer, meditation, or the laying on of hands. The channel is helping the person who seeks help in attuning to the Spirit within himself. When prayer is sincere healing is more than we can imagine. The laying –on-of-hands is highly recommended by Cayce's readings. If the recipient has enough faith there may be an instant healing. Although there are cases where healing is needed over a period of time. There is a pattern within each of us to be whole mentally and to function in a normal manner. These patterns in the body can be awakened in the higher centers of the body. Using patterns of imagery can awaken the mind. For the mind to be healed it must be uplifted, have a deep appreciate of others and self, as well as the continuance of forgiveness of others and our own mistakes. People need to have a healthy sense of humor. Music in our lives is a holistic approach to healing. The human voice can also be a tool for healing. The power of suggestion is strongly recognized in Cayce's readings and encouraged. Hypnosis and self-hypnosis is quick to help in the healing process. Deep meditation can raise our minds to find the creative forces themselves. Whatever the method of healing, a massage, or a castor oil pack, or a glass of water, the mind must be properly focused in a positive manner. (64)

Physical application for healing must be done consistently. Healing is characterized by circulation, as- simulation, rest, and elimination. Circulation includes exercise, massage, and adjustments. As-simulation is the belief that foods must be eaten in balanced combination with adequate amounts of water. Rest is needed to be healthy with time for recuperation, relaxation, and recreation. Eliminations are a proper diet, high colonics such as enema therapy, natural laxatives, and steamy baths, and other forms of hydrotherapy. Cayce's readings state that osteopathy healing should be a basis for all physical healing. Osteopathy is the adjusting of the spine and improving blood circulation. Adjustments provide an incentive for circulation to remove any blockages on the nerve forces. Massage helps the lymphatic system of the body. The application of oils to the body actually enhances the flow of the life forces in the body. Holistic healing is an awakening of the desire to be whole and inviting the Spirit to flow through for a higher purpose. We dwell upon this with the ideal of the mind. It is important to have a thorough healing rather than a quick healing. People must have patience or there is no soul growth and there is not a true healing. We must live as one with the Spirit of God. (65)

Edgar Cayce read the Bible from cover to cover every year of his life. His personal life was one of self-sacrifice. His work was Christ-centered supporting the work of Jesus. Cayce did not make any claims of the information he provided others, as he just wanted to help people. People from all denominations and religions, and many without any religious ties sought his help. His work was not accepted by the church because he spoke of reincarnation. We must remember that the Old Testament prophets, The New Testament apostles, and Jesus himself were rejected by the religious leaders of their times. There were people who rejected Cayce's readings as a challenge to spiritual growth. Cayce's readings addressed the differences in the mystical, the occult, and the psychic. The mystical experience is the awareness of Oneness. The occult is the use of the mind's powers without respect to purposes. The psychic is of the Soul, and the Spirit works through the individual and manifesting its gifts. (66)

There is a richness in discovering the Churches traditional versions of the Sacred Scriptures. The Clementine Vulgate was proclaimed the official Latin Bible of the Church after the Reformation. Educated Catholics throughout the world were familiar with the Vulgate. The Douay Rheims Bible is a beautiful translation of the Bible, having both the English translation and the Latin side by side. It is not difficult to understand and it is fairly easy to get through the passages and pick up a little bit of Latin. The Douay Rheims Bible has been used in the Church for over 1500 years, translated from the original Hebrew and Greek by St. Jerome (A.D. 340-420). In 1546, the Council of Trent declared the Vulgate Bible as authentic, in the 4th Session April 8, 1546. In 1943, Pope Pius XII stated that the continuous use of it made the Bible, "free from any error whatsoever in matters of faith and morals." (Divino Afflante

Spirtu (1943), paragraph 21). The preface states that at the Heart of the Christian faith stands the "Word made flesh", the incarnate Son of God, Jesus Christ. The Preface also tells us that the Old Testament prepared us for the coming of Christ through prophesy. The Church stands on this Bible as "All sacred Scripture is but one book, and that one book is Christ, because divine Scripture speaks of Christ, and all divine Scripture is fulfilled in Christ." Because of this the church has always instructed its children to read the Bible. This draws us closer to know the person of Jesus Christ more clearly. The Septuagint Old Testament and Koine Greek versions of the New Testament books served Greek speaking Christians. At the end of the second century individual books of the Bible were translated into Latin. Pope Damasus I (A.D. 384) in the fourth century, was a reforming Pope who decreed the canon of Scripture in the Catholic Church. He commissioned Saint Jerome to revise the Old Latin Bible to produce the Vulgate. Jerome drew upon the Septuagint and the Old Hebrew manuscripts, and the Greek Version of the Symmachus. The Vulgate has had much influence on the Western Culture. Since then translations have occurred such as a German Bible in 1466, Luther's New Testament appeared in 1522 and by then at least 16 editions of the Bible in German. An Italian Bible in 1471, and a Spanish Bible in 1478. The same year France had a New Testament that had been printed. The Bible was later translated into the King James Version of 1611. The New International Disciples Study Bible that I have used for years lacks the last six and a half chapters of Esther and has lost others books of the Bible. The Douay Rheims has been revised four times since its original version due to language changes in the people. (67)

Esther Ch. 16: 16 "And are the children of the highest and the greatest, and the ever living God, by whose benefit the kingdom was given both to our fathers and to us, and is kept unto this day." (68)

President Lorenzo Snow served as the President of the Church of Jesus Christ of Latter-day-Saints from September13 1838, to October 10 1901. Elder Lorenzo Snow was 21 years old when he met Elder Patten of the Church of Jesus Christ of Latter-day-Saints and felt a prick on his heart that had such a spiritual power that it would last his entire life. Oliver Snow married Rosetta Lenora Pettibone on May 6 1800.

They were both descendants of some of the earliest European settlers in the United States. English Pilgrims that had crossed the Atlantic Ocean in the 1600s to escape religious persecution. The family moved from Massachusetts to Mantua, Ohio into a settlement making them the eleventh family to move to this area. In June of 1836 Lorenzo Snow the son of Oliver and Rosetta was baptized by Elder John Boynton, one of the original members of the Quorum of the Twelve Apostles in this dispensation and was confirmed a member of the church. Lorenzo Snow knelt and prayed one night wanting to receive a special manifestation of the Holy Spirit and received a perfect knowledge that there was a God, that Jesus, who died upon Calvary, was his Son, and that Joseph Smith was a Prophet and had received the authority which he professed to have. This experience changed his world to testify to the whole world that by positive knowledge the Gospel of the Son of God had been restored. Joseph Smith was a Prophet of God whom God authorized to speak in his name. This experience strengthened him to become a missionary and he began his service in the state of Ohio in the spring of 1837. In his first meeting he got up to speak and the Holy Ghost rested on him with a message, filling his mind with light and communicating ideas and proper language to impart them. By the time he had left this area he had baptized and confirmed several people. (69)

Elder Snow's desire to preach the gospel led him to preach in Missouri, Kentucky, and Illinois. Elder Snow left for England to serve as a missionary for about four months. Many people were leaving Europe for the United States of America. Elder Snow administered the laying on of hands to an injured man on the ship Swanton and the man was healed. The sailors swore that it was a miracle. This in turn caused many of them to receive the gospel and become baptized. Plural marriages were accepted at this time and Elder Snow married two women, and later additional women. These pioneers made their way to Salt Lake Valley and Elder Snow was also called to serve as an Apostle of the Quorum of the twelve. The Prophet Joseph Smith claimed to have received a vision regarding plural marriage and felt that marriage was a commandment from the Lord. That marriage was an essential part of the heavenly Fathers plan of happiness. (70)

The ordination to the apostleship defined the rest of his life. An Apostle must possess a divine knowledge, by revelation from God, that Jesus lives and that he is the son of the living God. The second thing an Apostle must do is obey the Holy Ghost in revealing the things God makes known about his will and purposes. This must be leading by all truths and showing things to come as declared by the Savior. The third thing is to administer the sacred ordinances of the Gospel. President Lorenzo Snow is best known for his revelation on the Law of Tithing he received in May 1899. He shared this revelation to the members that the church should be built upon a strong financial foundation and to do the will of the Lord and pay tithes in full. Elder Snow promised the members that this would bring spiritual blessings and enable the church to break free from indebtedness. This revelation changed everything for the Church of Christ financially, from darkness to light. When Elder Snow prayed he would lift his hands and invoke the blessings of heaven upon the inhabitants of the earth. The idea of Mormonism is improvement mentally, physically, morally and spiritually. He believed that whatever experience and knowledge we gain upon the earth we take with us in the world to come. This learning requires faith, exertion, and perseverance, and the more knowledge and intelligence a person gains will be the greater advantage. We must gain knowledge before we can attain permanent happiness. Then, being enlightened by the gift and power of the Holy Ghost, we get the ideas and intelligence and blessings to prepare us for the future. This process can preserve the Saints from much trouble and vexation, gaining wisdom and intelligence day by day. Every circumstance which transpires may minister to our good and build our faith in the Lord God. People need an education of the Spirit. Spiritual knowledge is a great deal better than mere opinions, notions and ideas. Advancing ourselves in the principles of light and knowledge should be considered while we seek worldly wealth. Our minds must not be so one-sided in paying too much attention to acquiring earthly goods, to the neglect of spiritual wealth. People benefit from hearing gospel principles over and over again. When we gather to learn the gospel we need the guidance of the spirit. This is our privilege and our duty, for we have not come to earth accidentally. Jesus Christ set the example for us when he was baptized by immersion. In those days there was an order of the apostles to hear the gospel, belief on Jesus Christ, repentance, baptism by immersion for the remission of sins, and the laying on of hands for the reception of the Holy Ghost. When this order was understood and properly followed, power, gifts, blessings, and glorious privileges followed immediately. Baptism and the ordinance of laying on of hands should be done by one who has divine authority. This process opens a door that no man on earth can shut. The Holy Spirit communicates the mind of God to man. (71)

Mark 16:15-18. "He said to them, 'Go into all the world and preach the good news to all creation. Whoever believes and is baptized will be saved, but whoever does not believe will be condemned. And these signs will accompany those who believe: In my name they will drive out demons; they will speak in new tongues, they will pick up snakes with their hands; and when they drink deadly poison, it will not hurt them at all; they will place their hands on sick people and they will get well." (72)

John 3:5-8. "Jesus answered, I tell you the truth, no- one can enter the kingdom of God unless he is born of water and the Spirit. Flesh gives birth to flesh, but the Spirit gives birth to spirit. You should not be surprised at my saying. You must be born again. The wind blows wherever it pleases. You hear its sound, but you cannot tell where it comes from or where it is going. So it is with everyone born of the Spirit." (73)

Acts 2:38-39. "Peter replied, Repent and be baptized, every one of you, in the name of Jesus Christ for the forgiveness of your sins. And you will receive the gift of the Holy Spirit. The promise is for you and your children and for all who are far off, for all whom the Lord our God will call." (74)

The apostles before us are examples of faith and repentance before baptism and then the laying on of hands to receive the Holy Ghost. John the Baptist at Aenon because there was much water. So if sprinkling had been the mode all of Judea could have stayed where they were without performing a journey to Aenon. He baptized in the Jordan and afterwards the ordinances were administered to our Savior. To be buried with Christ would require to be completely covered in water. This also signifies being placed in the womb of waters and being brought forth again. There are several instances where Christ laid his hands upon the sick and healed them. This is where the example of laying on of hands comes to receive Gods heavenly blessings. President Snow taught about Christ in his commission to the apostles about the supernatural gifts that will be received that are fruits of the Holy Ghost. The supernatural gifts were the gifts of tongue, prophecy, and to lay hands upon the sick, by which they should be healed. With their gifts no person should have to rely on the knowledge of other people to the truth of religion, but should seek the truth for our self. So a person should not walk in darkness, but in the light and power of Gods free men. When we place ourselves under divine guidance we can enjoy happiness. He promotes to live humbly on our onward path and always have the Spirit of the lord to be your friend. The Holy Spirit can enable us to receive knowledge and suggestions that will help us on our onward path. Because we have divinity within us, we can become like our Father in Heaven, as we are all born in the image of God our Father. In our spiritual birth our Father transmitted to us the capabilities, powers and faculties which he himself possessed. As sons and daughters of God, we have the capacity for infinite wisdom and knowledge. The spiritual organism within the tabernacle or physical body has a divinity in itself that must be developed for improvement and advancing. As we have divinity within ourselves, we also have immortality within ourselves. The spiritual organism cannot be destroyed or annihilated. We will live from all eternity to all eternity. The gospel binds together the hearts of all who read and study the principles, with no difference between the rich and the poor. We have to reach a higher plane and love God more than we love the world. The law of the Gospel is honest and faithful in calling men and women to the everlasting Covenant. Who has any greater power or prospect than this? We are the children of the same Heavenly Father in the celestial worlds, and we have been sent into this world to bring goodness to one another for all time. Our happiness increases when we help other find happiness, as when we sacrifice for the good of others, we get heaven within us. We are all dependent upon Jesus Christ coming into the world to open the way and teach us the path, whereby we might secure peace, happiness and exaltation. (75)

The Church of Latter-day-Saints is still in existence today with the same mission as long ago, to bring souls to Jesus Christ. The same message of the angel in the fields that told the shepherds a Savior was born, Christ the Lord. The Mormons make Christmas cards to send to missionaries, single and elderly members. They volunteer with local community organizations, and give out copies of the Book of Mormon as gifts to all that will accept. Children follow the light to get to Jesus is still the sacred message. The Mormon Church is a Christian restorationist church that is considered to be a restoration of the original church founded by Jesus Christ. It is still headquartered in Salt Lake City, Utah, and has wards all over the world. It has over 85,000 missionaries and a membership of over 15 million. The National Council of Churches ranks the Latter-Day-Saints denomination as the fourth-largest Christian denomination in the United States. (76)

Chapter 3

HEALING TECHNIQUES

G enesis Ch. 9:12-16 "And God said, "This is the sign of the covenant" I am making between me and you and every living creature with you, a covenant for all generations to come: I have set my rainbow in the clouds, and it will be the sign of the covenant between me and the earth. Whenever I bring clouds over the earth and the rainbow appears in the clouds. I will remember my covenant between me and you and all living creatures of every kind. Never again will the waters become a flood to destroy all life. Whenever the rainbow appears in the clouds, I will see it and remember the everlasting covenant between God and all living creatures of every kind on the earth." (77)

Throughout the ages color has been associated with symbolism and ancient lore in the rituals of the church. Roger Lewis, an artist examined color symbolism and the science of color. He also studied Edgar Cayce's interpretation of various colors of a person's aura. Cayce's readings associated various colors with the seven spiritual centers in the body. Many theories have been written on the subject of how to use color for healing. People also use color for personality identification. Color harmony also relates to our wearing apparel and the environment. Psychologists and psychiatrists use color in the analysis of mental illness. There observations deal basically with the negative or destructive personality traits and emotions. We cannot live without color as it is all around us. Psychologists tell us that tasks which require muscular effort are best performed in an environment of warm colors because they stimulate and speed up the pulse. When a task involves mental concentration a calm atmosphere of tranquil blues and greens will be best. Colors can be separated into two basic groups. The vibrant red-orange-yellow group and the passive calm blue-green group. Individuals in the first color group are more likely to be extroverts which are easily influenced, impressionable, and social. The second group have more of an attitude of detachment. They show greater interest in themselves than in the world around them. These individuals are naturally quit, and more introspective. Introverts and conservative people often prefer blue, while extroverts prefer red. Intellectual people often choose yellow and well-balanced individuals choose green. Artistic or what is called ambiverts thrive on Purple. People react to color at an unconscious level and acknowledge color symbolism in the idioms of our language. Such as becoming entangled or feeling blue. The stop sign is painted red and also a sign of danger. Yellow is a color of caution or quarantine. People mourn in black associate green with medicine and purple with the law. We do not think about how much color influences our day to day existence. Scientists have found that humans receive all knowledge of the universe through electromagnetic radiation. What our eyes see is only a narrow band of the electromagnetic spectrum. The nature of light acts in a pattern of long and short waves. Electromagnetic radiation, or light fills space and is affected by powerful gravitational fields. Light can be bent or refracted, and reflects into the colors of the rainbow, causing violet, indigo, blue, green, yellow, orange, and red. (78)

Color does not actually exist, the energy is real but what we perceive is an illusion of energy. This is a sensation in our consciousness as what we see with our eyes is not the object, but various wavelengths of light, traveling at the same rate of speed being reflected from the light. The object is actually colorless. Some of the wave lengths are absorbed by the object while others are reflected. Man is surrounded by color and has a love for it. People express their emotions through color in every aspect of life. Color relates to both divine and human meaning, mysticism, the riddles of life and death and the ways of creation. We do know that all living things are reflected by visible light and color in one way or another. Visible light is necessary for the growth of plant life. Growth is restrained by ultraviolet and infrared wavelengths. Edgar Cayce readings tell us that the colors in relation to the seven endocrine glands allow us a choice that we can use each color vibration constructively or destructively. We can use color vibrations in harmony with the creative forces or use it for selfish reasons. Cayce's book on Auras is characteristic of the vibration of matter and our souls reflect it in the three- dimensional world through atomic patterns. People are patterns and project colors which are there for those who can see them. His readings reflect that the Creator himself is light and creative vibration. We can use this creative energy in a positive way or a negative way. Vibration is from the same source it is how we choose to manifest this vibration. Scientist are close to admitting that vibration and God are the same as they tell us that all knowledge of the universe is received through electromagnetic radiation. Cayce's readings state that creative vibration is God. (79)

Light that comes from within is not from the Sun or the Moon, but rather from the Son of Man. When that light is found and activated the Soul can express itself in any part of the universe. Within the physical body are seven glandular centers. The pituitary, the pineal, the thyroid, the thymus, the adrenals, and the gonads. Color and vibration move through the individuals centers when in meditation. Psychologists have devised tests such as the Luscher Color Test to chart a person's attitudes and emotions. The tests are believed to be able to mirror the individuality and personality. When the mental body is in perfect harmony with the Creative Forces the colors reach each center in the body in pure form. When light vibrations are received by the mind the first movement is to the pituitary gland. This gland has a controlling influence over the other endocrine glands. This is where the influence is of through which the old men may dream dreams and the young see visions. This gland is opened through meditation. The vibration of violet is changed to golden. This process works through the acceptance of the ways of the Creative forces. Our faults and inadequacies are overcome and the seven spiritual centers return to their original purposes and overcome the world. Wisdom is gained through the purification of the vibration of the seven centers as they become golden. Cayce's readings also tell us that the thymus gland is kept active in love and faith, there will be an abundance of white blood cells. The epithelial cells guard the body and keep it free from disease. When we neglect the community to love others as we love ourselves, the gland will fall from use. (80)

Selfishness is a sin and we must make a positive choice to love others so this gland will properly function. This gland activates the process to immunize the physical, mental and spiritual bodies against all disease. Growth, Forgiveness, and Opportunities come from love. The positive use of the color bright yellow can lead to the regeneration of cells and perfect emotional harmony. The positive traits of yellow are creativeness, inventiveness, constructivism, endless energy, forcefulness, powerfulness, courage, self-confidence, and strength of character. Without the motion of light or color we would have no awareness of the appearance of matter. It is said that all knowledge exists in the universe mind-force of light as an extension of God. We must become one with him to attain this knowledge. The body responds to color forces as it does to medicinal properties. The Creative Forces give us light to be in harmony with ourselves and with others, and so we may grow and evolve. To aid in the healing process a person needs to surround themselves in color and apply himself to the meditative process. (81)

Prayer is a concentrated technique of a promise necessary for the continuation of the covenant. God's faithfulness is absolute. We can find his fulfillment of this in 2 Chronicles 7:13-16 as he speaks to Solomon. The Lord appeared to him at night and said: "I have heard your prayer and have chosen this place for myself as a temple for sacrifices. When I shut up the heavens so that there is no rain, or command locusts to devour the land or send a plague among my people, if my people, who are called by my name, will humble themselves and pray and seek my face and turn from their wicked ways then will I hear from heaven and will forgive their sin and will heal their land. Now my eyes will be open and my ears attentive to the prayers offered in this place. I have chosen and consecrated this temple so that my Name may be there forever. My eyes and my heart will always be there." (82)

Alexander Lake had a fascination with prayer and if people's prayers were really answered. This became a life-long hobby of collecting prayer stories. His search began with discussions son to father as his father

Dr. John G. Lake was a missionary in Johannesburg, South Africa. Dr. John Lake was a treasure chest of true stories about prayer techniques for his son. One of his stories was about a farmer named Du Bois in French Equatorial Africa who had lost everything he owned as the desert encroached on his fertile acres. The situation seemed hopeless as his neighbors all fled the area. Du Bois stayed and prayed in faith for God to deliver him. Within a month poisonous snakes swarmed all over his land, and his family was afraid for their lives. Dubois prayed for a second time for an answer to his situation. Soon he learned to handle cobra snakes safely, and within two years he began to make a comfortable income selling venom to be used in making anti-snake-bite serum. Dubois's finances had been healed and many people are healed by the product that is made from what was at first glance a scary situation. The wisdom of God can transform any situation when we pray in faith. (83)

John and Jesse Fernald were both in there fifties and sold their Ontario farm when they saw a three-acre field on southern Oregon's coastal strip. They planted daffodil bulbs in hopes of harvesting them for a living. Heavy rains hit with thirty-four inches of rain in seventeen days. The daffodil crop was lost and Jessie Fernald began to pray over a fire that John made out of driftwood. Soon they realized they had a beach full of driftwood and came up with a process to make colored logs burn in people's fireplaces. This was a long process and they sold ferns that had grown on a hillside that the rains caused to flourish. The land also had a hidden treasure of wild huckleberry. John and Jesse learned that the answer to prayer does not come in a single revelation, but God reveals his plans to us as we are able to accept his ideas. The couple learned that no matter how lacking in opportunities an area may seem, God has an abundance there. We must pray for him to reveal and heal our situations in faith. (84)

Ovid Damasch had attended college in Germany, his family lost their money and he came to America almost penniless. He worked hard and operated a small contracting business, married and had a daughter. They lived at the foot of the Calico Mountains. After Pearl Harbor there was a materials shortage that forced him out of business. He found a job as a rigger in a Richmond, California, shipyard. His daughter became listless and grew weak. The doctors could find nothing wrong with her. Finally one day an old gray-haired physician, a Dr. Danskin, told Tilde, Ovid's wife to take the child to the Mojave Desert and she would get well with sunlight from this area. The old doctor told Ovid there were plenty of abandoned cabins in this area that they could stay in while the child recovered. He was correct and as the child took sunbathes everyday she began to get better. One day the child watched an ant playing and asked her parents for another ant. The father was so glad the daughter was getting better that he built her an ant house. A college student came by and wanted to buy the ant home so Ovid made him one. Orders started coming in for these ant houses and Ovid had an income for two years. This led to a job offer from an Agricultural Division of the United Nations in Germany. Tilde had always prayed, but Ovid realized he had stopped praying and began to pray again. He learned that God goes with us wherever men go and that happiness and security can only be found with God as our partner in life. God worked through the old doctor to bring about a healing for Ovid's daughter. (85)

In the book Mysteries of the Glory unveiled, Evangelist David Herzog talks about Alexander Lake's father Pastor John G. Lake. Pastor John Lake was a healing missionary to South Africa and had an encounter which is documented in his writings. Pastor Lake was alone in his room one night interceding for the healing of a woman who lived in another area. The next day the woman thanked him for coming to her house in the middle of the night to pray for her. This happened in the spirit and the woman was totally healed. He explained to the woman that he had been at home all night, although he was praying for her. The woman claimed she had seen him come into the room, pray for her, and then leave. The woman could not explain it, only knowing she had been healed. (86)

Sitting in a garden is a simple healing technique that brings you into contact with the healing power of nature. We struggle to achieve goals in our business, social, and emotional lives, and need time for relaxation and a place of sanctuary. Gardens, no matter what size, afford a place to release from the pressures of the outside world and helps to create a sense of personal fulfillment. Simple techniques can create real improvements to our environment and help us to lead healthier and happier lives. There is much more to our health than just being well fed and physically fit. The World Health Organization describes this as "the condition of perfect bodily, spiritual and social well-being and not solely the absence of illness and injury." Chronic illnesses and allergies are on the increase as we battle against environmental pollution. Chronic illnesses often considered incurable by conventional medicine most often respond to alternative methods. There is an increased interest in Holistic medicine as people are turning to complementary therapies like Aromatherapy, Feng Shui, Meditation and Herbalism. Cultures all over the world have stressed the importance of balance within the individual for good health. The basis of holistic medicine is rooted in the concept of treating the whole person. Our bodies' biochemistry is closely related to thoughts and emotions. The bodies' hormones, reproductive cycle, sleep pattern, moods, and metabolism are affected by our mental state. The system of endocrine, nervous, and immune, work together. Stress and emotional disharmony upset the balance of their systems. If all disease has negativity behind it then ailments can be cured by reversing the mental patterns that fuel them. A happy mind must be created to replace negative thoughts and emotions. This is done with positive life-affirming ones. Psychological devices such as relaxation and visualization exercises can be of great benefit. (87)

Conventional treatments aim for a speedy suppression of symptoms of illness, and acceptance of unpleasant side effects. Natural healing requires more patience and time for the body to heal itself. A holistic practitioner looks for the causes and the prevention of illness. In order to have a lasting cure the patient needs to accept responsibility for the healing process. A person's thoughts and feelings can be at the root of the problem as diet and environment are not always the influence. Two people with the same illness may have different causes and need to follow a different treatment path. Gardening helps you to get back to basics and provides an escape from everyday problems. Plants also attract wildlife and has a grounding effect on us. We were not designed to be isolated from a natural habitat. Getting into your own garden at every opportunity, day and night, can help you to be aware of changes in light levels and tones, the height of the sun, and the changing of the moon. Time dimension separates garden design from every other art form because gardens are never finished and change through the seasons. Spring is a time of planting seeds, cutting grass and a general clear-out. Summer brings the warmth of the sun and a burst of color. Fall goes out with fiery shades of reds, oranges, golds and russets. Winter has paler shades of green and weaker sunlight, but with a promise of rebirth and better things to come. A beautiful garden must have a caring touch and a person who works with nature rather than against it. (88)

Plants play a role in healing the planet as our gardens are a microcosm of the universe. We are creating improved conditions for the inhabitants of our gardens. Future generations are protected as we do our part in healing the earth. Gardens provide a rich sensory experience, as sight dominates, but other senses are awakened. Sight responds to color therapy, smell in aromatherapy taste in herbalism and holistic gardening. Touch and sound are also important for blind and sound are also important for blind and partially sighted. Touching plants and tree bark are important to gain sensations. Gardens can often provide a refuge from noise pollution. Sounds in the garden begin to come alive and generate a positive mood. Wind-chimes can bring pleasure and instill a feeling of tranquility. The sound of rain is also refreshing as we here a pattering sound. Installing moving water in the garden can create all manner of sounds. A gentle tinkling of a fountain or the gushing of a waterfall can be a pleasurable sound. The movement of wind through trees and shrubs produce refreshing sounds. Birds chirping and Bee's humming are a pleasant sound in a garden. Healthy earth and water are needed to produce healthy plants and support wildlife. We also take our place in the food chain when we grow fruit, vegetable, and herbs. Growing plants can improve air quality as air is affected by dust, fungal spores and pollen. Healing the earth means not using inorganic fertilizers, pesticides, and herbicides that are chemicals. Outdoor wood is pressure treated with creosote that contains heavy metals, copper, chrome, and arsenic that can promote problems in health. Organic gardens often used rich leaf mold and used mushroom compost, banana skins and old leather shoes to provide nutrients to the soil as they rot down. Well -rotted animal manure has always been used for a natural soil fertilizer. Deep mulch compost will also suppress weed growth and retain moisture. (89)

Growing your own edible garden is the only way to capture the true essence of strawberries, tomatoes or peaches which should be eaten straight from the plant. This is the only way to ensure a pesticide free stock of produce. Picking and eating apples or tomatoes is a simple pleasure. A thorn less blackberry or tayberry can be trained to grow across a trellis or over an arch for beauty and a source of food. Another healing technique is the concept of Feng Shui. Feng Shui is rooted in a spiritual practice of Taoism, a religion whose followers acknowledge the power of nature and seek to live in harmony with it. Feng Shui is also a creative and intuitive philosophy that blends common sense with creative design for a more balanced environment. This practice studies the way in which our surroundings affect our well -being, happiness, and success. The location and arrangement of our homes reflects our lives and can shape them, either supporting us or bringing about misfortune. This relates to problems such as global warming, sick building syndrome, and overhead power lines. People look for sites with good energy that will beneficially influence every aspect of life. Bad sites are avoided since they have the potential to bring about disasters including illness, divorce, or financial loss. Feng Shui is a practical way to specifically arrange your immediate environment to improve your life fortunes through an awareness of and alignment with the earth's energy lines. This is an invisible energy referred to as chi or qi, and is present throughout the universe in all living things and inanimate objects. This energy can be detected and utilized for healing. A Feng Shui master uses a special compass, or lou pan to indicate the potential of bath beneficial and harmful influences. Feng Shui also considers topography, psychology, and astrology. Feng Shui changes the way we see things and how we learn to live in harmony instead of conflict with the natural world. Chinese use the term chi or qi to describe the life force of the entire universe. Everything on earth such as water and the heavens has energy with the potential to affect us. We have not learned to measure wind and water as an energy. A balance of plant form, color and texture in a garden represents good or Sheng Chi. Un-kept landscapes with rough or sharp features would represent negative Sha-chi. Sha-chi is a destructive force that is naturally present in cold winds, still, dank air, stagnant water, and poorly drained soil. Fault lines in the earth's crust may also produce Sha-chi. Fast roads, power cables, tunnels, railroad tracks, and drains can also cause Sha-chi. The dualism of natural forces is described as the yin and the yang. This universal force contains both yin and yang energy in varying proportions. So in order for light to exist there must also be darkness. There cannot be heat without cold, as the entire universe has these components. Through their opposing qualities a flow of energy that is created that is a never ending cycle of change. This is a natural rhythm of cycles in life. The yin energy rules winter and the yang governs summer, and the two are balanced at the spring and autumn equinoxes. When the two energies exist in harmony good fortune is produced, as an in-balance occurs it can manifest in a misfortune. An imbalance of rainfall can cause a flood and destroy crops and homes. Severe enough accidents happen and lives may be taken. Chi is said to manifest itself actually and symbolically through the five elements of fire, water, wood, metal, and earth. One must strive to make sure the balance of all five elements is achieved. The central area of a space should be uncluttered, clean and orderly. Water needs to be clean fresh and always moving. This technique uses eight trigrams or Chinese characters of the I Ching. The direction of the compass, planetary influences, the five elements, and an individual's date of birth. It also incorporates a combination of metaphysical speculation, symbolic association, and complex calculation. The Feng Shui of a place is then interpreted through the placement of the Pa Kua symbol, the loshu square which is a magical square. This is an ancient numerological device, and the Chinese compass or luo pan. Each of the eight sectors has a different energy and the house, room or garden is divided into eight areas. Each of the sectors represents a key aspect of life, relationships, wealth, health, education or career. Improvements in one's life can be made by enhancing or strengthening the energy of a sector. (90)

Chinese herbal medicine has been practiced since at least 2500 B.C. and is still used in China today. The fundamental concept is that a life force or energy animates every aspect of the universe and will influence their state of health. The flow of chi around the body channels through meridians and is balanced through such techniques as acupuncture, diet, and herbal medicine. In Chinese medicine the cause of illness is not sought since disease is felt to be an expression of disharmony. This is an imbalance between yin and yang, opposite but complementary principles. Excess yin may present itself as a feeling of cold, dampness, or shivering. When yang predominates a patient may be hot or feverish. Warming herbs such as ginger are used to treat conditions caused by excess cold. Salty water herbs such as Chinese figwort are prescribed for fluid imbalances. Emotional characteristics may be caused by an imbalance of the five elements of wood, fire, earth, metal, water. Wood relates to what are called sour herbs that nourish yin. They refresh, aid in digestion and liver function. There are Chinese dogwood berries, hawthorn berries, rose hips, and schisandra. Fire applies to bitter herbs which are also yin. They are cooling, well drained systems, detoxifying, fight infection, and stimulate the digestion system. The herbs are burdock, dandelion, peony, and Chinese rhubarb. Earth relates to sweet herbs which are yang. They are warm, soothe, act as a tonic, and provide nourishment. These are ginseng, Chinese angelica or dong quai. Metal herbs are spicy and are yang. They have heating and drying properties and will improve circulation, stimulate energy and digestion, and relieve arthritic pain. These are cinnamon, ginger, peppers and cloves. Water herbs are salty and yin. They are cooling and moistening to support the kidneys and maintain fluid balance. These herbs are seaweeds, barley and Chinese figwort. Chinese medicine has gained credibility in the western world where the treatment of some disorders have proved difficult to treat with conventional drugs. An example of this is cases of people with eczema that have responded to herbal treatment. Using the principles of homeopathy plants in the garden may be enough to stimulate the body's self- healing powers. The Chinese have classified 6000 medicinal plants which is the broadest documentation known to man. (91)

The wonderful thing about research is the ancient secrets that you stumble across such as a garden to ward off evil influences. This is a six-pointed star that is an ancient symbol. The planting encloses seven plants which is a traditionally lucky number. Groups of mullein and lavender hedge bring the total number of plants to nine, another sacred number. St John's wart is placed in the center and provides the golden color of the sun, symbolizing the life force of daylight. The Christmas rose is placed in the first section, Vervain in the second section, Heartease in the third, Peony in the fourth, Chamomile in the fifth, Angelica in the sixth, and again the seventh the center St Johns Wart. The plants provide color throughout the ear with a golden gravel path. There are many other shapes and themes that can be built for gardens to enhance your property. (90)

Aromatherapy is a modern name for an ancient practice of practitioners who use essential oils extracted from plants. The principals that were put into place thousands of years ago still apply today. The movement of scent molecules through the body by the circulatory system was noted by the Greek philosopher-physician Theophrastus. Aromatherapy is used to complement other therapies and is used to treat a wide variety of ailments, from Rheumatism, Migraines to stress. Our present day knowledge is based on the use of essential oils in Egypt 5,000 years ago. The ancient Egyptians are regarded as the founders of aromatherapy. They used scented oils in everyday life. The essences from plants we extracted in a crude distillation process and used medicinally, in perfumes and beautifying potions, for massages, as fumigants, in religious ceremonies, as mood-altering incense, and for embalming. Hippocrates advocated a daily aromatic bath and massage to soothe away stresses and strains and to prolong life. The luxury of exotic fragrances was then taken up in Rome. The ancient civilizations of China, India, and Arabia used the fragrant plants before 2000 B.C. and demonstrated the healing properties of plants. The Ayurvedic medicine of India dates back to 1000 B.C. The Middle East and the Persian physician Avicenna is credited with the invention of distillation in the eleventh century. This led to the production of more sophisticated aromatic oils and floral waters used by Arab physicians for therapeutic massage and to scent the air and fight disease. (92)

French chemist, Rene-Maurice Gattefosse' had an accident in his laboratory when he burned his hand. He treated the burn with lavender oil and found the burn healed very quickly. He began to publish books describing the therapeutic properties of essential oils. A French army doctor Jean Valnet, began his own research and during World War II he began treating soldiers suffering from battle wounds and psychiatric disorders. Two Italian doctors in the 1920's demonstrated the sense of smell has a psychotherapeutic influence over the function of the central nervous system. A biochemist Marguerite Maury studied the use of oils when absorbed through the skin. This was the 1950's that she developed the methods used in aromatherapy today. This is a process of diluting essential oils and blending them in individual recipes and applying them through massage. Today biochemists have isolated dozens of active ingredients that account for some of the properties of healing plant essences. In Europe a therapists must also be a doctor with medical qualifications. The study of essential oils is included in many medical schools. In Germany and Switzerland essential oils as a treatment are accepted through health insurance programs. Aromatherapy works with the body and has rare side effects. Scent molecules enter the body through inhalation and/or absorption through the skin. Techniques are massage, bathing, inhalation and vaporization. (93)

Massage Essential Oils must be diluted in a carrier oil such as almond, hazelnut or grapeseed oil. This is to avoid any skin reaction. When bathing essential oils can also be added to a carrier oil and then dropped into the warm bath water. For the inhalation technique add 3 or 4 drops of oils to a large bowl of hot water and then cover your head with a towel. Inhale the vapors for a few moments while keeping your eyes closed. Vaporization essential oils can be used in a variety of burners. Also a few drops can be placed on a cotton ball and placed behind radiators. A scent can have a magical quality conjuring up distant and personal memories. People rarely forget scents as they stir deep emotions within us. We often recollect people, places or events in connection with certain aromas from our past. When inhaled scent molecules are taken into the lungs as they stimulate sensory cells in the upper nasal passage as they pass. These molecules diffuse across the lungs into blood capillaries into the bloodstream. The molecules of scent will tend to gather in specific parts of the body where ailments lie. These molecules are detected through nerve impulses in the area of the brain. The limbic system is on the right side of the brain which is primarily concerned with emotion, intuition, memory, and creativity. Smell is our only sense that has a direct link to this part of the brain. Once an aroma is detected the hypothalamus and pituitary bodies are stimulated to produce a response. There reactions affect the autonomic nervous system and hormonal system that govern heart rate, digestion, feelings of anger, fear and stress. This supports the concept of holistic health where every action, thought, and emotion is linked. A happy state of mind can have healing powers and strengthen our natural immunity. (94)

Medical science can now measure aroma with EEG instruments to record the electrical activity of brain and skin. Scientists have discovered that sweet essences produce alpha, theta, and delta brain wave patterns. Mimosa or chamomile fragrances relax a person and can help them to sleep. Rosemary induces beta brainwaves and produce a state of alertness. Lavender or geranium oils have a balancing effect and either invigorate or sedate according to the person's needs. When an aroma is not liked the body blocks any effect upon the nervous system. Research has demonstrated that the body's response may be ever more profound because the subconscious overrules the conscious mind so that we cannot fight the body's natural reaction. This discovery supports the belief of homeopathy and the Bach flower remedies that a reaction is brought about even when the essence is so diluted that only the energy pattern or vibration of the original matter remains. This means that certain plants just growing in their natural state have an active healing role. Through the release of minute quantities of essential oils through their leaves, flowers, or fruit. (95)

Essential oils are also called essences and are considered to be the life force or the soul of a plant. The oils are also called the DNS or plant hormones. The oils give fragrance to the plants and are used to attract pollinating insects, repel predators, and protect against disease. They are carried in the oil glands of the plant and flow through the petals, leaves, seeds, fruits, roots, bark and stalks of different species. An example of this is the orange tree which produces three entirely separate essences with medicinal properties. The neroli is the flowers, the petrigrain the leaves, and the orange is the rind. The whole plant essence brings about health benefits. A single oil can help with a variety of disorders, such as lavender acts as an antiseptic and an antibacterial, antibiotic, antidepressant, analgesic, decongestant, and sedative. All essential oils have been found to possess antibacterial properties and some are antifungal. Rosemary and Juniper are ant-rheumatic, and stimulate the blood flow and lymphatic circulation. This increases the supply of oxygen to affected areas and aids the elimination of the waste that causes pain. Many of the essential oils are expensive to make as it takes so many flowers to make one drop of the essential oil. The science of psychoneuroimmunology has shown that smelling pleasant fragrances can balance the mind/body equilibrium and help to strengthen the body's immune system. This will improve the body's defenses against viruses, allergens, environmental pollution, and stress. The holistic approach is strong at preventing the onset of illness with regular use of aromatherapy techniques. Long-term problems require full medical attention. (96)

Meditation is a relaxation technique used all over the planet. Through this technique adrenaline levels fall and potentially dangerous reactions to stress can be diffused. The aim of meditation is to reach a state where the body is relaxed and the mind is peaceful, but also alert. This is a beneficial state for healing as we are less likely to be distracted by the past or future concerns. There is a power in deep relaxation that can be detected by the electrical impulses of the brain. Beta brainwaves are rapid and denote an active state of mind. This is associated with the left side or the logical side of the brain. Alpha brainwaves become dominant when we relax and the electrical activity of our mind slows down. This alpha state causes us to become more receptive to our intuitive inner nature. During the daytime we constantly switch between these states as we approach different tasks. Through the practice of meditation we can learn to alter our thought patterns from active to passive and adjust our mindset to bring about controlled healing. The two other brain states that exist are theta and delta. They denote light and deeper sleep patterns. When in meditation a person retains a state of mind that is still aware. A basic stage in meditation is to relax and let go of everything in your mind. The release of tension brings about increased physical and mental energy. Improves concentration, freedom from anxiety, better sleep, inner peace, and the ability to face challenges and see things in a positive light. (97)

People find that the mind wonders as they try to meditate and they need to find a way to focus. It is easier to meditate on a subject or an object such as a statue, candle, tree, or flower. Some people concentrate on their breathing or a repeated word called a mantra. Choose a technique that works for you can also be to watch nature such as the passing of clouds, birds in the sky, colors of a sunset, water in rivers or oceans, grass moving in the wind, or rain falling. Many people meditate to the sound of music. People can meditate at any time of the day that is convenient to your schedule. Resting time is essential to healing the body and the mind. Meditation reconnects us to our inner energies and encourages us to keep with the sensations of our bodies and minds. We can more easily recognize early signs of illness and work on the problem before it becomes more serious. Meditation and relaxation assist the body's natural healing to create a better flow of blood to parts of the body that are deprived during stressful times. This aids the skin, brain, and digestive system. The airways opened which improves circulation and in of benefit to asthmatics and hay fever sufferers. Meditation helps the balancing of hormonal activity that affect the build-up of adrenaline and can cause infertility. The blood pressure is lowered and muscular tension is eased. Improvements are also shown for sufferers of insomnia, tension headaches, migraines, premenstrual syndrome, mild depression, chronic pain, allergies and irritable bowel syndrome. Meditation has been helpful to support a cure, such as a relaxation technique alongside the treatment for cancer, aids, heart problems and other conditions. This technique can help you deal better with your problems and the side effects of treatments you may be receiving. (98)

Visualization is a technique that holds the attention in a place of defined focus. It uses your imagination to experience it physically, mentally, and emotionally. All five senses are involved such as sight, scent, sound, touch, and taste are included in the imagery. Visualization leaves the person feeling relaxed and positive. The technique is very simple, as clearing the mind of other thoughts, relax and let your imagination take over. Imagine the smell of roses, birds singing, bee's buzzing, and the wind blowing your hair. When you feel ready just bring yourself back and stretch your body. (99)

Dreams, daydreams, and memories are all forms of mental imagery or visualization. This is a way of providing a healthy outlet for our imagination. Experts use guided imagery to harness our imaging abilities to counteract stress. Athletes also use visualization to enhance their performance such as a golfer forming a mental image of the fairway where he will place a shot. Researchers have used visualization to reverse the effects of a stress depressed immune response in the body. There are cancer specialists who are also using this approach against cancer. The technique of guided imagery has the person to picture the goal that they wish to achieve. Severely ill patients are urged to picture their internal organs as disease free or to picture a tumor shrinking. Visualization and relaxation methods often help to ease pain and lift depression. Elizabeth Manley, Silver medalist in the 1988 Winter Olympics used visualization to perfect a difficult ice skating jump. She would picture herself over and over in her mind until she accomplished the technique. Relaxation and breathing exercises help to calm her down. (100)

The ancient practice of Yoga is also an ancient philosophy as well as a system of exercises for physical and mental self-discipline. This form of exercise combines poses with deep breathing and meditation. Yoga was developed in India some 5000 years ago and aims to unite the human soul with the universal spirit. Yoga's simple exercises are excellent for relieving stress and improving overall physical condition. Yoga develops strength and flexibility, and can be done at any age. When the breathing techniques are mastered this becomes a powerful method to relieve stress. The importance of breathing is associated with Prana, the life energy that flows through the body. Yoga practitioners hold to the idea that breathing is the physical manifestation of prana. So by controlling one's breath, a person controls his energy. Meditation is another component of yoga as one reaches for a deep meditative state. Yoga students compare meditation to a vacation for the mind and daily practice can reduce feelings of anger, fear, and depression. In traditional yoga there are eight stages to reach a blissful state. One of these techniques is called Hatha-Yoga, which emphasizes poses and breathing techniques and reduces feelings of anger, fear, and depression. Visualizing a peaceful image like a meadow or sky can make the process easier. Many students report that the practice helps release powers of intuition and creativity and improves their concentration. (101)

The origin of Tai Chi Ch'uan is not known, but it has been practiced in China for centuries. Han Gong-yue taught the Nine Small Heaven method during the Liang reign, A.D. 502-557. Han Gong-yue taught the governor of the Anhui province. Other methods have been taught since this period. The Chinese National Physical Education Administration realize that growing numbers of people wanted to learn Tai Chi Ch'uan had the first national workshop in 1970 in Beijing where masters of different styles came from all over China to work together. They developed a simplified form of Tai Chi Ch'uan. This was thought to be a practical and simple way to learn this physical art. The elements of breathing, eye movement, and mental concentration are integrated with the physical martial arts. The movements appear light or soft, but they can exert a force that is hard and strong. Tai Chi Ch'uan is an invaluable treasure of Chinese culture. This ancient Chinese sport has been described as an exercise, dance, religious ritual, philosophy of life, method of achieving mental peace and relaxation. It is sometimes called shadow boxing. This is a philosophical exercise with the aim of harmonizing the mind and the body. This is suitable for children and older people. Some Chinese people have believed that mental and physical well-being depends on tai chi seen as the source of life. The exercises are suppose too hold in harmony the yin and yang energies that reside inside of a man or woman. (102)

All vital energies of physical and mental constitution interplay in the universe. According to traditional Chinese theory yin is passive and yang is active. They are two faces of the same coin. For good health the energies must be balanced. The exercises improve flexibility, strength, and balance safely for patients. The movement improves circulation, and supply blood to all organs of the body. Chinese people practice tai chi ch'uan to socialize and keep fit. They recognize it improves functioning of neurological, cardiovascular, gastrointestinal, and skeletal systems.

Lung capacity increases, digestion improves, muscles strengthen, and joints and limbs become strong and flexible. This technique is an aid in preventing heart disease and can help to regulate blood pressure. It is also recommended as relaxation therapy for the chronically ill. The movements are slow and graceful, so they can be performed without nervous tension. The practice also teaches people how to conserve energy, reduce stress, and relax. The person can tone muscles without strain. Holistic meditation can be practices with the goals of self-awareness, relaxation and enhances energy in mind. Tai Chi Ch'uan engages the whole body and the memory may improve since you need to learn the sequence of the moves. These exercises increase range of motion of the joints while strengthening them and improving balance. Flexibility helps older people to be less vulnerable to accidents and injury. (103)

Missy Vineyard is a master teacher of The Alexander Technique and Director of the three-year teacher-training program that she founded in 1987. She specializes in working with performing artists and children to enhance their artistic and athletic performance. The Alexander Technique teaches you to improve your movement skill in activities such as standing, sitting, walking, running, lifting, playing an instrument, hitting a ball, and jumping. To reduce tension and move with balance and coordination. By learning how to improve your body you also learn how to improve your mind. The Alexander technique teaches you how to better understand yourself physically and mentally. Having this deeper self-knowledge becomes a tool that helps you to recover from injury, maintain health, improve posture, learn new skills and have a deeper since of well-being. As you explore the mind-body connection you achieve self-mastery. How you use your mind and body tells how they interact to create your behavior. (104)

Alexander was an actor who had a vocal problem. He studied himself in a mirror and made discoveries about how our thoughts and movements join to create our unconscious way of moving that can create injury. This is a method of self-study to improve how you function. Well known students that have used this technique include John Dewey, George Bernard Shaw, Aldous Huxley, Kevin Line, William Hurt, Mary Steenburgen, Renee Fleming and Robertson Davies. Alexander teachers are employed at schools around the world such as Julliard, NYU, UCLA, and London's Royal Academy of Dramatic Arts. The method concentrates on inhibition which is a type of thinking that prevents unwanted tension, unnecessary emotional reaction and maladaptive behavior. Direction is a type of thinking that enhances our balance and coordination as we move. When you learn to play an instrument your fingers and arms must obey what your mind tells them to do. If this is difficult for you, then you must figure out why. When you exercise to strengthen specific muscles, you must also learn to coordinate the entire body as you move. We must understand our unconscious, harmful patterns of tension, and how to correct our self-conceptions. (105)

There is a realm inside of us where our thoughts, feelings, actions, and connection between the many aspects of our selves must be investigated When we do not succeed we often tell ourselves that we are the way we are because of genes or fate. The mind can misperceive the body's feelings where the body fails to respond to the mind's intent. Imagined fears can stop us in our tracks and lead us astray. We can learn the skills for restoration and reconnection and our conscious mind can be a tool for change. Theories have been formulated that the head leads and the body will follow. So it is important to learn how to use the head and neck as a primary control. The mind's interpretation of body sensations will then shift. (106)

You have a sixth sense of bodily sensation that comes to you from millions of sensory receptors spread throughout your body. These receptors send information to your brain to inform it of what is happening to you. The brain receives data from these receptors that you are bending your knees or swinging your arms. This also includes more subtle sensations such as the feeling that you know you are right or that you have forgotten something important. Self-awareness and self-reflection can be used to give us another option. We are able to think about our behavior and consciously choose another. We have a conscious choice also if a given stimulus in a threat or a warning. This gives us a conscious choice of whether we become defensive in a situation. (107)

Conscious Inhibition is an essential cognitive skill of the Alexander Technique to chase mental butterflies away. You learn to quiet your inner conversation with yourself. This gives your verbal mind a rest and allows you to keep your mind or track. Sometimes we feel and do not think. We are reacting to stimuli instead of thinking through the point of pain or the situation. You must learn to turn on your prefrontal cortex. It is practice to quiet the mind and body and let your attention shift to the prefrontal cortex. This is also called thinking from the attic. There are times our words lose their meaning. We blankly speak not thinking about what is said. We can learn to practice consciously summoning the meaning of words in your mind. There is power in the word no and many times we neglect to use our power. These exercises are cleaning up the attic of your mind. We cannot change our behavior until we clarify the meaning of our words. These exercises also are designed to let you discover your beliefs and what hold they have over your behavior. We acquire knowledge about everything except ourselves. The gift is within for conscious self-connection and self-mastery. (108)

Chinese medicine combined with Western thought and Western interpretation has an aid in the Organ Clock. This can be an early identification of energy disturbances that can lead to bodily illness or psychic ailments. The Organ clock can aid in specific conditions of illness that can be recognized and swiftly remedied. The organ clock is used for diagnosis and therapy since the beginning of modern crystal healing. This technique is easy to use for laypeople as well as for self-healing and preventive maintenance. The connection must be made between healing stones and the organ clock to identify the appropriate healing stones to be used. This process allows the problems to be identified at their origins. The Chinese philosophy and Chinese medicine is based on the principle of yin and yang. These two laws together form the basis of all existence from which all things originate. The idea of Yin and Yang is external change as all things emerge from opposites. In China all processes in life and nature go through five steps beginning, expansion, high point, retreat, and end. The phase of water is the beginning of everything. Expansion takes place in the phase of wood which reaches the high point of five. Metal is the phase of retreat, and at the end is water again. The fifth phase is the phase of earth between fire and metal. This is the phase of duration when things are steady and lasting in the world.

The harmony of this cycle is the basis for health in humans. When disturbances and disharmony occur illness occurs. There are phases of change which are the progression of the seasons and the passage of the day on the organ clock. Western medicine recognizes and addresses only the physical treatment of the function of organs and bodily structures as well as senses, emotions, psychic aspects and spiritual capabilities connected with them. (109)

The organ clock uses twelve functions. Each function uses its greatest strength for two hours only. The high points of activity are aligned with the Sun. Someone who wakes up often between one and three in the morning may have a disturbance in the function of the liver. A person who feels tired around 2.00 p.m. may have problems with the small intestine. Chinese medicine believes in prevention. In ancient China doctors were paid only when the patient stayed healthy. The organ clock teaches you which activities are best suited to which time of the day, and which should be avoided. This leads to an effective way to preserve good health to your old age. Healing stones can be applied to different parts of the body for balancing disturbances and thus preventing or healing illnesses. One of the simplest ways of using stones is to wear them as rings, pendants, collars, or bracelets on the ankle or wrist. Another way to use stones is to use them in water that you are drinking as a massage for health and healing. Healing stone water is distributed through the body with the stones information going through the whole body and energy system. There are books on Gem Water and how to use Crystal Waters for Therapeutic Treatments. (110)

When defining real local time our bodies define noon as when the sum is at its highest point in the sky. The Chinese begin the day with the time of the lungs. In Zen Monasteries monks often rise at 4.00 a.m. the high point of the lungs to begin breathing practice or meditation. This is there way of using the full strength of the living energy to meet the day and the world. Amethyst is a stone that releases feelings of closeness in the chest. Breathing is easier, freer and deeper. This stone promotes the exchange of gases in the lungs. Other stones that are helpful are apophyllite, aquamarine, blue chalcedony, fluorite, moss agate, rock crystal and rutilated quartz. Next on the organ clock is the large intestine. The intestine cleans the body in the morning by the passing of stools. The morning also brings the ritual of washing off nighttime sweat and secretions. Amethyst also improves elimination through the large intestine and skin. It is helpful for both diarrhea and constipation. Black tourmaline is also helpful for constipation. After cleansing it is time for nourishment in order to gain energy for the day. In Buddhist monasteries breakfast is the richest meal of the day. The stomach is for assimilating and for dealing with new things in life. Agate stones give a feeling of safety in facing life and experiencing new things. It strengthens the stomach and helps when worries disturb the stomach. There are also more stones that help such as amber, calcite, citrine, dravite tourmaline, imperial topaz and jasper. The spleen has the role of the everyday worker and corresponds to the everyday labor. Stones that help the spleen are amber, citrine, golden beryl, imperial topaz, jasper, mookaite, sardonyx and yellow tourmaline. The spleen enables the function areas of the body to work together. This ensures that other organs do not shift or prolapse. The spleen is responsible for the harmony of body and soul. (111)

The heart also has a time of rest. People who are early risers feel a need for a midday rest. This is due to a need for rest to be able to put your feelings into words. The heart is the ruler of emotions. This is crucial in how each individual will experience and perceive the world. Stones that are helpful are moonstone, morganite, pink chalcedony, pink opal, pink sapphire, pink tourmaline, rhodonite and rose quartz. The heart governs the brain and the five senses. The heart has a spiritual aspect of functioning to help you relax and get a good night's sleep. This leads to spiritual peace, inner strength, and strong perceptions. The small intestine functions as a filter and sorter of nourishment that is taken in and which parts are expelled. On the psychic-spiritual level this organ helps us to distinguish things from one another and acknowledge our own goals and wishes. Stones that are helpful are carnelian, fire agate, manganocalcite, pink agate, red agate, red chalcedony, sardonyx and topaz. Perception is connected with the ability to differentiate. (112)

The time of the Bladder is afternoon for working to get things done. The Kidneys partner with the bladder where energy reserves are stored. When we become distracted or discouraged difficulties arise. Stones that are helpful are blue apatite, blue tourmaline, cordierite, kyanite, lapis lazuli, pyrope, garnet, sodalite and sugilite. The ability to lead people and control them comes from the bladder. The Kidneys time of day is the evening and contains the beginning and end of life. The ability to reproduce belongs to the kidney function. So do maturity and old age. They are the ancestral energy that is passed on from parents to children. How strong we are and how we fight resistance to disease lies in the kidneys. Stones that help this function are epidote, hematite, nephrite, obsidian, scolecite, tiger iron and zircon. The pericardium is the sexual system which follows the organ clock at 3.00 every morning. This system functions also with the heart. The pericardium defends the physical and the psychic. Psychic attacks intentional and unintentional, such as hurt and disappointment will hit the pericardium function area first. Stones that help are the almandine garnet, fire agate, fire opal, heliotrope, precious opal, rhodochrosite, and sunstone thulte. (113)

There are three hot spots and in Chinese medicine inside the human body. The lower heater is the energy of the kidneys, the middle heater is the digestion and the upper heater the lungs where we breathe. The stones that help there three processes are carnelian, fire opal, mahogany obsidian, mookaite, pyrope garnet, red jasper, red tourmaline and ruby. This is the process in which body heat is produced, distributed and used. The body's defenses supply each area with the appropriate measure of energy and warmth. The time of the gallbladder is for sleep and regeneration. This organ recuperates best when the mind is still. It governs the ability to make decisions. The decision process mostly takes place subconsciously. The stones that are helpful are aventurine, chrysocolla, heliotiope, labradorite, and magnesite, periodot, serpentine and turquoise. The liver works best during the night when the conscious intellect is not interfering. The liver function is responsible for planning. The stones that help the liver are amazonite, aragonite, chrysocolla, chrysoprose, emerald, green fluorite, malachite and orbicular jasper. Meditation to ward off stress and tension have a strong healing effect on the liver. (114)

Chapter 4

GEMSTONES IN HEALING

As a child I attended Sunday school and first learned of gemstones in the Book of Exodus. We were taught that the 12 stones of Aaron were a spiritual symbol of God's family and his leadership as a loving father. The Book of Exodus has God giving Moses instructions for the Priestly Garments.

Exodus Ch. 39:1 "From the blue, purple and scarlet yarn they made woven garments for ministering in the sanctuary. They also made sacred garment for Aaron as the Lord commanded Moses." (115)

Instructions were also given for a Breastplate of twelve stones to be made for the Priests. The gemstone breastplate was given to the high priest Aaron to help him spiritually discern answers to questions brought to him by the people. The questions were to be asked of God while Aaron was praying in the tabernacle.

Exodus Ch. 39: 8-14 "They fashioned the breastplate the work of a skilled craftsman. They made it like the ephod: of gold and of blue, purple and scarlet yarn, and of finely twisted linen. It was square a span long and a span wide, and folded double. Then they mounted four rows of precious stones on it. In the first row there was a ruby, a topaz and a beryl, in the second row a turquoise, a sapphire and an emerald; in the third row a jacinth, an agate and an amethyst; in the fourth row a chrysolite, an onyx and a jasper. They were mounted in gold filigree settings. There were twelve stones, one for each of the sons of Israel each engraved like a seal with the name of one of the twelve tribes. (116)

The art of healing with stones is thousands of years old. Evidence that gemstones were used in healing can be found in most ancient civilizations. All gemstones originate from the hot magma inside the earth. They are formed from dust, sand, chemical substances and acids that have dissolved in water. Many gemstones are considered to have protective and talismanic properties to keep evil spirits away. Shamans and medicine men learned to harness the power of crystals in ceremonies and rituals and this ancient knowledge has been passed down to our time. There are early reports of gems healing properties to the fourth millennium before Jesus Christ. Writings of gems have been found in the Sumerian texts and Indian Vedic texts. Naturopathic medicine was known as Ayurveda meaning wisdom. Ayurveda writing describe in detail how to prepare elixirs, pastes, and powders made from gemstones. In India gemstones would be places on painful areas of patient's bodies to enhance their healing power as a channel for the light and warmth of the sun. Gemstone healing is part of the medical curriculum in Indian universities. The first Chinese medical book was written 5000 years ago by Shen Nung with detailed descriptions of gemstones and their influence on the human body. The Sumerians wore gemstones in leather pouches to protect themselves from evil spirits, sickness, and disaster. Roman soldiers also carried cut stones to ward off sickness and bad luck. The Egyptians wore amulets made of Amethyst, Hematite, Jasper, Carnelian and Lapis Lazuli. Stones were polished and hammered into scarabs, symbols of creation, and buried with the dead to protect them in their next life. (117)

In the ancient world gems were often used to treat the same ailments. The treatments varied among the Greek, Roman and Arabic doctors. These doctors would mix them with plant extracts, heated or pulverized them or treat them with chemicals. The art of healing with stones was revived in the middle ages by Isidore of Seville, Konrad von Meganberg, Albertus Magnus, and the Benedictine. Marbod and the Bishop of Rennes all wrote about them. Marbod wrote a handbook about sixty gemstones and their therapeutic properties. This handbook was translated into four languages and went through fourteen editions from 1511 to 1799. Hildegard von Bingen (1098-1179) dealt with gemstones both as an abbess and a mystic. She realized that physical and spiritual disorders could not be isolated from the environmental influences. The phases of the moon, inadequacies in diet and bad habits of living had to be recognized to determine a treatment plan for the patient. Some diseases called for a lifestyle change, others could be treated with herbs, powders, pastes and natural essences to be carefully balanced. Stones were placed on parts of the patient's anatomy and charged with energy. Drinks were made with powdered minerals and the essences of gemstones were prescribed for specific illnesses. (118)

Theophrastus Bornbastus von Hohenheim was a physician known as Paracelsus. He wrote on the healing properties of minerals and gems. Paracelsus distinguished between chemical formulae and the elemental powers that reside within stones. Pulverized rocks were used to treat symptoms, while their force attacked the root of the problem that caused the sickness and prevented their root reoccurrence. He states that the inner healer of the person has become weakened and obstructed through carless habits of living. To heal a person is to restore the healing power within that person. Stones come in all colors with different crystal structures and are part of the natural order. Diamonds have a colorful past as they reflect the light of all colors of the spectrum. Under certain circumstances they can mirror human passion and weakness. The Hope Diamond has many dark tales associated with this 112-Karat sapphire-blue-diamond. This diamond was originally the eye of a statue of the Hindu Goddess Sita. It was stolen by a high Brahmin and a curse was laid upon the diamond by the goddess. Unhappiness would follow all who posse's the stone and the curse can never be broken. Since 1958 the Hope Diamond has resided at the Smithsonian Institute in Washington, D.C. (119)

Volcanic stones with healing properties are jasper, porphyry and obsidian. Plutonic rocks are stones that remain buried within the earth's surface and take longer to cool. Minerals and stones are found in layers because the heavier elements sink and the lighter ones rise to the surface. Plutonic rocks crystallize directly in liquid magma, but some form from hot vapor and gas. Sometimes forced under pressure through cracks and fissures, already formed crystals can lose some material and combine with other chemicals to produce new materials. These stones include agate, amethyst, rock crystal, chalcedony, and rock quartz. Other healing plutonic rocks are Aventura, Olivine, Rose Quartz and Zircon. Healing stones that originate out of contact with water are Amazonite, Aragonite, Fluorite, Kunzite and Moonstone. Secondary stones that role and slide down river beds are calcite and pyrite. Tertiary stones are a further transformation of stones that end up as a hard marble. (120)

Rough stones are allowed to remain in their natural condition. They are distinguished by their simplicity as well as their beauty and healing power. Energy flows freely through them and they are thought to possess the greatest healing powers. Crystals are often used to make pendulums and are used for their therapeutic purposes. Energy gathers into small holes or pockets of these naturally developed crystals. Aggregate crystals have points that project in different directions. The two points dispense power so the balance of energy in their surroundings can be restored. These stones are used to restore other stones. Tumbles stones are put together with water and sand in a drum and then turned. This smoothies their points and edges causing rounded stones. They are also laid on the body for healing. In nature you can find round smooth stones in rivers where the water and sand have naturally worked on the stone. By holding and rubbing these stones their energy passes through the hand, and the entire body becomes infused with their power. Flat tumbled stones can be places under one's pillow or pressed onto a painful area of the body. Stones have a peaceful and calming effect. (121)

Jewelry made from different stones can have a positive or negative effect. The precious metals can increase their energy level. Skilled workmanship can also increase the healing power. Gold settings will enhance the power of the stone. Silver strengthens the vibratory intensity of coral and turquoise. People experienced in the therapeutic art of stones can tailor jewelry for an individual's health needs. There is a magic of gemstones and the art of astrology. This lore states that gemstones are intermediaries between the macrocosm and the microcosm that reside in each person. Astrological teachings of signs of the zodiac under which a person is born has a great influence on his life, his soul, his character and his general health. Each of the signs has its own characteristic qualities, and each corresponds to a specific area of the body and accounts for its strength or weakness. When a person suffers from chronic ailments a person should look for gemstones that address symptoms and serve one's basic personality type and counteract its weaknesses. (122)

The main gemstones for the sign of Capricorn are Onyx, Malachite, Tourmaline, Agate, Black Pearl and Moss Agate. Other gemstones for Capricorn are Rock Crystal, Diamond, Jasper, Obsidian, Smokey Quartz, Sapphire and Citrine. The main gemstones for Aquarius are Turquoise, Aquamarine, Labradorite, Amazonite, Falcon's- eye, Topaz, Fluorite and Malachite. Other stones for Aquarius are Jade, Chalcedony, Diamond, Moonstone, Opal, Onyx and Tourmaline. The main gemstones for Pisces are Amethyst, Opal, Blue Sapphire, Fluorite, and Suglite. Other stones are Garnet, Agate, Diamond, Jade, Carnelian, Rose Quartz and Citrine. The main stones for Aries are Ruby, Garnet, Carnelian, Jasper and Kyanite. Other stones are Diamond, Hematite, and Amethyst. The gemstones for Taurus and Rhodochrosite, Rose Quartz, Agate, Chrysocolla, Adventurine and Zircon. Other stones are Diamond, Malachite, Emerald, Obsidian and Citrine. The main gemstones for Gemini are Amber, Citrine, Carnelian, Yellow Sapphire, Celestite, and Apophylite. Other important stones are Aquarmarine, Rock Crystal, Chalcedony, Moss agate, Tiger's Eye, and Turquoise. The main gemstones for Cancer are Emerald, Moonstone, Aventurine, Chalcedony, Jade, Opal, Pearl, Olivine, Chrysoprase, and Chrysocolla. Other stones are Carnelian, Rhodochrosite and Sodalite. Leo has strength with Rock Crystal, Larimar, Diamond, Chrysoberyl and Topaz. Other important stones for Leo are Onyx, Yellow-gold, Citrine, Garnet, Peridot, Selenite, Tiger's Eye, and Tourmaline. The main stones for Virgo are Tiger's Eye, Gold Topaz, Jasper, Citrine, Carnelian and Ametine. Other important stones are Azurite, Hematite, Jade, Lapis Lazuli, Opal, ruby, and Sodalite. Libra masters the art of living with Smokey Quartz, Jade, Aquamarine, Sugilite, Star Sapphire, Chrysocolla and Tourmaline. Other important stones are Malachite, Turquoise and Diamond. The main gemstones for Scorpio are Hematite, Coral, Fluorite, Obsidian, Sard, Spinel, Tourmaline and Garnet. Other stones are Agate, Chalcedony, Jade, Malachite and Ruby. The main stones for

Sagittarius are Lapis Lazuli, Obsidian, Aventurine, Herkimer Diamond, Sodalite, Dumortierite, Apatite, Chalcedony, Spinel and Zircon. Other stones are Topaz, Moonstone, Amethyst, Opal, Rose Quartz and Tourmaline. (123)

Healing stones transmit their power through color and vibration. To experience this power one has to actually use the stones. Physical, intellectual and psychic processes, all sensation, thought and feeling result in chemical reactions in the body. They consume and create energy. By properly using color a person can regulate the body's energy level. This is why color appeals to people in certain situations. The color of healing stones work on the human organism and psyche. The play of light of gemstones can have a calming or stimulating effect and purity or heal. Stones emit frequencies of light that have a direct influence on the body's biochemical processes. Stones reflect the body's chemistry as crystals are the smallest singular component in the atom. We cannot see the constant motion or vibrational energy of the stones, as they appear to be solid. A person can react to the positive, negative or neutral energy. This is why we are more comfortable in certain environments. In ancient cultures people would paint themselves with bright colors to connect with the mysterious strength of the soul. Much of this ancient knowledge has been lost and is no longer taught. When these stones are used in connection with the body's energy centers called the Chakras health can be restored. When the energy flow is blocked, the body will not function properly. These blockages can arise from physical complaints or psychic conflicts. There are seven primary chakras in the human body vibrating at seven different frequencies. To influence the Chakras you would find a smooth flat stone whose color matches the chakra you want to affect. Laying the stone on the chakra for an hour a day can help. (124)

The first chakra is the root chakra and lies between the rectum and the genital area. It is said to absorb energy from the earth. This is the energy center for the body's hard tissue, bone, spinal column, teeth and nails. This influences the intestine and prostate, as well as blood and all formation. When the root chakra is disturbed it can lead to addiction, uncontrolled or diminished sexuality, digestive disorders and obesity. When this chakra is restored a person will feel a deep connection to nature. The stones that are recommended for treating this chakra are Garnet, Hematite, Red Jasper, Coral, Onyx, Rhodonite, Ruby and Black Tourmaline. The color for the root chakra is red and stimulates the life force. The second Chakra is the sacral chakra and lies above the pubic bone and opens frontward. This center controls the body's liquid elements of blood, lymph, sweat, digestive juices, sperm, urine and tears. When this chakra is disturbed it causes sexual problems. When this chakra is restored life becomes more open and enjoyable. Stones for this chakra are orange Beryl, orange Jasper, Carnelian and Citrine. The color orange is of nourishment and circulation. The third chakra is the navel or solar plexus chakra and governs the stomach, liver, spleen and gall bladder, the digestive system and the autonomic nervous system. Blockages of this chakra create discontent, restlessness and discouragement. Stones to treat this chakra are Tiger's Eye, Topaz, Yellow Tourmaline and Citrine. The color yellow corresponds to this chakra and stands for intelligence. The fourth chakra is the heart chakra and lies in the middle of the chest opening frontward. This influences the heart and circulatory system and the thymus gland and immune system. When the heart chakra is open people are considerate of others and have a highly developed sense of empathy. Stones for this chakra are green and pink. Green Aventurine, Chrysocolla, Chrysopras, Jade, Moss Agate, Olivine, Emerald and Tourmaline. Pink Coral, Rhodonite, Rhodochrosite and Rose Quartz. The color green has a calming effect. The fifth chakra is the throat chakra and lies at the base of the throat. It governs hunger and thirst, ear, eyes, nose and throat, and the bronchial passages, lungs, esophagus, vocal chords and speech. When energy is freely flowing people can express themselves and their beliefs. Stones for treating the throat chakra are Aquamarine, Chalcedony, Celestine, Chrysocolla, Moonstone, Opal, Pearl, Turquoise and Blue Topaz. The color for this chakra is blue. The sixth chakra is the forehead chakra or the third eye above the top of the nose. When energy flows properly a person can rely upon his own intuitive sense. The stones for this chakra are Sodalite, Amethyst, Sapphire, Rock Crystal and Fluorite. The color indigo is the color of mysteries and mysticism. This color banishes sickness and evil from the person's awareness and allows mental freedom.

The seventh chakra enters the body through the top of the head. This chakra leads to enlightenment. The stones recommended for treating the seventh chakra are Amethyst, Rock Crystal, Diamonds and Violet Fluorite. Three colors are associated with the crown chakra are violet, white and gold. All stones that are created naturally have healing powers, but they do not work with the same intensity. Different stones work on different problems. (125)

Keeping a collection of stones can help in cases of mild illnesses. The healing powers of nature is free and has no side effects. Stones are always available and can have a positive influence on our lives. Gold has always been a symbol of power and wealth. Governments all over the world have sought to obtain in their treasuries. This has been reflected in precious jewelry, amulets, death-masks, figurines, facings, coating of porcelain and even gold threads in fabric. Everything moves and depends on gold. The healing properties of gold have been overlooked as it carries a special energy. Gold increases the healing properties of the stones that are encased in this precious metal and increases the wearer's confidence. A negative effect of gold can be arrogance. The magical properties of gold are an association with love and faithfulness. It encourages people to accept innovation. Healing stones set in gold are thought to be powerful amulets. Through the many years and translations of the Bible we have lost what the exact Breastplate stones of Aaron actually could have been. (126)

The Greeks called the Ruby the mother of all gemstones for its beauty and rarity. Legend says that the ruby combines Eros, sensual love and Agape, spiritual love causing it to be known as Divine Love in Crystallized form. The Middle- Ages used the Ruby as a protection against the plague. If a Ruby turned darker it was a sign of infection. This stone promotes sexual energy when it is moved over the genital area. It strengthens the body's immune system against infections and diseases. The Ruby helps with the heart, circulation, low blood pressure, and eye infections. It is a good luck stone of love. The magical properties are vitality and passion. The Topaz is an ancient healing stone linked to Jupiter and considered a symbol of a ruler and bestows wisdom. The crown of England has nearly five hundred Topazes mined from the

Erzebirge Mountains. Ancient Mexico used the stones to see who was telling the truth as it would become darker. The stones stimulates the metabolism and digestion. According to ancient traditions the topaz staunches the glow of blood, promotes relaxation and eases tension. A Blue Topaz helps to promote artistic inspiration, where a yellow Topaz counteracts bad moods and calms irritability caused by lack of sleep. The legend of the Beryl stone originates from Mesopotamia and was worshipped as a magic stone by the ancient Hebrews. It is said that Beryl will protect the marital feelings of love, and help the person to reach high positions. As a healing stone beryl can be placed on the eye lids, used to alleviate stomach and bowel disorders, and to detoxify the body. Beryl can be used to relieve angina and placed on the neck to relieve stress and traveling. The magical properties of Beryl are protections while traveling. The Crusaders discovered Turquoise in Turkey. Native Americans have always considered this stone to be a holy stone protecting the wearer against harm. Objects of Turquoise were also discovered in Egyptian and Greek tombs. The stone was also used to protest a horse and the rider. Hildegard von Bingen used the stone in her naturopathic treatments. Turquoise has a wide range of healing properties. It helps with the treatment of throat and lung infections, it alleviates hyperpiesia, stomach aches, rheumatism and gout. It is said to cure infections, speed recovery after illness, alleviate pain and reduce inflammation, it has antispasmodic and detoxifying properties. Psychologically Turquoise lifts depression, gives self-confidence and promotes endurance. The magical properties of turquoise lifts depression, gives self-confidence and promotes endurance. The magical properties of Turquoise are to make women virtuous and loyal. (127)

The Sapphire is said to receive its protective powers from Saturn and is highly regarded by kings and emperors. Legend says this stone is the most protective stone. The stone helps with the nervous system and regulates the thyroid gland. Psychologically it strengthens the wearer's willpower and promotes strength. The Blue color represents the sky, loyalty, friendship, and faith. The Emerald is also a protective stone for travelers. The stone is associated with mercury the messenger of the gods and emeralds from the Red Sea were the foundation of the wealth of the Pharaohs. Cleopatra sought eternal beauty for herself through the reflection of emeralds on her skin. The fragments of emeralds are put in the corner of the eyes to stabilize the eyes. Emeralds can also help with headaches, promote mental growth, farsightedness and perceptiveness. The green emerald symbolizes hope and development. The Greeks used the stone for divine intuition. Jacinth is a stone of reddish blue or deep purple. This stone of reddish blue or deep purple is a stone that is said to aid to instill wisdom in the person. In history it is called Zircon or Hyacinth. The name came from a mythological character named Hyacinthus. Zircon has an antispasmodic effect on the liver and gall bladder. It has a calming effect on asthma and allergies. Helps to aid lung infections, bronchial problems and severe colds. The magical properties of Zircon helps the wearer overcome losses, heals mental disturbances and promotes common sense. The name of the stone Agate comes from the river Achates in Sicily. The healing powers of agate have been used during pregnancy for both mother and child. It is used to treat headaches, dizziness, impaired balance as well as skin problems. When placed on the heart or throat it combats feverish infections. The magical properties help the wearer to choose between true friends and false ones. The stone is said to avert storms and lightening, protect children from danger, bring prosperity and prevent miscarriages. (128)

The Greeks wore Amethyst for protection against magic, homesickness, evil thoughts, and drunkenness. Wine was served in amethyst beakers. Buddhist monks in India use Amethyst to help them meditate. Placed under ones pillow prevents nightmares. Amethyst can also alleviate migraines and nervous headaches. An Amethyst stone can also improve concentration. The magical properties of Amethyst is said to attract justice and protect against burglars and thieves. It also wards off danger and violent death. Chrysolite is also called peridotite or olivine. It can be yellow to green in color. Olivine was imported from the volcanic island of the Zebirget in the Red Sea. Legend says that Moses wore an olivine in his cuirdass as protection. Olivine strengthens and protects the organs in the thorax, especially the heart and lungs. It also improves the immune system by stimulating the thymus gland. The stone protects against dehydration and brittleness. Olivine creates inner harmony, combats envy and resentment. The stone reduces anger, encourages admission of one's own faults and helps a person to make amends. This stone transforms negative feelings such as selfishness and coldness into positive feelings. The magical properties of Olivine symbolizes cheerfulness and promotes friendship. (129)

Onyx has been used for years in healing eye disorders. It must be laid on the body or worn for a long period of time because its powers develop very slowly. Onyx heals infected wounds, fungal infections, inflammation, and sunburn. Onyx also deflects negative energy, increases stamina, and creates inner harmony. Onyx is used as a magical stone all over the world, its power is further increased by magic inscriptions. These can be found by the graves of American Indians, and ancient Greeks, and Romans. Ancient Egyptians wore Jasper scarabs as amulets believing that the stone increased sexual energy. Massages with a round stone are said to have an aphrodisiac effect. Indians in Asia and Native Americans see Jasper as a magical rain stone that heals the kidneys, liver, and gall bladder. Drinking Jasper water one hour before meals is said to promote weight loss. This can also help with constipation and menopausal symptoms in women. The magical properties of Jasper help with will power. (130)

Across the globe people have a fascination with stones and pick them up when they catch our eye. Sacred stones are all around us that focus, store, transmit and transmute energy. Monumental structures, both natural and man-made are regarded as holy. There are stone circles at Avebury in England, natural rock formations at Uluru in Australia, standing stones in the Cotes Des Megaliths in Brittany, France. The Sonoran Desert has petroglyphs etched on rocks. The most sacred stones of all are the two tablets of Lapis lazuli on which the ten-commandments were written. Technology in the 21st century has electrical machines guided by the piezo and pyro-electrical properties of quartz crystal, which has been associated with ancient healing and mystical powers. Small pebbles of blue Preseli stones from the original monument at Stonehenge, England are found all over the ground. These stones were used for healing on wounds and chakras on the body's energy systems. The Bible has over 200 references to crystals and gemstones and their powers as well as Chinese and Indian Texts. Native Americans call these stones, the Stone People. They are always ready to help us in the natural world. Rivers are also linked with sacred sites as the Kennet River in Avebury, England is regarded as sacred. The Druids would cast items of value into rivers and lakes to appease the gods and ask for their support in a project. The Romans had a strategy of religious conversions of conquered people by adding statues of their own Gods to the people's temples. The people would continue to go to the same places to pray and be praying also to the Roman Gods. As Christianity spread throughout Europe many churches were built on ancient Pagan sacred sites. Sacred sites throughout the world are built where they are because people are drawn to the place by its natural energy and the conjunction of energy lines. These places of energy were found by dowsing crystals and sticks or rods used. A crystal pendulum is easier to start with because the crystal helps to focus the energy. Dowsing rods are made from a forked twig or branch. Metal ones can also be bought. This practice can help you to map energy lines as this is how the rocks were placed at Avebury. When using a pendulum it is wise to hold a hematite stone in the other hand to ground yourself. Drinking water or clapping your hands will also ground you. Many of the Holy wells have had churches built near them. Cote Des Megaliths is the largest Neolithic site in Europe, covering 15 miles of the Brittany coastland around the town of Carnac in France. This is one of the major Celtic centers in the world with over 3000 standing stones, but also dolmens and tombs. (131)

Different legends are associated with these stones such as the great Celtic Wizard Merlin, to a Pope working magic on pagan warriors. There are tales of Christian Saints mystically acquiring the powers of existing Pagan Gods. Folktales of Nature Spirits, Fairies, King Arthur and Merlin are still told. Carnac France is also thought to be an astronomical observatory where alignments with the sunset at the solstices were held. Petroglyphs are images carved or etched in stone. Many are drawings of objects, events, or animals. Symbols are often found representing ideas or concepts, such as Gods and religious beliefs. Along with paintings found in caves they are an original form of rock art. Mythical creatures have been found in these drawing that may have once existed or are part of a belief system that once existed or are part of a belief system that once existed. The petroglyphs in the Sonoran Desert were mostly carved by the Hokam people an ancient Pima Native American people who have vanished. Uluru (Ayers Rock) is a massive red sandstone rock almost 6 miles round in Australia. It is perhaps the most sacred and mystical place on the continent. Ancient stories revolve around wars between ancient beings that created this landscape. The Anangu tribe believed that the ancestors still inhabit this sacred site. The Uluru at sunrise and sunset glows from grays to browns, reds, oranges, and yellows as the light alters. Kata Tjuta is another ancient rock site about 19 miles away from Uluru. This site has 36 rounded domes of rock. Legend of the Wanambi Tribe are of a great snake king who lives on the highest summit, Mt. Olga. His rainbow colors support his life-giving gifts as the seasons change. People look for rocks along beaches, rivers, or paths as if they are a long lost friend or treasure with a story to tell. Some stones have a purpose in our lives and help us with being creative, healing ourselves and others. When you are unsure of your environment picking up a stone can help you to focus on your feelings. The double terminated quartz crystal is also called the talking crystal. This comes from the idea of the Native American concepts of talking sticks. The stick is passed around the room and each person has a moment to express themselves while they hold it. Some of the traditions say one must speak the truth or the stick will curse you. The crystal turns hot and cold, vibrates, and causes sensations in a person's body. The stone helps a person to see the hidden answers that they seek. (132)

Rock painting is an ancient art and form of communication. Prehistoric paintings often told stories of hunters, which could have been used to teach techniques to young hunters. Magicians also painted the walls and illuminated the walls with fire in sacred ceremonies and rituals. This is still a leisure activity to decorate walls and places where people live. The whole process of painting is therapeutic and very enjoyable to people. Painting rocks can draw you back to your childhood where rules of getting messy or dirty have no meaning. Stones are magical in our minds for what we need at the time to release. They were a place to paint a prayer, symbol or sacred picture to pass on to future generations.

The Native Americans painted arrows on rocks representing different things to other tribes, generally messages of strength, leadership, and protection. The heart-line is the path the breath takes, compared to the life-force energy of the animal spirit. The arrow represents the movement of force and direction. There are stories, tales, legends and folklore surrounding crystal skulls found in South America. A powerful band of wizards and magicians are said to have lived in Atlantis or possibly originating from an alien world. They held fantastic powers and were adept healers. The magicians eventually died and thousands of years later the crystal skull was discovered. There are 13 of these crystal skulls of which have astonishing healing qualities. There is also a theory that if all 13 crystal skulls come together the whole planet will be healed of its ills and wars will end. (133)

Deut. 11: 26-29 "I am setting before you today a blessing and a curse- the blessing, if you obey the commands of the Lord your God that I am giving you today; the curse if you disobey the commands of the Lord your God and turn from the way that I command you today by following other gods, which you have not known. When the Lord your God has brought you into the land you are entering to possess, you are to proclaim on Mount Gerizim the blessings, and on Mount Ebal the curses." Life under the God of the covenant had two options. Loyal obedience would lead to covenant blessings and dis-obedience would lead to covenant curses which involves suffering. Suffering could not be blamed on God it was the sin of the person. Any culture that did not conform to the commandments and decrees of the Old Testament was considered Pagan and worshipping a foreign God. (134)

From ancient civilizations up to the present stones have been employed for protection and to contact spirits in some way. They were worn as talismans and amulets as the stone Jet or Black Amber was used for protection. It was thought to ward off the evil eye and remove the effects of negative forces, such as witchcraft and curses from evil beings. This stone was also thought to have the power to chase away melancholy. The stone Jet was very popular in the Victorian times in mourning brooches. Crystals were placed in ancient graves to protect the deceased from evil spirits. Lapis Lazuli was commonly used to assist the person unto the next world without mishap. The Jade stone is often carved into animal shapes and thought to protect the wearer from untimely death. The stone Turquoise is said to detect poisons or sickness by changing color from dark to light. The Quartz Crystal is said to be the "most powerful crystal," the "grandfather crystal," and "Chief of the Stone People." Ancient Greeks believed the quartz crystals were frozen light from heaven, or holy ice. Whoever possessed this stone was sure of having their prayers granted, as the gods cannot withstand its power. Biblical tradition associates Agate with the lion. A brave man would carry this stone for courage. (135)

The Cherokee Indians have legends that are passed down to future generations. One such legend states that the animals became unhappy with man and his destruction of the environment. The animals each brought a disease into the world. So the Plant Tribe and the Stone people had compassion on mankind and brought remedies for the animals' illnesses. Each plant had a healing force embedded within its growing structure. Man would be made aware of this and honor the plant to gain its healing properties. One plant became the chief of the plants named Tobacco. This Tobacco plant did not cure any particular disease, but it would help people return to the sacred way of life when smoked or offered with prayers and ceremony. If this plant was smoked for pleasure only it would cause the worst disease of all. The stone people also agreed that each mineral would have a spiritual power and a subtle vibration that could be used to regain perfect health. A Ruby worn as an amulet would heal the heart. Emerald would heal the liver and eyes. The chief of the mineral tribe Quartz Crystal was clear like the light of creation. A quartz crystal can help to heal the mind and help the human being see the origin of disease. This stone brings wisdom and clarity in the person's dreams. When humans gaze upon this stone they see the way to harmony. (136)

There is always a grain of truth in legends and tales. We have to find the truth for ourselves. They are not just stories from the past but they hold a bit of wisdom or knowledge from past experiences. The mystery is seeking, asking questions, and researching until we find the key that unlocks the door and we gain insight. Holey stones are created by the process of erosion caused by water or wind and are highly sought after.

The Holey stone is known as the Odin stone, after the Norse god who transformed himself into a snake to crawl through a hole in a stone in order to steal the sacred drink that inspired poetry. Another name for the Holey stone is the Fairy stone. With practice you can look through the whole to see the faerie folk. This is a way of explaining second sight or clairvoyance. The larger stones are said to heal when you pass through the hole. The men-an-tol or crick stone in Cornwall, England was thought to heal rickets in children. The gift of pregnancy was given when a woman passed through the whole seven times backward at a full moon. Holey stones are thought to boost your powers of perception and intuition and are helpful aids in meditation. The stones help with eye problems. Worn around the neck the stone protects you from harm on all levels such as physical, emotional, mental, and spiritual. People hang them in doorways or by windows for protection to a home or business. They are also placed over beds and pet's beds to ward off nightmares and keep them safe. In rituals they represent the veil between the two worlds being the earth plane and the spirit world. Power bracelets also called Buddha bracelets are made up of 21 beads. The bracelets are used to keep track of the rhythm while chanting or meditating as attention came to them because the Dalai Lama wore them. Famous celebrities such as Robbie Williams, Richard Gere, and Madonna began to wear them believing in the mystical powers of the gemstones. (137)

Native American medicine bags are compact and made of leather. They are worn around the neck and are kept for a lifetime. A person will carry unique items to protect the wearer against all manner of evil spirits and bad luck. It can contain small stone crystals, feathers, and special herbs. A medicine man or woman often traveled with the hunters to give predictive or intuitive assistance in finding a herd of Bison. Stones from the medicine bag were laid out and consulted. In today's world people often carry a medicine bag to work to keep the atmosphere calm or consult to solve problems. Wearing the bag promotes good health increases vitality and strength. People also keep bowls of crystals around there homes for good energy. They can be a conversation piece to get to know people who enter your home as visitors often have a fascination with crystals. (138)

In ancient times transformational gems and metals were placed inside the Turban and later the crowns of Kings and Queens to enhance spiritual wisdom, knowledge and power. Stones resonate electromagnetically with the body. This often is the extent that beneficial effects are manifested. The human heart has been documented as the strongest generator of both electrical and magnetic fields in the body. The heart is 100,000 times stronger than the electrical impulses of the brain. Science tells us if we can change the electrical and magnetic fields of energy we can literally change the atoms in our body and the world. The human heart is designed to do both, which is why forgiveness is so important. (139)

Chapter 5

WHO WAS JESUS AND HOW DID HE HEAL

The Book of Matthew gives us insight into the teachings of God's Holy Son, Jesus Christ. Chapter 5: 13-16 "You are the salt of the earth. But if the salt loses its saltiness how can it be made salty again? It is no longer good for anything, except to be thrown out and trampled by men." "You are the light of the world." "A city on a hill cannot be hidden. Neither the people light a lamp and put it under a bowl. Instead they put it on its stand, and it gives light to everyone in the house. In the same way let your light shine before men, that they may see your good deeds and praise your Father in Heaven." Heaven is a place of rewards for service on earth. Rewards are bestowed on deeds, while access to heaven is only through faith on the basis of grace. Jesus taught us to use our abilities and opportunities to further mankind and know our Heavenly Father rewards us for faithful service. Christ's followers had a difficult message to tell people that were estranged from God and desperately needed salvation in Jesus Christ. Christians that are faithful to their evangelistic possibilities are often persecuted and Jesus called upon them to be faithful and trust God. (140)

Matthew 5:17. "Do not think that I have come to abolish the Law or the Prophets, I have not come to abolish them but to fulfill them." Jesus Christ was the greatest gift of all time. This is how God showed his love among us. His son fulfilled all that God had done for, given to, and promised Israel. His teachings did not replace the Old Testament, they represented the completion of the Old Testament. Jesus lived out what he taught and was an example of what people shall be. His motivation and intention was to call people to join God's kingdom and be like God. Jesus was a pure likeness of God and had a godly character. The scripture laws of the Old Testament were not merely intended to regulate a list of specific actions. They motivated an attitude of reverence of life, reconciliation with other people, commitment to marriage and family, hatred of sin, honesty, servanthood and sacrificial love. (141)

Matthew 6: 22-23. "The eye is the lamp of the body. If your eyes are good, your whole body will be full of light. But if your eyes are bad, your whole body will be full of darkness. If the light within you is darkness, how great is that darkness." Jesus took our needs seriously and taught that material things are not bad in themselves. They become bad when we devote more time to acquiring them than time spent with God. Money must not dominate life. God's sustaining care allows Christs followers to serve him without anxiety. Prayer and meditation relieve anxiety as we ask God to open doors of opportunities for our needs. (142)

Faith, religion and spirituality are still an interest in today's times as the world is driven by confusion, fear, famine and war. Technology has not been able to solve these problems. Institutionalized religion professes a particular faith although the institutions have lost followers in the fundamental way they practice it. The Church keeps its members involved when there is a tradition such as christenings, weddings, confirmations and funerals. Many people are no longer familiar with the contents of the scripture, the New Testament or the interpretation of the Word. There is an esoteric side of Christianity and much to be taught about the life of Jesus of Nazareth. Insights into Jesus life can be found in the Church Fathers, the Christian mystics, the Greek and Russian Orthodox traditions, the apocryphal scriptures, the Dead Sea Scrolls and the Nag Hammadi Scriptures. One of the keys to Jesus teachings lie in the Essene's community and the Aramaic language spoken by Jesus and his contemporaries. The Aramaic New Testament is called Khaboris manuscript and is thought to be one of the oldest written accounts of Jesus and his teachings. The manuscript focuses on what Jesus wished to communicate. Jesus was called Yeshua and was one of the initiated people from ancient times who possessed an insight and knowledge beyond our understanding. There are mystery traditions of ancient times that come from the Essenes and therapists from Alexandria. Jesus was the most outstanding exponent of the hands on metaphysics that healed the incurable and raised the dead. The ancient mystery schools agreed that the universe is controlled by an intelligence called Alaha, God, or The Heavenly Source. (143)

Through Aramaic studies the author Lars Muhl began to understand that there is an inner archaic knowledge that humanity has always possessed needs to be awakened in order to function and heal the sick. Many people do not understand this process and this is one of the main reasons for the spiritual destitution that prevails in the world. John 14: 12. "Follow my example and you will be able to perform even greater wonders than I." As we understand Jesus words will find an ancient energy field of healing and insight is open to us. This energy field has always been open to us since the beginning of time, but it demands an awakened consciousness to gain access to it. An insight into the Aramaic language can be of use to us. This energy field has always been open to us since the beginning of time, but it demands an awakened consciousness to gain access to it. An insight into the Aramaic language can be of use to us. (144)

John 8: 31. "To the Jews who had believed him, Jesus said, 'if you hold to my teaching, you are really my disciples. Then you will know the truth, and the truth will set you free." (145)

Jesus was a Semite and an ancestor of Shem the oldest son of Noah. Jesus Jewish name was Yeshua is translated as YHWH saves. Jesus parents Mari and Yoasaph were both Essenes and possess an insight into scriptures and the overall meaning of life. The Essenes dressed in white, lived as vegetarians, practiced an economy where by everything was held in common, opposed the custom of animal sacrifice, tilled the land, took ritual baths, studied and copied the holy writings, interpreted dreams, new astrology and the prophetic sense, knew about herbs and crystals, and most of all were outstanding healers. When the stars appeared in the heavens the event had been anticipated by the Essenes as the event had been anticipated by the Essenes as the constellation of Melchi-zedek, the three oldest and wisest of the congregation to find the new incarnate. Melchizedek incarnation in the same way new lama incarnations are found in the Tibetan Buddhist Tradition. From scrolls that were found outside of the Essene University at Qumran by the Dead Sea one of the most revered books of the Essenes was the Book of Enoch. According to Edgar Cayce, Jesus was an incarnation of Amilius an etheric spirit identity in Atlantis and the first incarnated man on Earth, Adam. The incarnation line of Jesus is the true order of Melchizedek a line of the first true soul. Jesus was born in a cave between Jerusalem and Bethlehem in today's Talpiot. He grew up in the Essene's colony east of Mount Carmel where present day Nazareth lies. The Essenes oldest university was called the School of the Prophets was on Mount Carmel. This school was established by Elizah who was a Nazarene. Nozrei means initiated in Aramaic or the one with insight. Jesus was also initiated into the Nazarene branch of the Essene's tradition when Yohannan the Baptist baptized him in the River Jordan. In Aramaic yeheeday means the firstborn, the unique, the Eldest One or the Chosen one. This can also be interpreted as Jesus being the first Soul on Earth, Adam. (146)

The New Testament tells us that Jesus was a rabbi, a teacher with knowledge of the Torah (the book of the Moses), the books of wisdom, the Prophets, Enoch, Isaiah, Jeremiah, Ezekiel, and Daniel. There were many writings found at the old Essenes University at Qumran by the Dead Sea. Jesus was the Messenger of God to show us why we are here and how we learn to love unconditionally. The Essenes knew that the physical world we live in and the cosmos are a part of an endless system of worlds and planes of consciousness. The book of John 14:2. "In my Father's house are many rooms; if it were not so, I would have told you. I am going there to prepare a place for you." These other mansions, worlds and planes of consciousness are mostly ethereal and not material and are all connected. These levels can only be experienced by those who have reached the necessary levels of consciousness. The highest planes are the ones that vibrate the quickest. The higher the vibration is the way to accumulate more light. The whole of creation is built on the law of light. This secret lies hidden in every universe, cell, in every atom as a seed of consciousness that awaits for our actions. Man has a free will and the Law of light represents an ethical choice that is made with our every breath. People choose darkness or light and the result is the karma that we experience, many times years later without recognizing how it came to be. This is a great challenge that every human being must pass and learn the lessons life offers. (147)

The Essenes believed that mankind's body returned to the soil as compost but the Soul is eternal. The Souls return to the Oceans of Paradise where all Souls have a basic matrix. After a period where the Soul contemplates its actions it incarnates again not always on Earth. Our souls are God's ambassadors that gain experience, create and transform. What came from dust returns to dust and what belongs to God returns to God? Mankind was given freewill as a baptismal gift, so when our life spirals out of control it is caused by our own actions. When the world experiences agitation it is a reflection of the agitation inside of human beings. In nature we are seeking harmony because there is a cause and effect response to every stimulation. This also causes a psychic reaction to good or bad within the individual and within their spiritual system. As we go through life we cause other people pain though our intentions may be for goodness. Mankind seldom acknowledges what it means to be both victim and executioner. The Law of Light helps to stir the heart of man to open to others needs. In the ancient mystery schools their ceremonies and words of power served to bind together what was detached, isolated and tune the mind. A person who lives in the outer world will become a victim of loneliness and separation when the inner life is neglected. Working with spiritual matters is to create a connection between the planes of consciousness into the very cells of our bodies. Religion comes from the Latin word religare, which is to unite. Religion is a spiritual path to reunite with god. Along line of church fathers from the early centuries, Ephiphanius, St Jerome, Papios, Origenes, Eusebius and Clement of Alexandria referred and quoted from the original Nazarene Gospel written in Aramaic. This manuscript circulated among the first Christians as the Gospel of the Hebrews. The Gospel according to the Egyptians and the Gospel of the Holy Twelve. This was later known as The Aramaic Gospel according to Matthew which laid the ground for other gospels around the time of Papias (AD

60-130). The Bishop of Hierapolis in Asia Minor states that Matthew wrote his gospel in Palestinian Aramaic. The Nazarenes were a mystery school that came out of the Essene Brotherhood on Mount Carmel and by the Dead Sea. The Nazarenes practiced abstention from eating meat and drinking spirits. These people did not abuse or sacrifice animals. Women played an equal role side by side with the male teachers and disciples. Like many other holy men of the time Jesus traveled healing and prophesied wherever they went. Aramaic was the main language through which Jesus the Nazarene communicated with the Kingdom of Heaven, taught, healed and prophesied. According to the Nazarenes God in pure creative energy of unconditional love. Love is the language throughout the universe as the language of the angels is empathy and prophecy. For humans language is signs and symbols. These signs and symbols are dependent on mankind's ability to raise its consciousness towards love, empathy and prophecy in the world. When this process is avoided evil is released. (148)

Namosa D' Noohra is not only the Law of Divine Light but the law of Heavenly Sound. Both the Alexandrian Therapists and the Galilean Nazarenes worked with sound and song in connection with their rituals and ceremonies. Therapists are discovering through the Source of Sound and understanding of man's own voice can achieve healing when we sing. Music and tones can balance the bodies' energy system. This helps with meditation and healing. Over periods of time it develops intuition and our abilities to trust what is inside of us. The key to finding the mysteries of Jesus are inside of ourselves and not our outer circumstances. This is also the key to understanding the mystery that Jesus was Gods son and was crucified for the sins of the world. The key is a way of thinking, that transpersonal psychology, gnosis or wisdom of the heart is found in the language that Jesus healed and passed on his wisdom. The Assyrians still speak the Aramaic language and they say it was the angels who brought it to earth in order to widen mankind's consciousness and he would be able to communicate with the divine world. This special language can be traced back to the beginning of recorded time. It is the language of the Persian Empire, Zoroastrian religion and of the Chaldeans. The church Jesus founded was Aramaic and survived for centuries and then disappeared. These Jewish Christians were called Nazoreans, Ebonite's and Hebrews. Today Aramaic lives on in the Assyrians, Chaldeans in Syria, and in Iraq and the United States. Aramaic uses the concept Alaha for God. Alaha is the heavenly father/mother, the heavenly parent. He is the Source that makes up the great heavenly unity. Alaha is the first creative principle in the universe that contains both the masculine and feminine aspects. (149)

The discoveries of a Gnostic library at Nag Hammadi, Egypt, by Muhammad Ali Al-Samman, an Arab peasant, in 1945 and a fragment of a "Secret Gospel" of Mark in the Judean desert at Mar Saba by Morton Smith 1958 strongly suggest that early Christians possessed a larger body of writings and traditions on the life of Jesus Christ than what has been handed down in the New Testament. Scholars believe that Jesus and his father were both carpenters as the Gospels record. There is no proof that Jesus grew up as a working carpenter. Apocryphal writings say that while Jesus was growing up in Egypt and Palestine. Records here tell of many more healings and miracles he performed. In one instance he commanded a serpent that had bitten a boy, Simon the Canaanite to "suck out all the poison which thou hast infused into that boy." The serpent obeyed and then Jesus cursed the serpent and it burst asunder and died. Jesus touched Simon and his health was restored. In other passages of the scrolls, Jesus healed the foot of a boy, carried water in his cloak, and made a short beam longer for his father Joseph. He also made twelve clay sparrows and clasp his hands bringing them to life. People of his time were religious, but not very academically inclined. The early Christians were not interested in history or advancing in the spiritual life. Dr. John C. Trevor director of the Dead Sea Scrolls Project of the School of Theology at Claremont, California believes this to be true. Nowadays we study history because we want to know what happened, or what caused the situation. Dr. Trevor theorizes that early Christians were expecting Jesus to return so they did not write as much down. (150)

In 1894, Nicolas Notovitch a Russian journalist published a book, La Vienonnve de Jesus Christ, which challenged people's thoughts on where Jesus was in the Last Years. He found a copy of a manuscript while traveling in Ladaker (Little Tibet) in 1887. This ancient Buddhist manuscript states Jesus was in India. Notovich was told by a lama that in the archives at Llasa, capitol of Tibet and was the home of the Dalai Lama. There were several thousand ancient scrolls discussing the life of the prophet Issa, the Eastern name for Jesus. Some of the principal monasteries had copies. Notovitch determined to find the records of the Life of Issa traveled to the great convent Himis tucked away in the hidden valley in the Himalayas. According to a lama there, the documents were brought from India to Nepal and there to Tibet. They were originally written in Pali the religious language of the Buddhists. The copy at Himis had been translated into Tibetan. (151)

Two large bound volumes were read aloud to Notovitch and an interpreter translated as he wrote the stories about Issa. In English the text is called, The Life of Saint Issa: Best of the Sons of men. Some of it talks of the Egypt and captivity, the deliverance of the Israelites by Mossa, the backsliding of the Israelites followed by foreign invasions, subjugation by Rome, and the incarnation of a divine child to poor but pious parents. God speaks by the mouth of the infant and people come from all over to hear him. Issa left his parent's home at around 14 years old with a caravan of merchants. Traveled east to perfect himself in the "Divine World" and to study the laws of the great Buddha's. They say he was 14 when he crossed the Sind. This is a region in southeast Pakistan. There is a reference to "Aryas" which means Aryans who migrated into the Indus valley. His fame spread and he went to Juggernout where he was received by the Brahmin priests. There priests taught him to read and understand the Vedas and to teach, heal, and perform exorcisms, Issa spent 6 years studying and teaching at Juggernaut, Rajagriha, Benares, and other holy cities. He became embroiled in a conflict with the Brahmins and the Kshatriyas by teaching the Holy Scriptures to the lower castes, farmers, merchants, peasants, and laborers. These people were limited in being able to hear the scriptures. (152)

Issa left Juggernaut and went to the foothills of the Himalayas in Southern Nepal. He finally returned to Palestine at the age of twenty-nine. The account of what took place in Palestine is similar to the Gospels. The difference is that John the Baptist does not appear in his life or the resurrection. Pilate condemns him, while the Jewish priests and elders find no fault with him. Pilate fears Issas popularity and the possibility that he might be chosen king. Pilate gives Issa's body to his parents for burial. So many people came to pray at Issa's tomb that Pilate sends guards to remove Issa's body and bring it elsewhere. The following day the people find an empty tomb. The story was suppose too have been based on accounts of merchants who had witnessed the event. There is an argument of whether Buddhist records were of greater value than Christian ones. (153)

We know that the apocrypha's were so numerous in the sixteenth century that the Latin Council of Trent was forced to curtail a great number of them. This would also avoid controversies and they reduced the Book of Revelation as not to reveal to the common place mind. The Nicene Council also reduced the books of the Bible as to reduce transcendental truths. Stilicho, a general of Honorius also caused the Sibylline Books to be burnt in the year 401. There books overflowed with moral, historical and prophetic truths of the highest order. Appendices of the Bible were rescued such as the Book of the Pastor of St. Hermas, the Epistle of St. Clement, and that of St. Barnabas, the Prayer of Manassas, and two books of the Maccabees. God belongs to all of us and we have a right to the books that contain the truth. The llama of Tibet believed Jesus soul was incarnate being God himself come to earth in this child. He choose him to help those who had fallen into evil and to cure those who suffered. Jesus exhorted the souls of those gone astray to repentance and the purification of the sins of which they were culpable. They taught him to read and understand the Vedas, to cure by aid of prayer, to teach, to explain the Holy Scriptures to the people, and to drive out evil spirits from the bodies of men, restoring their sanity. Issa taught that God the Father makes no difference between his children who are all equal. He taught that God was the Eternal Judge and the Eternal Spirit, the one and indivisible soul of the universe, which creates, contains, and vilifies all. (154)

When Issa entered into Persia the priests became alarmed and forbade the people to listen to him. The villages welcomed him and listened to his sermons. Orders were given to arrest him and bring him to the high priest, where he was put through an interrogation. Issa was told that only Saint Zoroaster was admitted the privilege of communion with the Supreme Being. (155)

John 1: 32-34. Then John gave this testimony: "I saw the Spirit come down from heaven as a dove and remain on him." "I would not have known him, except that the one who sent me to baptize with water told me." "The man on whom you see the Spirit come down and remain is he who will baptize with the Holy Spirit." "I have seen and I testify that this is the Son of God." (156)

After this Holy event between Jesus and God, he spent 40 days in the wilderness where he was tempted. Each time he overcame the temptations with the words, "It is written" (Luke 4). The word Christ translates to "the Anointed one and his anointing." Jesus was anointed because he was the Son of man. God choose to operate on earth through the body of a man. We are able to manifest the miracle anointing of God because we have authority on earth. The authority of having a body gives you and me the opportunity to manifest miracles, but the anointing of the Holy Spirit gives us the ability to manifest miracles. When Jesus left the earth he transferred this anointing and authority to us. (157)

Matthew 28: 18-20. Then Jesus came to them and said, "All authority in heaven and on earth has been given to me. Therefore go and make disciples of all nations, baptizing them in the name of the Father and of the Son and of the Holy Spirit, and teaching them to obey everything I have commanded you. And surely I am with you always, to the very end of the age." (158)

We serve the Anointed One, Jesus, the burden remover, and yoke destroyer. This means if we call on him then we are not destined to be bound by the burden of addiction or negative words spoken over our lives, such as you will never amount to anything or your loved ones will never be saved. The anointing is not an idea or a philosophy. It is not natural. The anointing can be supplied, imparted, and withdrawn. The Holy Spirit anointing is not a man-made power, or something that will just barely get you by. Once this is understood how the great men and women of the past walked in this tangible anointing. We can learn to release God's miracle anointing in every area of our lives. We will then know that God within us, like wearing a garment. The anointing that destroys yokes is not in the name of anyone else, it is in the name of Jesus Christ of Nazareth. When people see a sign it is an instrument that points individuals to something beyond itself. People all over the world are suppose too look at the church, which is you and I, and find their way to Jesus. When people look at us we are suppose too be a sign and a wonder of the anointing of God. A wonder is a display of a mighty act of God that only he can accomplish. (159)

Mark 16: 15-18. He said to them, "Go into all the world and preach the good news to all creation. Whoever believes and is baptized will be saved, but whoever does not believe will be condemned. And these signs will be condemned. And these signs will accompany those who believe: In my name they will drive out demons; they will speak in new tongues; they will pick up snakes with their hands; and when they drink deadly poison, it will not hurt them at all; they will place their hands on sick people and they will get well." (160)

If you have ever had resistance in your life, ask God to give you the anointing to overcome the motion against you. There is something living inside of you that is bigger than all of your problems and all of your fears. It is the anointing of the Holy Spirit. When a person is oppressed there is something ruling over an area of their life. Throughout the ages God's power has always been shown through this anointing. (161)

Luke 4: 17-18. "The Spirit of the Lord is on me, because he has anointed me to preach the good news to the poor. He has sent me to proclaim freedom for the prisoners and recovery of sight for the blind, to release the oppressed, to proclaim the year of the Lord's favor." (162)

Jesus work in Galilee was empowered by the Spirit. This is similar to the work of the spirit in the lives of ancient leader such as King David. The major aspects of Jesus ministry were preaching, teaching, healing, and exorcism, which the Gospels all attribute to the Spirit. Jesus demonstrated what God's kingdom is. The kingdom is not pride in prosperity and power. It is helping the needy enjoy life's necessities. It is not greater wealth for the rich but deserved reward for the faithful. Jesus and his kingdom overcome the injustice and evil of this world. His ministry is the model for our ministry. Faith is necessary to recognize revelation. God works where people are ready for his action. (163)

1 Corinthians 12: 1-12. "Now about spiritual gifts, brothers, I do not want you to be ignorant. You know that when you were pagans, somehow or other you were influenced and led astray to mute idols. Therefore I tell you that no one who is speaking by the Spirit of God says, 'Jesus be cursed,' and no one can say, 'Jesus is Lord,' except by the Holy Spirit. There are different kinds of gifts, but the same Spirit. There are different kinds of service, but the same Lord. There are different kinds of working, but the same God works all of them in all men. Now to each one the manifestation of the Spirit is given for the common good. To one there is given through the Spirit the message of wisdom, to another the message of knowledge by means of the same Spirit, to another faith by the same Spirit, to another gifts of healing by that one Spirit, to another miraculous powers, to another prophecy to another distinguishing between spirits, to another speaking in different kinds of tongues, and to still another the interpretation of tongues. All these are the work of one and the same Spirit, and he gives them to each one, just as he determines." (164)

The gifts of the Spirit are the weapons of our warfare to destroy any force of evil used against the body of Christ. We need to always be ready to minister to the whole world. Through a relationship with the Holy Spirit we will gain a firsthand knowledge of the operation of these gifts. This is why prayer and meditation are so important. The Holy Spirit can bring you knowledge that no one else may be fortunate enough to have. The spiritual life and the faith that is needed is within your heart. Modern times have not changed the gifts of the spirit. Accepting the truth that is revealed in your heart is a key that opens a door. God still wants to accomplish his work supernaturally through people on the earth plain. The Holy Spirit is not new, he has been working with human beings for over 4000 years prior to the Christian era. We find this truth all the way back to the book of Genesis. (165)

Gen. 1:1-3. "In the beginning God created the heaven and the earth. And the earth was without form, and void; and darkness was upon the face of the deep. And the Spirit of God moved upon the face of the waters. And God said, Let there be light: and there was light." (166)

The Spirit of God was functioning here with Sound. The Sound of

God's voice was used in the creation process. The Holy Spirit brought order out of chaos that existed in the beginning and he brought the cosmos. When God spoke his word had to be obeyed. The Spirit of God brought forth that which was beautiful on earth for God and man. You cannot escape the presence of your spirit inside of you or the Holy Spirit. When you are trying to run away from your convictions God can follow you over and over until he has your attention. The Holy Spirit is universal in the fulfilling of his operations, he possesses all power and is everywhere. The gifts of the spirit will work everywhere on earth. The Holy Spirit strives to bring man into a place of reconciliation with God. The Holy Spirit has a ministry to cause men to come to God. Jesus spoke of the Holy Spirit being a comfort to us and that he would relate things from heaven to us. The Holy Spirit will bring us messages from God. He is our guide into all truth and the revealer of things to come. (167)

Jesus had a union with God. His statements in the Upper room were "Abide in me as I abide in you"; "I am the vine, you are the branches"; "I have said these things to you so that my joy may be in you, and that your joy may be complete"; "I ask... that they may all be one; as you, Father, are in me and I am in you, may they also be in us". (John 15:4-5-11; 17-21). Our final goal is a union with God. Meditation will not bring divine union, neither will love, nor worship, nor your devotion, nor your sacrifice. It takes God to make a union a reality. Our union with God does not mean the loss of our individuality. Union brings about full personhood and we become all that God created us to be. Contemplative prayer is the process that puts things into motion. We receive his love and return the love. The message you find is that God loves you. He is present in you, lives in you, dwells in you, calls you, saves you, and offers you an understanding and light which you will never find in books and sermons. Divine Love leads us to purity of heart. The pure and the impure can never be united. God's wisdom burns away all the impurities in a man to make him divine. As we wait before the Lord we have a teachable spirit. This brings us to a listening prayer where we experience God in our everyday lives. Spiritual ecstasy can happen as God's spirit rests upon us. (168)

Christian meditation uses the most basic approach to Meditative

Prayer. This is to fill the mind with discipline by Scripture and enter into the presence of holy in unmediated communion. In Meditative Prayer the Bible becomes "wonderful words of life," that lead up to the words of life. The written word becomes a living word addressed to us. Meditation is pondering the words of Scripture. It is a practice usually done in half-hour silent meditation upon Scripture. In this kind of meditation the past parallels and intersects into the present as we place ourselves in the shoes of Abraham to sacrifice his son Isaac, or an Angel telling Mary she is with child. Some people can experience God through abstract meditation alone, but most of us need to be more rooted in the senses. The Scriptures are a wonderful aid to use. This technique uses the imagination which brings the emotions into the equation, so that when we come to God it is with mind and heart. The person sees images we know and understand to teach us about the unseen world that we know so little of and find it difficult to understand. In meditative Prayer God is always addressing our will. Christ is present to heal us, to forgive us, to change us, and to empower us. The technical word for this is lectio divina (Divine reading). (169)

Healing Prayer is a normal part of the Christian life. God cares for our bodies as well as our souls. He can bring healing through doctors, modern psychiatry, psychology, angels, the laying on of hands and other methods. The ancient Hebrews would minister to the spirit and the body when there was illness. The aid of prayer and the aid of medicine should be pursued at the same time, for both are gifts of God. Jesus is the only person we know of that could heal in every instance. The laying on of hands is found throughout the Bible as a tribal blessing, the baptism in the Holy Spirit, and the impartation of spiritual gifts, as well as in healing. Most often people will also anoint with oil while praying for healing. We are open conduits for God's flow of energy. This flow will stop if we have a spirit of hate or resentment, or un-forgiveness. Prayer is a privilege not a quick answer, it can reach to Heaven and change the world for the better of humanity. Jesus work in Galilee was empowered by the spirit. This is similar to the work of the spirit in the lives of ancient leaders such as, King David. The major aspects of Jesus ministry were preaching, teaching, healing, and exorcism, which the Gospels all attribute to the Spirit. Jesus demonstrated what God's kingdom is. The kingdom is not pride in prosperity and power. It is helping the needy enjoy life's necessities. It is not greater wealth for the rich but deserved reward for the faithful. Jesus and his kingdom overcome the injustice and evil of this world. His ministry is the model for our ministry. Faith is necessary to recognize revelation. God works where people are ready for his action. (170)

God exists in community and has existed as and will into eternity remain three persons in one. God was incarnate in Christ Jesus, who offers a model you cannot ignore. Jesus dreams of oneness for all people and can provide a vision for group and churches. God created us in his image and we all live in communities. There is a call to gathering in groups which is God-created and a God-directed ministry birthed out of his very nature. People don't come to church simply to satisfy spiritual needs. They come internally wired with a desire for connection. They see a church as a place to discover God's involvement in creation and in their lives. People hunger for togetherness and to be a part of something beyond themselves. You don't have to be a Christian or a churchgoer to understand that people need each other. Prisoners know the pain of being away from friends and loved ones. Being subjected to extended aloneness kills the spirit, induces insanity, and destroys a person. Some of us need more solitude than others do, yet we all need the companionship of other people. Humans are relational as we seek each other out, meet, court and marry. We define life by the community of family. Jesus' entire public ministry models what it means to live in community. His pattern of small group relationships is an example. When the crowds were to large Jesus would withdraw with his disciples. He healed many and the crowds would push forward to try and touch him. Jesus did not work the crowd he would pull away from it. He knew the masses had great needs, but would spend most of his public ministry together with his community of disciples. He invested most of his time with these 12 disciples teaching them how to heal and spread the word. Jesus followed the divine pattern of gathering a few so that he would transform many lives. He has existed from all time in the community of three in One, the gathering of a few. This was Jesus nature and identity as he became incarnate as a human being. (171)

God has a dream for us and our churches. We are called into community to form networks of small groups to weave real community into the fabric of church life. God created you to crave relationships and embrace small group life. Brotherhood or unity is part of God's created order. This view of humanity applies to people at creation, after the fall, and in our lives today. We are God's image bearer created for community and designed to seek God and enjoy interdependence with him. This helps us to generate spiritual life in others. The Bible reminds us that as human beings we have a natural dependence on God and cannot exist apart from the sustaining gift of life he gives us. Relationships with small church groups give us strength for life's storms, we receive wisdom for making important decisions, experience accountability which is vital to spiritual growth, and find acceptance that helps us repair our wounds. These relationships become attractive to everyone they touch. We do not know when trouble will appear in our life and often need a place to turn. Small groups provide wisdom when we face important decisions. They can help us make the right decisions. We live in an era of corporate downsizing and people lose their jobs every day. To be suddenly without a paycheck, job title, familiar routine, or workplace social network can be traumatic on the entire family. We need friends to hold us accountable and offer acceptance while we are making changes. When we are vulnerable and tell the truth friendships can grow. The church is one place where most people, whether introverts or extroverts, have a reasonable promise of finding accepting relationships. People in churches need to see themselves as members of one body. (172)

Jesus led his group into spiritual community by creating moments, seizing moments, and marking moments. These moments had the active presence and power of God at work in the life of the individual or group. Creating moments, means designing an experience that leads your group to a decision or response to God. When we invite the Holy Spirit to work in us we build a creative atmosphere. In the Upper Room, Jesus created a holy moment. He invited his group to the table. Tables are often a plane that can alter history, such as marriage proposals, family celebrations, peace negotiations and spiritual friendships. In the table in the Upper Room Jesus seized the moment to speak the truth. He showed the disciples service, which showed them a different side of God. Jesus was interested in more than meetings he wanted to see people change and their lives transformed by truth. Prayer of blessings, confession, hope, and intercession should be a mark of small groups. (173)

People all over the world and thru time have wanted to know the secret of how Jesus, Christ healed. Dr. Mikao Usui (1865-1926) was a learned scholar who taught in a Christian seminary in Japan. He was challenged one day by one of his students if he believed the stories in the Bible of Jesus healing. The student asked Dr. Usui when he was going to be taught how to heal. Dr. Usui dedicated the rest of his life to finding out how Jesus and the Buddha had been able to heal. He traveled and learned other languages researching both Christian and Buddhist teachings. At a Zen Buddhist Monastery he was advised to meditate to find the answers. Dr. Usui did a 21 day fast and was struck by a great light revealing the sacred symbols of Reiki. He came to understand these symbols, receive spiritual empowerment and became enlightened. (174)

Reiki is a holistic healing therapy that has now been taught in Japan since the 1920's and in the west since 1938. This is an ancient way of channeling healing energy. This is a safe, gentle, nonintrusive healing technique to be used on oneself, other people, animals, plants, and the environment. This is more than a physical therapy it is one holistic system for balancing, healing, and harmonizing the body, mind, emotions and spirit. The channeled energy promotes relaxation, a sense of wholeness, well- being, self-awareness, personal growth and spiritual development. You cannot teach yourself Reiki, you must go thru the spiritual attunement process with a qualified Reiki Master. Reiki is one of the simplest and easiest holistic healing methods available. Anyone can learn Reiki at any age, gender, religion or origin. Children need permission from a parent or guardian. There are three degrees of Reiki to learn. In Reiki one the class can be taught over 2 to 4 days. It is traditional to receive four separate attunements to open up your inner healing channels and allow Reiki healing energy to flow through you. Some Reiki Masters use one-simple integrated attunement instead of separating them out. The first level of Reiki places an emphasis on self-healing and learning the basic hand positions. Students are taught about the history and origins of Reiki and also how to use it on animals and plants. (175)

Reiki two is regarded as a practitioner level and many people decide to practice professionally. It is usually a two day course, but can be taught in one day. One more attunement is done. You learn the three sacred symbols, which are the power, mental/emotional and distant symbols. Ways of using the symbols are taught for self-treatments, treatments on other people and animals. A form of distant treatment is also taught where you can send a Reiki treatment to anyone, anywhere, at any time. Reiki three is the level of a Reiki Master or teacher. The training varies from one Master to another. The training will include the empowerment symbol and one or two attunements. Some advanced healing techniques, plus training in how to carry out the special attunement processes for each level of Reiki. This is an opportunity for a lifelong commitment to the mastery of Reiki. Each level of attunement to Reiki the frequency or rate of vibration of your energies is raised. For this to happen one must have a clearing of old, mental, emotional, spiritual patterns and thoughts. This is like a spring cleaning that breaks down the blockages in your whole energy system. As Reiki helps to flush out toxins you may have to go to the toilet more. It is wise to do a treatment on yourself every day. (176)

Reiki can be described as a word, as an energy and as a holistic healing system. Reiki should not be regarded as a cure for all conditions, or a religion or a belief system. As a natural form of healing it can support other forms of treatment, such as conventional medical treatments and alternative therapies. When experiencing a treatment of Reiki people often feel a warmth or tingling. Reiki can also help you to channel energy into creativity. Mentally Reiki can help you to let go of negative thoughts, concepts and attitudes, replacing them with positive thoughts, peace and serenity. It can also help you to enhance your intuitive abilities. Reiki helps you to accept and love yourself and to have a nonjudgmental approach to humankind. The way to go about accessing Reiki is to undergo the process of attunements. This is sometimes referred to as an initiation. Energy follows thought so thinking you want to use Reiki switches it on. (177)

There are five principles taught in Reiki: 1) Just for today, do not anger, 2) Just for today, do not worry, 3) Honor your parents, teachers and elders, 4) Earn your living honestly, and 5) Show gratitude to every living thing. There is a general belief that these principles were originally written by Emperor Mutschito the Meiji Emperor. Just today highlights the need to live in the moment and be aware of what is going on around you. Anger is a destructive emotion, and a conscious choice. It is a habit that you develop to a given set of circumstances. People learn to worry about the future and the unknown. We feel that we may not be able to cope with situations. Often we worry our future will never happen. Worry is fear based on negative beliefs about life or the world. Be appreciative for the many blessings in our life. We have a great deal in western society. Work on your personal and spiritual development with Reiki. Be kind to every person you meet. Honor and respect the people you interact with in your life. You have to learn to trust that Reiki is doing what it needs to do. It is an act of love to give yourself a Reiki treatment every day. It takes time to rid yourself of years of blocked or stagnant energy. When practicing professionally you should show total confidentiality as Reiki is a spiritual energy guide by the recipients Higher Self/Soul to go to those areas of greatest need, whether physical, mental, emotional, or spiritual. We aren't promising any miracle cures so a code of ethics should be practiced. (178)

Whatever level of Reiki you are it is useful to include regular energy protection and cleansing into your daily self-healing routine. Being attuned to Reiki raises your body's energy vibrations. Your energy field becomes faster and lighter as you gradually become more "enlightened." This increases your spiritual awareness and your whole energy field can become more permeable to denser, negative energies. Negative energies can impact your energy field either internal or external. You can protect yourself by using your thought energy which is very powerful. Visualize protective barriers around you, and you can use Reiki with or without the symbols. Imagine yourself in a bubble of white light and only love, light, Reiki and positive energy can come in. If you feel threatened surround this bubble with a ring of fire and mirrors to reflect the negative energy back to the sender. With level two of Reiki you can draw the power symbol in the air and step into it saying its mantra three times. As well as protecting yourself from negative energy it is necessary to cleanse your whole body every day. The Reiki Shower technique can be used for cleansing, centering yourself, raising your consciousness and bringing you into a pleasant meditative state. Place your hands in a prayer position and then intend to use Reiki to cleanse and activate your whole energy field. Lift your hands above your head and turn palms downward facing the top of your head. Let the energy flow down and remove any negative energy. Let your hands flow down your body and the energy flow down into the earth. As you breathe blow out any negativity. (179)

Reiki works on the physical level through the warmth of the hands and on the mental level through the thoughts of Reiki symbols. The Reiki system works on the emotional level through the love that flows with them. On the emotional level through the presence of an initiated person, as well as the Reiki power. Dr. Usui also had an Intuitive Reiki ability. He had reached a level of enlightenment where he recognized that the rules on earth could hinder us and would no longer fulfill their purpose. He was able to work in an intuitive manner. Dr. Usui taught a very intense Reiki class to his students. They met once a week to meditate, apply Reiki together and practice scanning the body until they succeeded in reaching a type of energetic diagnosis. Then the part of the body that needed treating was done. Some students are successful immediately and others require a few weeks or months of practice. Reiki energy finds its own path to where it is needed. Besides the five principles of Reiki Dr. Usui taught what is called Gassho, Reiji-Ho and Chiryo. Gassho is a form of meditation that he did before practicing Reiki. Gassho can be done alone or in a group. In group meditations the energy can increase far beyond the people participating. With hands placed together and eyes closed focus your attention at the point where the two middle fingers meet. Relax and then return to where your two fingers meet. This is a very simple but effective method. Reiji-Ho is a breathing method done as a ritual before treating a client. Fold your hands, pray for the health and recovery of the client and fold your hands in front of your third eye and ask the Reiki power to guide your hands to where the energy is needed. We cannot always see what is happening on the etheric level and must learn what others have researched before us. Masters have practiced these techniques to develop the intuition. Chiryo means treatment in English. This is the method of how you treat a client on the floor or a massage treatment. The methods help us to become attuned with the universe and find the divine within. The laying on of hands is one of the most natural things in the world. (180)

In all esoteric traditions there is an important message between the body and the consciousness. The breath is the energy of life. Every skin cell is capable of breathing and does this function without our conscious mind. Dr. Usui taught students a breathing technique called Joshin Kokyou-Ho. This is a method that you breathe through your nose and through your crown chakra. With practice you will begin to feel the energy flow through you. The tandem is the center of the body and the seat of a person's vitality. Hold your breath and the energy you have drawn in for a few seconds. The energy will spread throughout your body. Exhale through your mouth and the breath and the Reiki energy will flow out of your hands, finger tips, mouth, toes and foot chakras. This is how you become a clear channel for Reiki. (181)

Chapter 6

PASTORAL COUNSELING

Pastoral counseling offers psychological thought and method with religious training to address psycho-spiritual issues. Spirituality is an important part of recovery for people. Getting through the Valley's in life can be difficult and finding the right healing process can often be found in our prayer life. This was discovered by Robert Schuller in the beloved twenty-third Psalm. The twenty-third Psalm can be helpful in breaking down barriers to healing, such as self-pity, guilt, fears, and the inability to forgive. "The Lord is my shepherd I shall not want," is a step to look at your life in a positive way. Where am I and where am I going emotionally and spiritually. Remember how God has helped you in the past is a key to knowing he will help you now. Make a decision to keep moving forward to get through what you are going through. "He makes me to lie down in green pastures," is a step to look up when you are down. Praying a prayer of petition can be a comfort knowing that God is listening. We are allowed to pray for ourselves especially when we are hurting. Jesus Christ is the son of God and our intercessor as we are promised our needs will be met. God often comforts people through other people. All of the people who follow Jesus around the world are a church together. The church is here to comfort and not here to condemn. We can't see God or touch him, but often we can feel his presence. Many of us become bitter about the struggles we face and turn away from God instead of toward him. (182)

"He leads me beside the still waters. He restores my Soul," leads us to think of God as your partner. Everyone follows some kind of philosophy in life, like materialism, humanism, Buddhism, or Christianity. People need guides and instructors in life and the guides we choose can make a huge difference. People that follow materialism can crash like the stock market or fall into bankruptcy. Humanism is an ancient philosophy focused on man's free will and the creation of ideals and values. Sometimes these free thinkers believe they are the complete masters of their fate and believe God, does not exist. There are people in churches that believe God exists but does not respond to prayer or interfere in human's lives. They sometimes think God has abandoned them. Christianity is a religion that offers the assurance of life and salvation. Whoever believes in Jesus Christ as the son of God will not perish and have everlasting life. Men who resist adopting a religious perspective of faith in God often are lead into spiritual darkness. A path to a dead end and despair. It is a huge weight to believe that all of our decisions and problems must be ours alone. No matter how dark life may become, it is never as dark as living with the knowledge that God loves us and can intercede. No one person can prove the existence of God, but we can look at his influence around us and the word of the Bible prophets. Knowing that God loves us unconditionally has a healing effect on people and their lives. It is a choice to surrender our wills to the guidance of God and make him our partner in life. (183)

"He leads me in the paths of righteousness for his name's sake," is a step to replace guilt with gratitude. The feeling of guilt can be overwhelming on our consciences when we have done something wrong. There are times we contribute to the failure of our marriages and family life. Maybe we have stretched the truth to achieve some personal gain. God can cleanse us from our feelings of guilt. God is always willing to forgive you and me. A simple prayer of confession washes away the burden of guilt. Expressing an attitude of gratitude for God's love and gift of salvation can make us desire to live up to God's laws. "Yea though I walk through the valley of the shadow of death, I will fear not evil," can help us to face our fears with faith. There are times we need to leave a vision, put our faith into action and allow God to carry us. Facing problems of incredible magnitude can be challenging. Having a vision can move us forward to meet the challenge. All of us must overcome criticism, fear, and ignore negative comments. "For you are with me," reminds us that God will never leave us in our search for truth God and love are the only truths that exist through time and space. Forgiving others for the harm you think they have caused you. Pictures of experience that have hurt us play on our subconscious mind, influencing everything we do. Our minds store fragments of old memories causing us to not see the present as it really is and repeating these memories. Positive prayer helps us to build self-esteem. When we scream "Why Lord?" negative prayer is never answered. Fear can be a barrier to feeling God's love and purpose for our life. (184)

The Hebrew people of the Old Testament believed that God lived in the Ark of the Covenant and put their trust in the ark instead of God. We have a personal God who will walk beside us in times of trouble. People have forgotten we have to ask God for help in prayer. "Your rod and your staff, they comfort me," is the step to hold and hope. The United States has a court of justice relating to crimes as our parents teach us discipline to respect authority, to love God, to appreciate other people, to obey rules, and to mind our manners. "You prepare a table before me in the presence of my enemies," is a guide to follow your heart and stay the course with God. Jesus is our way shower to trust in God when the path is steep and we can't seem to find our way. People's daily lives feel like soldiers fighting a trench war. Wars cause grief to all families, as it only takes a moment to change the course of events for all time. Our enemies are people that also have tragic circumstances. Spiritual healing comes in praying for peace on earth for everyone. "You anoint my head with oil. My cup runs over," and our future can be fruitful. Good health involves more than a fit physical body, but a healthy mind also. We can never, really be healthy until our Souls are in tune with God and allow him to heal us. In Biblical times olive oil was one of the main ointments for soothing a wound. This was also an ointment used on animals for their healing. Jesus and his disciples healed the sick in biblical times with the energy of God and faith. The best kind of medicine is the preventive medicine of a positive mental attitude and daily prayer. Oil was also used as a preventative medicine. Reading the Scriptures is a protection of our minds like taking a vitamin. Daily contact with God keeps us from temptations. God can heal our minds by us taking these direct actions. When we eliminate negative thinking, we are striking at the case of many illnesses that affect the body. The subconscious mind lies beyond our conscious mind where we store our pain and sorrow and our joy and happiness. The magnitude of God's love and healing power is beyond our own comprehension. (185)

"Surely goodness and mercy shall follow me all of the days of my life. And I will dwell in the house of the Lord forever." Happiness is a decision and a state of consciousness. Personal happiness is something each of us is responsible for in our daily lives. Problems and sorrows will come our way, but we must be determined to meet these challenges. Christianity does not make you a better person than your neighbor. Christianity builds your faith and Christ purifies you to meet your maker. You are not going to feel happiness every moment of your life, but you will be able to face your problems with force. God helps us to see the person we have become. All of the goodness the world has to offer would be worthless without Jesus teaching us to live in harmony with God. Our everlasting lives transcend physical existence to spiritual existence. The strength of the twenty-third Psalm is that through Christ we know where we are going to the Promised Land. Forever is a long time. (186)

In order to be a counselor of people we sometimes need to know a history of them and where their belief systems are coming from. New DNA studies show that Native Americans came from West Eurasian people linked to the Middle East and Europe, rather than from just East Asians. This theory came from a genome sequence done on the arm bone of a three-year-old boy from the Malta site near the shores of Lake Baikal in South-Central Siberia. These are the oldest genome of humans ever sequence. This was also found in a second individual genome sequenced from material found at the site, which means humans occupied the region of Siberia. This study shows that Native Americans did not derive from just East Asia, but from a people related to present day western Eurasians. A land bridge formed the way to America which united East Asians and Western Eurasians. This is what formed Native Americans as we know them. This is a great migration mystery that has occurred with many remaining questions unanswered. Such as when and where did the mixing of West Eurasians and East Asian populations occurred. This could have been in Siberia or in the New World. The only way to find out is to find more skeletons of North Americans and also Siberians. The Siberian child found was buried with all kinds of cultural items, Venus figurines, found from Lake Baikal west all the way to Europe. So we know this individual is Western Eurasian. (187)

The wisdom of Native Americans has traveled through time by word of mouth and on the hearts of these people. The Native Americans and the white man are two distinct races with separate origins and separate destinies. There is little in common between the two. The white man's religion was written upon tablets of stone by the iron finger of God so that man could not forget. The Native American religion is the traditions of their ancestors. Dreams given to men in the solemn hours of the night by the Great Spirit, and visions given to the people. The common belief that these two races share is that the earth is a spiritual presence that must be honored, not mastered. The Native American people were grounded in the truth of nature and part of the daily life and experience. Native Americans did not carry on dialogues when discussing an important matter. Each person listened until it was their turn to speak. The person would rise without interruption and speak. The Native Americans realized that the white man's way of life based on commerce and nationalism, and they would need to adjust to survive. He had to accept this as the workings of the Great Mystery. The spirit of the native people has never died and lives in the rocks, forests, rivers, and the mountains. Chief Seattle believed that all things are connected and whatever befalls the earth befalls the children of the earth. This great Chief looked upon the beasts of the earth as our friends who keep us from becoming lonely. Whatever happens to the beasts happens to man. (188)

The Lakota were true naturalists that loved to sit on the soil feeling close to a mothering power. Birds, insects, and animals filled the world with knowledge beyond our comprehension. The Lakota practiced silence as a meaningful practice being polite as thought should always come before speech. Silence was the mark of respect and more powerful than words. A person who talked too much could not be trusted or taken seriously. Native Americans had an education of how to survive in the woods, be a good runner, and bear either cold or hunger. They could build a cabin, take a deer, or kill an enemy. They were hunters, warriors, and counselors. Children were taught not to pass between the fire and an older person or a visitor. They did not speak while others were talking or make fun of a crippled or disfigured person. When a child acted up he was taken aside and talked to in a quiet voice. If a person injured or caused inconvenience to another the word mistake was spoken. Children sat on the ground and became conscious of life in its many forms. (189)

The Onondaga (Iroquois) people opened each council by greeting their cousins and experiencing gratitude to them. They then would offer thanks to the earth, where all people dwell. The Native Americans accepted the message of Christ and new that Love is something you and I must have. Our spirits feed upon it, or will become weak and faint. When we do not have love our self-esteem weakens and our courage fails. Love helps us to live confidently in the world. When we lack love we turn inward and begin to feed upon our own personalities. This causes us to destroy ourselves. The heart cannot fill up with joy unless we have love in us. The benefits last forever and cause our face to shine with joy. A heart that laughs with joy is beautiful to behold. There is a comfort to feel safe with a person and not have to weigh our thoughts or measure words, but to pour out our words with a breath of kindness. This is how the sun of peace shines forever. (190)

Chief Joseph, Nez Perce, questioned the ways of believing. He felt that churches would teach people to quarrel about different beliefs. He had been told the only way to heaven was by baptism. If a man was good and never offended God, and died without baptism, would he go to a place called Hell. This did not make sense to him as God was supposed to love all people. God was supposed to exist before the creation of heaven and earth. So where did he live if there was no heaven or earth? The missionaries declared that those who got to hell do not come out of it, so how do people who are damned appear on earth. He could not understand why angels and the devil did not repent and God would be merciful to them. The Native Americans were told that the virgin mother of Jesus Christ is not God, and never offended God. Her son redeemed all men and atoned for all men, but Mary did nothing wrong so how could her son atone for her. The white man called themselves Christians, yet they practiced cruelty to the Native Americans. The Native Americans say the Catholics and Protestants quarrel about God and felt this was wrong. (191)

Native Americans had a kinship with all creatures of the earth, sky, and water. This was an active principle that the animals had rights of protection, the right to live, the right to multiply, the right to freedom. The Native Americans did not enslave an animal, and spared all life that was not needed for food and clothing. This gave Indians an abiding, love, joy, and mystery. It gave him a reverence for life and made a place for all living things. All creatures on earth were made by the same hand and filled with the Great Mystery of God. From the earth they inherited secrets never told or revealed. Indian faith sought the harmony of man with his surroundings. The world was full of beauty and the Native Americans new the heart would grow hard away from nature. There was a secret influence of nature upon their children keeping the heart soft. The land does not belong to people it belongs to the Great Spirit. (192)

The Native Americans held their breath as their way of life passed away. A great deal of timber, pine and oak was sent to foreign countries, which brought a great deal of money. The buffalo died and an advance civilization was built. What is past cannot be prevented or grieved for, misfortunes happen in everyday life. The passing of the old ways are gone forever and the Native Americans mixed their blood with the white man to survive. My grandmother passed herself off as a white person as she was Native America and my Grandfather was a white man. It is only passed on by word of mouth who has Native American blood. Many of the Native Americans took white names to cover their tracks. (193)

Chief Luther Standing Bear, Oglala Sioux, speaks about the transformation of the Indians by the white man, and the chaos that has resulted in society. He regards the chaos as the white man's disobedience of a fundamental and spiritual law. Civilization and reservations were thrust upon his people with no sense of justice, or the rights of the Native American life. He states that after all the great religions have been preached and expounded, and revealed by brilliant scholars. They are still confronted with the Great Mystery of God. Men must be born and reborn in the dust of their ancestors. If the white people continue to contaminate the land they will also pass and suffocate in their own waste. The Great Spirit made all men brothers and the color of the skin makes no difference. It is not the color of the skin that makes men good or bad. The Great Spirit must shed light on each person's path.

"When you see a new trail, or a footprint you do not know, follow it to the point of knowing." Uncheedah, The Grandmother of Ohiyesa. (194)

The worship of the Great Mystery was in silence, solitary, free from all self-seeking. The Native Americans new God in nature and that he was inside of all men. The souls of the ancestors ascended to God in quiet adoration. There are no priests authorized to come in between us and our Maker. None can exhort or confess or in any way meddle with the religious experience of another. We are all created children of God and conscious of our divinity. Faith cannot be formulated in creeds. There is no preaching, proselytizing, nor persecution, neither are there any atheists. The religion of Native Americans is an attitude of mind, not dogma. There would be no need for a temple or shrine, since God is everywhere in creation. Silence is the balance of body, mind, and spirit. Silence is the Great Mystery. It is the Holy Science to hear God's voice. The fruits of silence and self-control, true courage, endurance, patience, dignity, and reverence. Silence is the cornerstone of character. Guarding your tongue in youth means as you mature you may have a thought that will be of service to your people. The Spirit of God is not breathed into humans alone, but into the whole created universe shares in the perfection of its maker. The elements of lightning, wind, water, fire, and frost are regarded as spiritual powers, but secondary in character. The spirit pervades all creation and every creature possesses a soul in some degree, although not a soul conscious of itself. This is why the force of nature should be shown reverence. This is why the souls of the animal kingdom are regarded as sinless and pure as children. The Native Americans have a faith in the instincts of the animals and believe they have been given a mysterious wisdom from above. They accepted the sacrifice of their bodies to preserve their own, but pay homage to their spirits with certain prayers and offerings. The original white conquerors despised the Indians for their poverty and simplicity. They did not understand that their religion forbade the accumulation of wealth and the enjoyment of luxury. It was clear to them that virtue and happiness are independent of wealth and luxury. (195)

Spiritual power would be lost when to close of contact happened with one's fellow man. Daily prayer and recognition of the unseen and eternal was their duty. The Indian people have always divided the mind into two parts, the spiritual mind and the physical mind. The spiritual mind is strengthened by spiritual prayer and the body is subdued by fasting and hardship. The physical mind is concerned with all personal matters such as success in hunting, relief from sickness, or the sparing of a beloved life. All ceremonies, charms, or incantations to avert danger come from the physical self. The rites of the physical worship are symbolic, such as Sundance's and other ceremonies. The Indians do not worship the sun, it is a symbol of the light, as the cross is a symbol in Christianity. The Sun is a symbol for Father-God as the earth is a symbol for Mother-God. Each soul must meet the morning sun alone and the Great Silence alone to pray. When food is eaten the woman utters the words "Spirit, Partake," as a prayer of thanks. Flowers are for our soils to enjoy and they must be left alone to live out their lives and reproduce themselves. The trinity of the Native Americans is Silence, Love, and Reverence. (196)

Self-hypnosis is more than a set of words and a relaxing procedure. It is a technique to create the reality you want for yourself now and into the future. By quieting your mind and learning to induce a state of hypnosis you can visualize what you dream of. This is a technique that enables you to achieve this altered state of consciousness. You are able to direct your attention to specific goals in order to achieve them. In hypnosis your mind adjusts to the alpha frequency range. Your mind is directed to specific goals such as quitting smoking, dieting, improving self-image, overcoming fears and phobias and improving memory and health. The list is limitless to what can be achieved. Hypnosis is one of the most valuable tools in the world to enrich your life. You can break bad habits, create desirable habits, deal and resolve every sort of human problem. You can replace unhappiness with true happiness in your mind. Hypnosis does not work as an exercise of control over other people. Many people do not engage in daily self-hypnosis due to lack of education and knowledge. Most people lack good information about hypnosis. There are few places that teach about hypnosis, it is not taught in public schools or most colleges. Self-study is the main way to learn this course of study. To be a good hypnotist you need to be honest, have integrity and dedication. You must care about humanity. Learn the techniques and practice. Hypnosis takes advantage of the brains ability to cycle down into alpha waves without going to sleep. In this alpha state the subconscious mind is open for suggestive input. With hypnosis you can suggest to your subconscious mind, and it will accept and respond to make these suggestions a reality. (197)

A hypnotist does not have magical powers. He is an ordinary human being who has mastered the skill of using the power of suggestion to bring about desired results. A person cannot be hypnotized and made to do things against his or her will. Many people use self-hypnosis every day to give themselves constructive suggestions. Hypnosis can help you to visualize your aura and strengthen it. Your aura radiates from you with the strength and colors that you decide by your mental, physical, and emotional condition. You choose to be in such a positive healthy state that your aura is clear and brilliant with beneficial energy you desire. Hypnosis can aid in the healing process when you are injured. Place your hand on the area on your body that needs healing and visualize that area being flooded in healing white light. Picture the area being healthy and normal. Healing energy from your hand will penetrate the area. A healthy thinking mind will create a healthy body. If you do not give directions to your subconscious mind someone else will direct it. This will impress upon you that you are not a worthwhile person. Your mind becomes programmed. Self-hypnosis can help you direct your own mind. Practicing every day can make your dreams become a reality. This may be a self-enrichment tool that changes your world. (198)

Matthew 11: 11-15. "I tell you the truth: Among those born of women there has not risen anyone greater than John the Baptist; yet he who is least in the kingdom of heaven is greater than he. From the days of John the Baptist until now, the kingdom of heaven has been forcefully advancing, and forceful men lay hold of it. For all the Prophets and the Law prophesied until John. And if you are willing to accept it, he is the Elijah who was to come. He who has ears, let him hear." (199)

Matthew 17: 11-13. "Jesus replied, "To be sure, Elijah comes and will restore all things. But I tell you, Elijah has already come, and they did not recognize him, but have done to him everything they wished. In the same way the Son of Man is going to suffer at their hands. Then the disciples understood that he was talking to them about John the Baptist." (200)

Regression Hypnosis is a trip to an earlier period in your life or a past life. A regression can be a traumatic and unpleasant experience and should be done by a Spiritual Counselor, Minister or Therapists. Certain kinds of situations involved in the treatment of various mental, or emotional disorders may cause the subject to experience pain, torment, fright, or whatever. This is the domain of a trained psychiatrist, psychologist, or medical doctor. Hypnosis should always be handled in a safe, helpful, and professional way. When a person is told there is no cause for your pain. Regression Hypnosis may be the answer to find out why the experience is happening. Counseling may teach the person how to cope and solve problems. Sometimes a previous life experience has a direct relationship or a current life. Regression Hypnosis can transform your whole perspective about life. One can bring knowledge to the current situation. Regression requires much preparation on the part of the operator. Thought needs to be given as to the purpose of the regression in advance. You may have to improvise on the spot for whatever direction the events take. Do not impose your own ideas or concepts on the subject. It is possible to go back to previous lifetimes because you have always existed as an intelligent energy. All experiences that have ever existed are recorded somewhere in time. Our human perception of time makes it seem as if the past is gone. You are always in control and can always direct yourself in or out of any experience. (201)

The mind of God created the Christ Consciousness and then the Angelic Hierarchy was manifested to assist in the overseeing and structure of creation. Angels are pure energy that manifest in a way that is most meaningful to the recipient. Nine levels of Angels exist in the mind of God. Cherubim assist in the structure of the Earth plane and are sometimes referred to as "elementals." In nature they maintain the structural integrity of plants, animals, and minerals. In human beings they help the physical body in maintenance of the cellular structure and bodily structures. Their main color is red and they help in creating pregnancies. The second level of Seraphim focus on human emotional conditions. Seraphim Angels appear during times of extreme crises. They have a concern with the transmutation of one form of energy to another. They are associated with the color orange and are helpful in discerning the truth. Thrones are the third level of Angels and they have access to your thought forms and mental structures. The thrones provide you with answers to perplexing problems. They are highly intelligent and help humans digest information about themselves. These Angles are sometimes labeled "elevated masters" or "Ascended Teachers," and their color is yellow. They also assist people with mental disorders. (202)

The fourth level of Angels are called Principalities and are talked about in the New Testament by Jesus Christ. People struggle with their thoughts and are actually in communication with this group of Angels. They bring ideas from the astral level into physical manifestation. People are often in battle with their ego and the principalities. Their color is green and they help us with beneficial change. The fifth level of Angels are called Powers and provide the pathway to the future. They help us to decide which path to the future will exist. They assist us in opening DNA to who or what a person is. Their color is light blue and they help with all forms of communications. The sixth level of Angels help with the flow of time as it relates to linear reality. They help to keep us from confusion with time. Their color is royal blue and help people who are creative with their time. The seventh level of Angels are Dominions and are in charge of the activations in the physical plane and complete the process of Salvation. They open the codes and seals of DNA and mind-patterns that lead to people's true self-realization. The Dominions assist the soul personality with its identity. Their color is violet and they are occupied with unconditional love and knowing. The eighth level Angels are the pure energy form that seek purification of all life forms. These Angels communicate through light, music, and beautiful visions. They operate at a very high frequency. The color associated with them is silver and they assist the God-mind with judgement and atonement. The ninth level of Archangels are the right hand of Christ directed by Father God. They assist with all intelligence and bring entire frequency bands into the proper alignment. They activate the Christ-mind in all people for the sake of logic, sanity, and to end error. They help us with the battle between good and evil. (203)

World famous clergyman Billy Graham researched and wrote a Book on Angels as God's secret agents. People have always had a fascination with Angels appearing in our world. The powers of evil in the world system seem to be preying on their minds and it can be disturbing and frustrating. God is all powerful and omnipotent and he has provided us with offensive and defensive weapons. We are not to be fearful, distressed, deceived or intimidated. It is good to be on our guard, calm and alert. We have assistance for us in spiritual conflicts. Throughout the Bible it is mentioned that God has countless Angels at his command. These Angels can help us with our struggles on the earth plane. This should be a source of comfort and strength for us in every circumstance. Spiritual forces and resources are available to all people and the Bible can be a resource guide to us. (204)

Colossians 1:16. "For by him all things were created: things in heaven and on earth, visible and invisible, whether thrones or powers or rulers or authorities; all things were created by him and for him." (205)

Billy Graham stated in his book he had never heard of anyone preach a sermon on angels. This is a great biblical teaching that has often been ignored. Man relies on scientific discovery, where God has the market on spiritual revelation. Man can only know what God reveals to them about the spiritual and the supernatural. There is nothing we can know about Angels apart from revelation. Through revelation in the Bible God has told us a great deal about Angels. Angels belong to a uniquely different dimension of creation. Our minds have a hard time comprehending something we cannot see. God has given angels knowledge, power, and more mobility than us. They are God's messengers whose chief business is to carry out his orders in the world. They have the capacity to bring his holy enterprises to a successful completion. (206)

Angels have the ability to change their appearance and shuttle in a flash back and forth from heaven to earth and back again. Hebrews 1:4 calls angels ministering "spirits." They are able to take on a physical body when God appoints them a special task. Angels do not reproduce or marry. They are in the ministry of helping sometimes through visions. Angels are also God's chariots of war when needed and the book of Revelations speaks of Angels. (207)

Rev. 5:2. "And I saw a mighty Angel proclaiming in a loud voice. Who is worthy to break the seals and open the scroll?" (208)

God placed Angelic sentinels called cherubim at the east of the Garden of Eden. Genesis 3:23-24 "So the Lord God banished him from the garden of Eden to work the ground from which he had been taken. After he drove the man out, he placed on the east side of the Garden of Eden cherubim and a flaming sword flashing back and forth to guard the way to the tree of life." (209)

Belief in Angels is a general phenomenon in the history of virtually all nations and cultures. Ancient Egyptians would make tombs of their dead very lavish as they felt angels would visit them in succeeding ages. Islamic scholars have proposed that at least two angels have been assigned to each person. One Angel records the good deeds and the other records the bad. Our world has been made more aware of occult and demonic powers. We should be grasping the eternal dimension of life and conscious of the good angelic powers who are real and are associated with God himself and work on our behalf. Angels rejoice when we pray to our Father in heaven. (210)

The Book of Daniel and his Vision is a Revelation given to Daniel as a message of truth from God.

Daniel 10:13-14 "But the prince of the Persian kingdom resisted me twenty-one days. Then Michael, one of the chief princes, came to help me, because I was detained there with the king of Persia. Now I have come to explain to you what will happen to your people in the future, for the vision concerns a time yet to come." (211)

Angelus Occidentalis describes any celestial servant of the leader of a monotheistic religion such as Christianity or Judaism. In Judeo-Christian literature angels predate the creation of earth. The first War in Heaven occurred previous to the seven days that God created the world that we know. St. Thomas Aquinos states besides the nine orders of Angels there are Angels of Contemplation, Angels of the Cosmos, and the Angels of the Earth. Angels of pure contemplation oversee the entire universe and are concerned with manifestations of divine grace within creation. They concentrate on God and do not interact with humans in a direct way. They are Seraphim angels and no one is able to look upon them. They are mentioned in the Book of Revelation. The Angels of the Cosmos are the second house of Angels and are focused on the celestial balance. The Virtue Angels are in this house and bestow Heavenly Miracles upon the world and Holy Blessings upon those individuals whom God chooses to favor. The Angels of Earth are involved with the affairs of earth. Their presence is constant in our daily lives as they listen and influence us. The principalities specialize in working with large groups and creating positive energies. They offer us inspiration and bring structure to the abstract. Most of us know of the Archangels who are known through the Holy Scriptures and bring the answers to prayers. The presence of an Archangel is a signal of great change. (212)

There are innumerable angels who watch, record, and influence the happenings of the worlds of creation. Angels dwell with God in Heaven which is also home to the souls of the just. The Book of Enoch or (Henoch), an apocryphal book of the Bible describes Heaven as seven realms. Angels are in seven spheres of influence that directly influence mankind. Angels of Power teach humans how to channel and release their spiritual energy. Prayer is the act of transforming energy between God and Man. Angels of Healing assist men and women in avoiding illnesses and disease. They help to heal us when we are sick. Healing Angels work closely with a person's Guardian Angel to discern a person's emotional, mental, and spiritual sickness. Guardian Angels of the home protect our homes against dangers, disasters, and ill fortune. Building Angels help humans to separate fears and pain that prevent us from truly being enlightened beings. They help us to strive for perfection of the physical, the mental and the spiritual. Angels of Nature oversee the elemental processes of earth, air, fire, and water. They help to balance and educate humans about organic methods. Angels eat and drink like humans. Angels eat Manna which is thought to be a bread-like substance. Native Americans generally practiced shamanism also believe in winged beings that act as messengers and assassins for the gods. Their angels always have bird-like aspects, like an eagle or a raven. Some are helpful to their tribes and others are evil and take their lives. Native Americans at separate ends of the country share in these similar beliefs on Angels. (213)

Daniels prayer to understand his vision is answered by Arch-Angel Gabriel. Daniel: 9: 21-23. "While I was still in prayer, Gabriel, the man I had seen in the earlier vision, came to me in swift flight about the time of the evening sacrifice. He instructed me and said to me, 'Daniel, I have now come to give you insight and understanding. As soon as you began to pray, an answerer was given, which I have come to tell you, for you are highly esteemed. Therefore, consider the message and understand the vision." (214)

Ministries given by Christ to his church have a common purpose to prepare people for the work of ministry. Pastors, evangelists, and teachers all have a place to share in ministry. The major task of the Bible colleges and seminaries are to produce professional clergyman and to train people who can train others for their ministry. The growth of any ministry is involvement of all believers in the Church of Jesus Christ. A priest is someone who offers up something to God. Followers of Jesus Christ offer up ourselves to God in service and ministry. We offer up all that we have and all that we become. We are fortunate that we have been chosen to make known the wonderful redemptive acts of God. We are all valuable to God and are part of a special kingdom to be set apart for ministry. Theology is the study of God and every sincere believer has a desire to know more about God. Christology is the study of Christ. Soteriology is the study of salvation. Hamartiology pertains to the doctrine of sin. Eschatology is the study of the church. Much of what we do is determined by what we believe. If you believe there is a ministry of laity you will do certain things to further the cause. If we have a clear theology of lay ministers, we will respond like a lay minister in our everyday lives. We need to have a place in our minds that include the important place of the layperson. Throughout history the ministry of the church has changed and will continue to change. Jesus made the meaning of ministry clear as he stated "He did not come to be served, but to serve." The incarnation began with Jesus and God continues to dwell in human flesh today. In the body, the body of Christ and the church. Incarnational theology means when we reach out and touch other people, it is not we who actually touch, but Christ who touches through us. (215)

Light is a guide and there are times when followers of Christ serve as a guide to the world. The world does not have a long-term purpose for living. We are involved in a movement that is bigger than ourselves, that will outlast ourselves. Light sometimes gives a warming like a lighthouse. Our holy lives stand in judgment upon the world as a warning of the earths own self-destruction. The church is the transformer of the current culture. Society depends on the church to have a relationship with the environment and teach holiness of mind, body, and spirit. I am one of the people of God. This is a rich, Biblical statement that is positive and honorable. Within the body of people, the Laos, is a group of people whom we call clergy or "specialized ministry." Such a person is groomed for teaching, preaching, administering of the sacraments, baptism and the Lord's Supper. There are people who are gifted administrators and needed by God's people for chapels and churches. (216)

Ephesians 4: 11-13. "It was he who gave some to be apostles, some to be prophets, some to be evangelists, and some to be pastors and teachers, to prepare God's people for works of service, so that the body of Christ may be built up until we all reach unity in the faith and in the knowledge of the Son of God and become mature, attaining to the whole measure of the fullness of Christ." (217)

Wings and halos showed up in Christian art around the time of the Roman emperor Constantine (A.D. 312). Constantine converted from roman paganism to Christianity after seeing a cross in the sky before a major battle. The pictorial image of wings and halos provided believers with a focus and an icon to follow. These messengers from God are meant to bring up closer to achieving heaven on earth. It is easy for humans to visualize angels with wings. The Yoga Sutras of Patanjali is an Indian meditation teacher who taught how one could contact "celestial beings" by meditating on the light inside of your own head. These beings help us to make the connection between the human and the divine realm. (218)

Lord Aster (also known as Zarathustra-628-551 B.C.) wrote in great detail in his Avesta about encounters with Angels. He stated that angels are extensions and projections of God toward humanity. He believed they were not separate beings standing between God and humanity. Zarathustra showed God presiding over a court of angels. They were oversized humanlike figures both male and female that reflect God's radiance. Heaven is a realm of joy, lightness, happiness, unconditional love, laughter, and beauty. (219)

Angels exist in heaven as a higher divine power in the universe who send information and loving thoughts through our higher self to inspire and guide us. These wonderful beings have the properties of light, speed, brightness, the power to heal and to obliterate darkness. Angles help you to connect your higher self with heaven so that you can be happier here on earth. Heaven is where miracles originate, love exists as pure unconditional healing energy, and humans are regarded as a protected species having free will. Angels do not control us or learn our lessons for us. They can step into protect us when they know we want their help. Angels can coach us to bring love, beauty, and peace into our lives. Many people do not take angels seriously as humans are consumed with seriousness. When minds are free of seriousness we can perform amazing creativity with our minds. This is also when we can heal ourselves from disease, mental and physical by changing the way we think. Angels know of the great number of higher possibilities humans are blessed with. They teach us the way of lightness where human potential becomes human reality. Free will gives human beings tremendous creative power. With this freedom of choice we can choose any spiritual or nonspiritual path that we desire. Humans are influenced by many cycles such as our natural biorhythms, the seasons of the year, energy waves, astrological movements and more. Low points are a natural part of life and we can learn not to be distraught by them. Angels can teach us emotional balance so that our emotions come into harmony with your higher self. (220)

Spiritual guides are angels of basic teachings that give us new insight and new creativity to bring us into harmony with our higher self. Spiritual guides teach us about spiritual values that are unfamiliar to us. Different guides come to us when new lessons are to be learned. If your guide is a Zen Buddhist you may have a lesson concerning losing your ego for a while, developing intuition and learning to be. This may teach you a new way of being. In order to heal the body we must begin with healing the mind. The mind must be supplied with what it needs to be healthy and happy. Negative beliefs hurt our health and need to be replaced with positive healing thoughts in order to heal the body. By changing your attitude toward yourself and towards life can help. Healing involves repairing and making whole after a separation or break in one's life. Healing is the act of cleaning up messes left over from the past. Angels can help us by channeling healing rays from God. Angels can also help us to settle our conflicts with other humans. They can help us relay messages of forgiveness and reconciliation to other people. We must first be willing to forgive and forget. Angels can reach people that are no longer alive. You can meditate and ask angels for insight into what thought patterns are blocking integration. You can ask angels to release learned pain and transmute it. All angels are healers and messengers. Healers are able to call on angels for extra guidance and love. With the help of your own imagination angels can rearrange your cells on a microscopic level. Visualization technique can help you program your immune system and charge it up with energy. Sometimes people get so sick that they are no longer in control of their own healing energy or they go into a coma before it is there time to die. Healing angels are sent from heaven from God to take charge. These angles purify the atmosphere around those that are very ill or unconscious. They provide a barrier against unwanted and sickening influences. They purge the atmosphere of negativity inside this barrier. This provides pure, clean and comfortable energy. Healing rays are then able to have direct access to the person. Angels do not compete with hospitals or doctors, they are there to help. Healing is a simple concept of balance of the body, mind, and spirit. If we are not resistant Angels can appear and rescue us when we are in danger. Only on occasion we can become our higher self and act as an angel of the moment. We may not be aware of what is going on or what we are doing. (221)

Cupid is called the roman God of love and the son of Venus. Cupid is a young angel with wings. True romantic love is one of the greatest gifts given to us. If you go looking for love you will not find it, love has to find you. Love involves other humans and this can cause us trouble when we expect them to provide us with happiness. Love has a way of coming to those who already possess it. Love must come and multiply enough to create an abundance to be able to give some away. We attract what we feel that we deserve. As we learn to love others we must set them free to come and go. This process includes releasing them with forgiveness when they do something we do not like. The angels know you personally and can be of service in helping you to find a partner. Angels are also prosperity brokers that can teach us the true essence of wealth and abundance. We must see our own life as its own fortune, rich and plentiful with enough to go around. Know that the universe will take care of us. Angels help us to convert time, energy, and ideas into negotiable commodities. They can also help us to enjoy our wealth with more love. Angels do not interfere with our thought processes and patterns unless we ask. We are in charge and must make a conscious choice to let the Angels in to eliminate the negative out of our lives. Visualization and positive thinking are techniques that help us to eliminate negative belief systems that cause you to feel undeserving of your highest good. If you allow your Angels access to your brain and mind they can go into your brain like a technician and improve your programming. They can discard negative and stale programs. This process can give you a mission of greatness in life. Dorothy Maclean, in her book To Hear the Angels Sing, wrote that the mythological gods of ancient Greece were actually members of the Angelic world. (222)

Jungian psychology studies the effect that archetypes have on the human personality. These archetypes are inherited from universal ancestors such as the gods and goddesses of ancient Greece, India and Rome. Archetypes are lodged in our unconscious mind as patterns of ideas, thoughts, and physical images. Angels would then be the original models from which human personalities are designed. This gives us a deeper understanding of ourselves and our drives. This information is a key to our personalities and how to strive for greatness. This is also a clue to changing certain behavior patterns. The astrological signs are also archetypes that have a planet associated with one of the archetypal gods and goddesses of ancient Rome. The study of Jungian psychology is a place we can go to consult books on the subject. An optimist expects good results and a mystic seeks union with God. So when you combine them you have an optimistic. This creates a positive environment for a spiritual quest and for enlightenment. Good things can happen and wishes can come true. A wish is also a blessing and a way of expressing desire. With practice an optimistic can interpret everything in a good light. (223)

Iyanla Vanzant is a Yoruba priestess and an ordained minister in Christian New thought. She is the founder and director of Inner Visions International and the Inner Visions Institute for Spiritual Development. Her father's lineage was Native American and her mother was African. This combination helped her to grow in cultural sensitivity, diversity, respect, and knowledge. The Youruba spiritual beliefs and practices opened her heart and mind to the meaning and presence of the spirit of God in all of its forms and manifestations. Yoruba is defined as a pagan religion because its traditions are not like Christian, Jewish, or Islamic. Interpreting spiritual phenomena is different from an intellectual perspective. Our intellect is programmed and tends to discount what it does not recognize or cannot explain. Many of us were raised in religions and spiritual communities that did not honor the contributions or the presence of women. The traditional African and Native ways have a place at the universal table of spiritual knowledge. The concepts and principles of living a Spirit-directed, Spirit-filled life have not changed since the beginning of time. The methods and techniques have changed and evolved. We all must discover and share the true meaning of love. We must learn to forgive all things and all people. This also includes ourselves. We must find the true source of our joy and share it with all people, walk harmlessly and peacefully on the earth. We must all acknowledge, embrace, and honor God who is the creator of all life. Life is the simple flow of events, circumstances, and people. We can make it difficult by cutting off, holding on and trying to control the flow of our breathing and our love. We need to be conscious of the presence of God in all people and situations. Learning to let things flow like breath will let life do the rest. It is sometimes difficult for people to accept that all people are divine. The key is to "believe" you are divine, and to accept that you have spiritual rights. Spirit and spirituality are an essential aspect of your basic nature. You are not undermining God by developing your spirit. What you are doing is trying to make contact with the powerful force that is God within you. What we are seeking and searching for has always been inside of us. Spiritual growth, development, and empowerment is a conscious choice. We have to learn how to make the divinity within us work with and for us. (224)

Principles are what we call tradition and culture. These mediums are what our ancestors developed as a standard of behavior, a code of morality, ethics and values, which govern thought and actions. Our ancestors determined five principles that will reap positive spiritual and physical results, truth, order, love, faith and patience. When these principles are followed as the foundation of our actions and decisions it will put us in touch with the highest universal forces. When we do not follow these principles our lives become chaotic, disorderly, and stagnant. People tend to lay blame and seek solutions outside of ourselves. We have to use the key of within to figure things out and why they are not working. Tapping the power within us means to connect to the beauty, power, wisdom, love, and divine intelligence that exists at our own core. The conscious awareness of the divine within is the ultimate and common goal of all religious beliefs and spiritual traditions. Spirit is universal and our Soul is unique to each human being. (225)

Our physical life here on earth is a learning process that we are spiritually purified. The purification takes place as a result of our experiences in life. The learning is a spiritual process where we are refined in order to be of greater service to other human beings. To do this we must bring our soul and physical mind into alignment with the laws of nature. The Creator established these natural laws. The laws are what we humans call seasons, causes, effects, righteousness, and order. We are constantly provided with the opportunities to bring ourselves into alignment with natural law. This will lead us to be of greater service to other human beings. To do this we must bring our soul and physical mind into alignment with the laws of nature. This will lead us to a more peace-filled and purposeful sense of living. (226)

Our greatest challenge to this process is our mind. The mind expresses our will and ego. It is developed as a result of experience, emotions, and intelligence. When the mind and ego are not in alignment with natural or spiritual laws, they are concerned with how things appear to be. It takes a conscious effort to infuse the will and ego with energy and power of the spirit. People often function without the guidance of Spirit or elders. This is called being hardheaded or stubborn. This means we are not listening internally to the voice of Spirit or to wisdom and we are not in alignment with the laws of nature. What we think and feel will create our reality from the inside to the outside. The Creator is sustained in us by the breath. When you know what to do and how to do it, and why you are doing it, you are more in control. You learn lessons and create divine order in your life. Purification prepares your spirit for its path of evolution. (227)

When our spirit leaves our body in the experience we call death, our soul ceases to exist except in the memory of those who encountered it. Our spirit remains connected to God as he never dies. The spirit changes form to an invisible presence. This is what supports African spiritual philosophy, culture and the practice of ancestral worship. Spirits are connected to the Creator and take on various forms at different times to fulfill a mission. Ancestral spirits are people in the family, community, race, or nation who no longer have a physical form, but whose energy is still among us as a result of their having lived. Ancestral worship is a large part of the Yoruba spiritual culture as a method of staying connected to those who have laid the foundation for our lives. In calling the name of, giving praise to, or honoring an ancestor you are not worshipping the person. You are connecting to the person's spirit. Spirit is energy no longer a personality. When your spirit leaves the body it is no longer hindered by the physical nature, character flaws, personality disorders, or emotional imbalances that were present during the individual's lifetime. The individual spirit moves into a new level of experience and enlightenment. The prayers and mental energy that is offered to the spirit of an ancestor lift the energy of that spirit to a process of evolution.

Your lesson in life is to practice forgiveness and acceptance in life. African spiritual philosophy recognizes ancestral spirits as being vital to spiritual growth and evolution. This is not considered primitive, irreverent, or antichristian. Jesus Christ is considered to also be a powerful ancestor. His energy should be praised. Ancestral altars are a place where one can praise the ancestors daily in the heart and mind. In African culture every person is born with an "Egun," which is a guardian spirit. When you follow the thoughts of your guardian you can overcome many challenges and obstacles. The Catholic faith refers to the guardians as "Saints." Others may call them universal spirits or earth spirits. Prayer is the best method to communicate with your Egun. Iyanla Vanzant is also a certified life coach. She teaches students about the Divine Nature of every individual through knowledge and integration of universal laws and spiritual principles. These ancient principles are incorporated into daily living. (228)

The pressures of ministry and spiritual work can be felt at all areas and at all levels of ministry. This is true of different kinds of ministers, pastors, musicians, educators, youth ministers, administrators, evangelists, and missionaries. All are affected at different times. In many situations ministers have a loss of privacy, poor pay and unrealistic expectations. Depending on the size of the church or spiritual center more ministers own their own homes, have a base salary and a written job description. There is a growing awareness that the minister cannot carry on the work of the church single handedly. There is also a rise in clergy divorces which is a reflection of many factors such as attitudes about marriage, acceptance of divorce, and self-realization philosophy. Divorce is more accepted by society, although still quite disruptive to most families and more so to the clergy family. With this realization more clergy attend seminars and seek professional counseling. (229)

Five general areas of counseling are often used to discuss conflict. The crises of authority, the crises of identity, the crises of priority, the crises of integrity, the crises of dependency. These are aspects of life that can create unique burdens. The crises of the church comes from the flow of humanity of the church. Our self-centeredness can thrust its way into the structure and foundation. Jesus is thought to be head of the church and we often do not want to submit ourselves to another person exercising power over us. People often point to God's Word as our authoritative document, as we put our own spin of interpretation on it. Battles for control are often fought as we try to give leadership to volunteers. There are three common battlefields being the contest of control which is who is running the show? The question of direction of God's Word versus man's ideas, and the issue of ownership of protecting the sacred shrines. The next is the contest for control as growth happens, influence, spiritual power, and changes. Many want to hold onto the past. A church or a center that is growing must adapt to change. Staff needs to feel confident about those being given responsibility and power. Recommendations of newer people should be considered and any negative feelings taken into consideration. There are always people silently at work manipulating those under their influence who may need to be acknowledged and worked with. Ministers with a low-self-esteem may feel threatened and unable to give power to anyone else. (230)

Another conflict in Centers and Churches may be the place of the Bible in the beliefs and practices of the church. The ministers and the congregation may have differences about the role of the Scripture and its proper interpretation. A minister may feel as a theologian that his interpretation is the only one. This can be a difficult dilemma. People's belief systems often hang in the balance. "It is the written word the authoritative revelation of God or not?" Ministers and staff need to look to see if there is any place for human ideas or truths from nonbiblical sources. A minister must separate his own need for authority from issues of doctrine. Sometimes people use biblical interpretation as a battleground to establish personal power. This can lead to struggles of arrogance, pride, and judge mentalism. A Counselor must be able to help the minister identify his feelings and face conflicts over biblical authority. Territorial disputes are also a common area of conflict. One of the greatest areas of conflict is when a minister trespasses on someone's territory. It is easy to invade someone's sacred space without knowing the boundaries. When we are going to an established church or spiritual center we need to respect and ask, before we make changes.

An old church organ may have many memories and needs to be worked around. (231)

As we grow up each of us must find his own identity. We must discover the boundaries between the self and the universe. Most people introduce who they are and where they live. The next most common exchange is what you do for a living. We are identified with our vocation and each person has defined our role with their own expectations. Pastors, Ministers, Spiritual Counselors are usually expected to also preach, teach, administration, counseling, public relations, fund raising, accounting, law, and computer technology. A ministers' family life is often disturbed by someone's emergency, funerals, and mealtime interruptions by listening to someone's problems. Their own family often feels left out and hurt. This is also a source of guilt for many ministers. The clergy is caught in a no-win situation. The expectations of the church must be met, and this requires time management skills of the minister. The demands of the congregation can be expressed on various levels. The minister is to participate in the direct worship services on Sunday. He is to keep certain office hours for counseling and administrative functions. The sick are to be visited as well as church finances are to be promoted, building expansion supervised, and Christian education directed. The minister conducts weddings and funerals and also participates with church committees. Saying no produces not only guilt of not being a good servant, but also fear of rejection. We have common expectations such as to be tireless, to be above being hurt, and to be excellent at every task, to be emotionally self-sufficient, to be free from material needs and to be spiritually perfect. (232)

There is a crisis of integrity of trust of Christians and Churches in our communities. People point out the sinfulness of church members, the emphasis placed on money, and the inability of Christians to love each other, or unbelievers. Some of this is based on our culture or some personal incident that has happened in their lives. The financial appeals of the TV ministries do not help this problem. Ministers must learn to change negative attitudes to positive changes in the spiritual lives of people. The discrepancies between the teachings of Christ and the ministers working this out in his own life can be overwhelming. Ministers must also find a balance between finances and materialism. This can be trickery as there are always opposing forces at work in the world. There are people who receive inheritances and use it for Gods work, receiving only a small fee. Yet these people receive criticism for their life-style. Critics often do not know how much these people give to Spiritual causes. They only see what kind of car they drive. This can cause a loss of integrity where materialism is concerned that should not happen. Another area of integrity is the ministers own spiritual discipline. Ministers know to maintain an active life of prayer, meditation, and Scripture study is an essential way to a growing spiritual life. We all go through dry periods in life and these practices can feel like drudgery. This doesn't change the truth of their usefulness. (233)

We need to encourage these practices in others because God loves us and wants to spend time with his children. A minister must also maintain his integrity as a Prophet and a Priest. This can be done as a prophet by forcefully saying "Thus saith the Lord." A message from God or the Holy Spirit must be passed on to people as any piece of information can help us win the battle. We are here to love and help each other. There can be a crisis of dependency when counselors and ministers fail to ask for help and try to do it all. We are here to serve people but we must know our limits. This is not a weakness to reveal problems or needs. As people advance in responsibility a degree of isolation occurs and a person can feel alone or fearful. Suffering in silence can result in a crises point. Recognizing the pressure in ministry and hearing them with compassion will ordain you as a pastor pastorium. Pastors also face job insecurity as there is a growing number of forced resignations and congregations sometimes ask their pastor to leave and another position is not always available. Pleasing everyone as a pastor is impossible and church politics sometime give power to one or two people. Even churches with appointive systems can fire or jeopardize a pastor's well-being. Disgruntled people are not forced from the church and often stay to demolish several pastors in a row. This is one of the challenges of being a pastor that can go the distance. Pastors often feel as if they are in a no-win situation and are convinced that holding on to anger is un-Christian. This can lead to denial of negative emotions. Sometimes you can see denial or suppression in a Pastors leadership style. Ulcers, colitis, low back pain, and headaches are common. Unspoken anger is often expressed through depression. Pastors frequently suffer from financial stress as many are underpaid. They must accept their realistic financial needs and learn to negotiate better salaries. You cannot be of help to others until you can help yourself and solve some of your own challenges. To be a good counselor you must also learn money management techniques. (234)

There are basic principles of counseling that can be taught to ministers, therapists and Spiritual Counselors. Some people have inborn qualities and are sensitive to feelings and compassion for those in emotional pain. Without these qualities the position would be more miserable as a profession. There are some areas where skills can be taught such as the knowledge of the problems faced. An understanding of the areas of resistance, and an ability to offer acceptance. Each person brings a uniqueness into their counseling as they are unique and need to know their own self. You have to accept yourself and know that God loves you. He has given you your gifts, life, and uniqueness to help others. There are times when counseling a person that you may not understand a problem or have the answer to a question. This is when it is essential to say so and be honest. Answers come in time as we walk our path and learn our life lessons. (235)

I think that everyone has been Scripture-whipped by a self-righteous person at some point in their lives. This is not a good counseling technique. I have never felt the need to confess my sins to a person or tell all of my prayers to one. Respect a person's right to privacy between themselves and God. If I need to confess and change, the Holy Spirit knows he can do this in a way as not to humiliate me in front of others. We are not stone throwers qualified to judge other people's sins or negative thoughts. People under severe stress need all the love we can give them. We want to bring people into a positive state. Counselors are not here to show how intellectual they are at figuring out problems. Giving another person our undivided attention is a gift of love. Listening to the person provides an opening for making interpretive remarks. What a person believes, how he feels and acts must be brought into line with what the Creator intended. We can counsel people about sins, poor choices and bad habits. Damaged emotions and thinking can come under the healing power of the Holy Spirit. The universal laws are spiritual and need to be understood. People dream every night and their dreams can be a source of understanding areas of conflict. Individuals can usually make meaningful interpretations using their own unique symbolization. As a counselor you will discover a wide range of spiritual practices and religious beliefs. The opportunity to apply spiritual principles in calling people back to God. That is what is called Godley counsel. People often forsake meditation because it brings them face to face with themselves. Things are brought into our mind during meditation that leads to confession and cleansing of the mind. The workings of the Holy Spirit are a guide to all wisdom as the fruits of the Sprit, love, joy, peace, patience, kindness, goodness, fidelity, gentleness, and self-control. (236)

Prayer acknowledges before God who we are and that we know who he is. It is an act of faith that brings us into direct, personal touch with God. Ministers are like professional prayers no matter where they are. Praying can become a performance for the people gathered. Ministers can end up neglecting their own personal private lives of prayer. This connection needs to be maintained to provide us our needs. When you stop believing there is a God who cares. When we do work in our own power we begin to fail and miracles go unheard. People reach a point of despair. Prayer isn't a way to change God, it is a way to change ourselves. Restoring a person to a private life of prayer and meditation can be a key to recovery. Scriptures are often used in therapy to bring hope to the hopeless. The mind must have something to hang onto so that healing can occur. Scriptures can be of reassurance to renew one's faith and restore hope. We want to use Scriptures that describe God's love. The beauty on the mountains are the feet of those who bring the gospel of peace. (237)

The road to the future runs through the past. We are drawing wisdom from the past and translating these insights into the present and future life of the church, its faith, worship, ministry, Spirituality. Ancient texts are a tool to help us to do that. Interpretation of the Church fathers, the creeds and practices of the ancient church are sources to be studied and we must look at the culture of the past and how it affects us today. The historical origins of the Christian-Spirituality have deeply affected the spiritual lives of many generations. It is God who establishes a relationship with us through the work of Jesus Christ. God became man to do for us what we cannot do for ourselves. As incarnate God incarnated in Jesus Christ, paid the penalty for sin, overcame the power of evil, destroyed death, and began the new creation. This restored our relationship with him. The Holy Spirit, whom the Nicene Creed calls the "Giver of life" helps us to embrace disciplines that express our relation to God. Living a Christian life is a path of ancient discipline for living in the pattern of Jesus. It has the power to call ethical behavior into conformity left to us by Jesus. The focus of light is the incarnation of God into our history to rescue creatures and creation. Spiritual practices work on some aspect of our character and inner life. They are tools in developing an inner life. Therapy is an adventure in healing where recovery comes from insights, feelings that change, and new behaviors. When you are freed from the spirit of fear, a person gains power and the ability to love and be loved. (238)

John Izzo, PhD is a former minister and has taught at major universities and advised at many companies. He emphasizes that knowing how to use this one life here on earth requires more wisdom than knowledge. Knowledge is the accumulation of facts where wisdom is the ability to discern what matters and what does not matter. In order to find true meaning in our lives we must discover what matters to us. Dr. Izzo's first profession was a minister in the Presbyterian Church. He spent a good deal of time with people who were dying and discovered that individual human beings die very differently. Some people have lived full lives with great purpose and no regrets. Other people look back with bitterness at having missed what really matters. He realized as a young man that some people find the secrets to life and some do not. Having conducted dozens of funeral services and sat with many people in their final days. He discovered this intimacy with mortality to be a great gift as he began to search for the secrets to living a purposeful and fulfilling life. The two things humans want most are to find happiness and to find meaning. This does not mean feeling good brought on by pleasures such as good food and sex. I t means that every human being wants to experience joy and a deep sense of contentment. We want to feel the rapture of being alive. This is not a permanent state of bliss, but a day to day contentment and joy that create happiness. This must include meaning in our life as we discover our purpose. Meaning is finding a connection to something outside of ourselves. This also includes not being alone, but connected to something and someone beyond the self. Our mortality causes us to want to be connected and know it matters that we were here. Many of us stumble through the journey of life learning as we go and discover wisdom when we are old and most of our life is behind us. We need to discover those secrets before we die and while we are still climbing the mountain. A secret is a formula or a plan known only to the initiated or the few. Knowing a secret is not enough, we need to put it into practice. This is like eating a balanced diet because it leads to good health. Confucius tells us that the three methods that we may learn wisdom are by, reflection, which is the noblest, second by experience, which is the bitterest, and third by imitation, which is the easiest. (239)

It is a gift to take an interest in other people. If we could identify people that had lived a long and happy life we would try to learn their secrets. Wisdom can come from listening to the stories of other people. When people find happiness and meaning others around them notice. Older people are a wealth of life experience. They share a common core of wisdom. One of the first secrets to happiness is to be true to yourself. Some people would call this following your heart and know what matters to you. A happy person also lives with intention. You do not want to get to the end of your life and realize you did not follow the path that was your own. This means reflecting again and again whether your life is going in the right direction, and making adjustments to get to the life you desire. Many people live day to day and never reflect on the path they desire as if they are leaving their life up to fate. We should not compare ourselves to others everyone is different and has their own dreams and desires. There are things that make you unique so you would never need to imitate others. A happy purposeful life is the accumulation of many happy days. A wise person knows what a good day for them is. We need to reflect on the elements that contributed to contentment. People lose track of time when engaging in a hobby that is enjoyable. (240)

A person must have the discipline to listen and the courage to follow what their dream or goal in life may be. Sometimes we get so busy we hardly have time to hear the voices of our own souls. Sometimes the universe makes us listen. We catch a cold or an illness that stops us in our tracks and we know we must change. It is a secret in life to have no regrets. Then when it is our time we can accept death with grace. We must move toward what we want rather than move away from fear. At the end of our lives we must not regret risks that we did take and they did not work out as hoped. Our mistakes are often the greatest lessons we learn. Success is never guaranteed in our lives. Anything you attempt holds the possibility of failure. If you fall in love you may risk rejection. Taking even a small risk can have far reaching implications. We must keep moving forward in life toward the direction of what we want. When taking a risk begin by imagining the highest possible good that would occur by taking the risk. Then imagine the worst that could happen and ask yourself if you can handle it. The third secret to life is love and if you miss love you miss life. The giving and receiving of it, is the fundamental building of a happy purposeful life. A great secret is to be a loving person. It is a choice to be a loving person as we also choose to love ourselves, family, friends and others. It is a choice to become love in all of our interactions. One of the most important ways we choose to love the self is to be careful about what we feed ourselves. We can also get hypnotized at an early age with a toxic view of ourselves. The subconscious treats every thought as a prayer. We have control over what we feed our minds. People that focus on the development of deep personal relationships in their lives become happy. A BMW car doesn't come to visit us in a nursing home. Choose to see others with kindness. Continually look for the "red roses" in those we love, focusing on the things that are good about them. It is our power to change at each moment and choose to become love and affirm one another. When we choose love and kindness as our way in the world happiness finds us. (241)

We believe we have forever but we need to live in the moment to find happiness. Then each day becomes a great gift. It is of no benefit to live in the past or the future. Life is to be lived now and not planned for continually telling ourselves we will be happy when. Planning for the future is a good thing as we enjoy the moments of today. When you are walking your dog you can tell he is enjoying the moment. The dog is not trying to get through the walk he is enjoying the moment with his human friend. The present moment is the only moment we have power. How we act in the present moment may influence the future. When tomorrow comes we can embrace it with our full energy as we have done today. To live in the moment we must train our minds over a number of years with the practice of meditation. The practice of silence and focus of meditation is present in most spiritual traditions such as the Christian monastic tradition and Buddhism. You must tell your mind over and over to live in the present until it learns to obey your command. When you have taken control of our mind you are then able to train your mind. Your mind is not a slave to external circumstances. Happy people realize that we are in control of our minds. The capacity to create a good feeling is within you, as you choose the power to shape your thoughts. This means choosing to be in a place of gratitude. (242)

The last secret Dr. Izzo tells us is to give more than you take. What you leave behind really matters to people that your life has touched. My father worked for over 50 years as a Barber listening to the stories of others whose hair he cut and was of service to. Ask what life expects of you and you will never throw your life away. We cannot always control what we get in life, but we can control what we give. We have the power to give kindness without limit. Something inside of humans longs to make a contribution while we are here. Giving connects us to something larger than ourselves. There is a connectedness in the universe we don't fully understand. The universe is too large for any of us to have full knowledge of it. God is called the great mystery to which we are all connected as human beings. Being of service and of being charitable is a way to give life meaning. We make changes in our lives by a natural learning process. Humans learn by naturally watching, listening and experimenting. We then move forward by what we hold in our awareness. (243)

Chapter 7

FURTHER RESEARCH AND CASE STUDIES

A fourteen-year-old girl Bernadette Soubirous witnessed eighteen miraculous appearances of the Virgin Mary, who called herself the Immaculate Conception. These apparitions were authorized by the Roman Catholic Church and a shrine was built to Our Lady of Lourdes. This event took place between February 11, and July 16, 1858, and now more than a century later thousands of people flock to this remote village in Southern France for a miracle healing. There are many mountains and rivers in the world, but God chose this place for people to gather, pray and praise him. This is a place of kindness and hope that a secret exists beyond this world and one where these are no strangers but only people desiring more of God's Divine Love. The secret is not one of only physical healing as only a few are really healed, but one of spiritual healing of the heart. Many people travel at great personal sacrifice and are forced to take a look at their real faith in God. People return to Lourdes year after year, even when the cure they seek does not take place. They want an intimacy with God, a moment of joy of a heavenly place. Their Soul is touched in some way and their faces begin to shine. Lourdes is rich with spiritual miracles. The fruits of this God-intimacy are what despair that has been buried inside of the person, how one perseveres in one's faith, the lessons of patience and of acceptance. People endure their suffering even though they may not understand it and to be inspired to love their neighbor. It is often the sick that love with the love of God. Every kind of human frailty shows up in Lourdes and no one is turned away. This trip is a look into the life of God and is unforgettable. If one is open to the experience it is a very special encounter with Christ the Lord through the guiding of the spirit of Our Lady. This experience is worth it if we can see our neighbor as someone always in need of love. People often complain about their human rights, and everyone is entitled to them, but without the cross we have no resurrection. Everywhere in Lourdes there is a contradiction of the cross that is made manifest. Love and suffering and joy come together, a role to play in missions of the whole people of God in the church and in the world. (244)

Mary was a hidden soul, who did her work and went to temple. She was lowly as her husband worked with his hands. What distinguished her from other women of Galilee is that God chose her to bear his son. Mary was innocent and whole. She was clear-eyed and clear-thinking and a complete person. Mary was filled with God's light and stood the scrutiny and presence of God at all times in her life. She accepted and endured all things as her strength came from God. She did not escape suffering and only God could have healed her heart when her son died. Mary was an example to her son who was the perfect man. Mary helped to bring out the perfection in her son. She guided him through his boyhood and adolescence. Mary had the likeness of God and was hidden in the background of her sons' life. Mary's peace was in God as the world brought her anguish for her son. Mary knew that through her son victory over death becomes a possibility for all of us. People give thanks to the Virgin Mary and now ask for her progress at the hour of their death. (245)

The Hallmark Channel captures the heart at Christmas in the Romantic movie The Christmas Card starring John Newton and Alice Evans. A U. S. soldier visits the town where an inspirational Christmas card was sent to him by a church group that mails cards out to servicemen as a goodwill effort. John Newton had a profound awakening in his twenties and realized he had gifts of healing. He is able to enter a state of pure consciousness and help to relieve negative content, burdens from your life and clearing of ancestral lineage. John used the money from his acting career to study healing techniques from around the world. He works to help humanity end suffering. As more and more people were helped from his gift he knew he had to switch careers. His work compliments the care of medical professionals. John's clients have reported benefits in the areas of headaches, back and joint pain, arthritis, weight issues, high blood pressure, digestive disorders, auto-immune disease, relationship concerns, financial uncertainty, addictions, fears and phobias, low self-esteem, and clarity of purpose. He also shares the Ancestral Clearing techniques in a workshop modality. He teaches others how to use these techniques in their professions. (246)

John Newton's Inspiration: "The irony of this is that we are only truly able to put others needs first, when we have handled our own- much like putting our oxygen mask on first as they say...So much of our past experience goes unresolved only to keep affecting our present. The Ancestral Clearing work that I offer allows one to make peace with the past. To be able to connect with one's higher power and truly be able to come from the heart to create a life worth living not just for ourselves, but for everyone we share this delicate planet with." (247)

Most doctors have one or two stories about spontaneous healing. Few medical researchers seek them out and study the cases as a source of information about the bodies' potential to repair itself. Modern medicine has become very expensive straining the economy and putting medical care beyond the reach of much of the world's population. Politicians all over the world argue about how to pay for health care. Doctors maintain that health requires outside intervention of some kind. Natural practitioners maintain that health results from living in harmony with natural law. Because doctors rely on technology medical care is very expensive. Scientific medicine is identified with external agents of disease. The discovery of antibiotics has been the weapon against diseases caused by bacteria. China has explored ways of increasing internal resistance to disease, so that no matter what the harmful influences you are exposed to, the body can remain healthy. Infectious-disease specialists throughout the world are now seeing untreatable plagues of resistant organisms. Antibiotics are rapidly losing their power and some infectious-disease specialists are beginning to think we can no longer rely on them. Hospitals have had to rely on methods that were used before such as strict quarantine, disinfection, surgical drainage and other processes. Resistance has not developed to the tonics of Chinese medicine, due to the fact they are not acting against the germs, but act with the body's natural defenses. This helps the body resist all kinds of infections. Antibiotics are of no use in diseases caused by viruses. Methods that take advantage of the body's natural healing abilities are far cheaper than the intensive interventions of technological medicine. Few doctors have looked for examples of spontaneous healing as a concept of an internal healing system. The more we embrace healing concepts from within the less reason we will have to use medical interventions. Healing oriented medicine would serve humanity and be less damaging to the body. (248)

Modern medicine does not get to the root of the disease process and promote healing, but suppresses the symptoms of disease. It does not teach us how to prevent disease and not get sick in the first place. The categories of drugs we use in today's society begin with anti. We use antispasmodics, antihypertensive, antianxiety agents, antidepressants, antihistamines, antiarrhythmic, antitussives, antipyretics, and anti-inflammatories. Modern medicine also uses beta blockers and H2-receptor antagonists. This medicine can be suppressive to the healing process, they are meant to be used on a short-term basis for the management of very severe conditions. Corticosteroids are very powerful anti-inflammatory hormones that conventional doctors do not dispense without much thought for the harm they can do. Topical steroids are very effective suppressants of skin rashes and are now sold over the counter in the United States. When this counteractive force is removed the disease process soon returns. People who take drugs like prednisone for months or years for rheumatoid arthritis, asthma, autoimmune and allergic disorders commonly suffer weight gain, depression, ulcers, cataracts, weakened bones and acne. One of the greatest threats to the body is toxic overload from the multitude of harmful substances in today's environment. Traces of pesticides are found in organic and non-organic foods. In 1985, (Alicarb) an extremely toxic pesticide was used on watermelon. This led to the largest reported epidemic of food-borne pesticide poisoning in North America. This has an effect similar to nerve gas. The melons had to be destroyed and an inspection program imposed. Long term use of pesticides and other environmental toxins can cause cancer, immune dysfunction and a variety of chronic ailments. Exposure over time can come from many sources of toxins. Our bodies are able to naturally defend against a certain amount of injurious agents. Cancer risks from radiation over a lifetime with other manmade radiation can overwhelm the body's defensive capabilities. (249)

The body's ability to eliminate unwanted substances depends on the functioning of four systems such as the urinary system, the gastrointestinal system, the respiratory system and the skin. The body discharges wastes through urine, feces, exhaled air, and sweat. The liver processes and breaks down compounds to simpler compounds that can lease the body by one of the four routes. These four systems must remain in good order. Drinking enough pure water helps the kidneys maintain a good output of urine. Eating enough fiber ensures regular bowel functions, as regular exercise clears the respiratory system. Exercise, saunas or steam both help as to sweat out toxins. People come into contact with toxins in the workplace, from the air we breathe, the water we drink, food we eat, and other sources. Taking vitamin C three times a day will give you added protection against toxic overload. Eating fresh fruits and vegetables is also essential. Vitamin E is a second powerful nontoxic antioxidant. It is naturally present in grains and seeds. Selenium is a trace mineral with antioxidant and anticancer properties. (250)

In the home there are a number of electromagnetic hazards that may interfere with healing. Electric blankets and heating pads should be avoided as they generate large electrical fields. Electric blankets and heating pads should be avoided also as they can also dehydrate the body of fluids and in the elderly this can happen quickly. Electric clock radios are dangerous near your head as you sleep at night. Computer supply dealers can also provide screens for the computer that eliminate any electromagnetic transmissions. Tonics are natural products that increase the probability of spontaneous healing. Ginseng is a natural product that if used regularly can increase energy, vitality, and sexual vigor, it improves skin and muscle tone. Garlic is another rich tonic and a source of healing. It is a powerful antiseptic and antibiotic. Ginger is also a spiritual tonic as it is valued for the ability to stimulate digestion, settle upset stomachs, and relive aches and pains. It strengthens the lining of the upper GI Tract and protects against the formation of ulcers and intestinal parasites. The national beverage for Japan is Green Tea which the catchins lower cholesterol and improves lipid metabolism. Green tea also has anticancer and antibacterial effects. Milk Thistle is a tonic that protects the liver and is nontoxic. Astragalus is a tonic herb that is a good treatment for colds and flu. The fibrous roots of this plant enhances the immune function. (251)

There are four activities of the mind that interact with the healing system. The four are belief, thought, mental imagery, and emotion. Our system of belief in healers, miracle shrines and drugs influence our responses to spontaneous healing. Our beliefs also influence perception and determine what we see as we move through the world. One technique therapists use to help the body heal itself is to repeat affirmations. Other strategies are to seek out people that have experienced healing so their reality can become yours. Addiction is thought to be seen as a major obstacle to enlightenment. This is due to the fact that when our attention is focused on thought we cannot experience what is reality. Thought can take us to the here and now and into the past, the future, fantasy, which are unreal realms. Thoughts are a source of anxiety, guilt, fear, and sadness. Emotions can obstruct healing and cause anguish. It is not possible to stop thought unless you have advanced levels of mental training. It is possible to disengage attention from thought. By focusing on sensations from the body one can disengage. Our bodies are anchored in the here and now, while our minds are concerned about the past and future. When we pay attention to sensations in the body we are in the present. (252)

When the mind is overactive it withdrawals from thought and puts it into the here and now. Breath is a natural focus and meditation is a safe way to accomplish this for thought. When you have disturbing thoughts instead of stopping them move your attention to your breath. Manage unwanted thoughts by changing them, as thoughts will cancel each other out. This also works with mirror-image sound waves that cancel each other out as noise elimination. Meditation is a technique to break an addiction to thought. It is a form of directed concentration. By being quiet and focusing concentration on an object, the breath, body sensations and visual image, a person learns to control attention and keep it in one place. Meditation is a practice that helps to change lifelong habits of letting the mind wander into different thoughts. The practice of meditation helps you to move through the world in a calm manner. The mind's eye has a great deal to do with healing. The cerebral cortex is located at the back of the head and is devoted to vision. This part of the brain processes information from the retinas of the eyes. When this action is disengaged and turned inward it becomes a channel for the mind/body as an information tool. When the visual cortex is not processing information from the eyes it can connect the mind and will with the controls of the autonomic nervous system. It can also cause spontaneous healing. People often engage this system in mental imagery of sexual fantasy. This involves interplay of imagery, highly charged emotions and body responses. This is one of the best examples of the power of the mind to affect the body. Learning to control the processes could activate the healing process at will. (253)

Hypnotherapists, visualization therapists, and guided imagery therapists can help you learn methods to take advantage of the mind, body connection through the medium of visual imagination. Once you have mastered a technique you are able to practice on your own. A visualization therapist can explore which images elicit the strongest emotional responses. Breath is the movement of spirit in the body which is a central mystery that connects us to all creation. This would then cause working with breath a form of spiritual practice. How we breathe would naturally impart health and healing as we influence the state of the nervous system. We can regulate the heart rate, blood pressure, circulation, and digestion by consciously changing the rhythm and depth of breathing. It is a basic form of meditation to concentrate on your breath, relax and a way to harmonize the body, mind and spirit. The Science of conscious breathing is not taught in medical schools, but as an esoteric subject. More often it is passed on as an oral tradition. Few books are written on the subject. Many healing systems in the east and west practice this and make use of energy transmission through the use of hands. This can be done with or without touch contact between giver and recipient. China and Japan use systems such as Reiki, Jin shin, Johrei and our culture uses therapeutic touch, a form of healing taught and practiced by nurses. Mystics and spiritual adepts have always taught that it is possible to raise spiritual energy and increase the body's vibration. (254)

People travel all over the world to place themselves in the vicinity of places with high spiritual energy. These include mountains, groves, shrines and temples that they feel uplifted, renewed and recharged. There are also people that make us feel happier, better, and more positive. Our spiritual selves resonate with other people, as human connectedness is a most powerful healer. This positive energy can neutralize many harmful influences that are on the material plane. When you do get sick you must decide what course of action to take to recover your health. If you do not decide this someone else will decide for you and you will not have choices. You must decide if conventional medicine will help or reduce the possibility of spontaneous healing. You must also want to look to see if any alternative treatments exist. Conventional medicine can help in managing a trauma such as a car accident. Once out of danger other sources may speed healing. Conventional medicine is also good at diagnosing and managing a crisis such as hemorrhage, heart attack, pulmonary edema, acute congestive heart failure, bacterial infections. Symptoms that are persistent need to be investigated. Common sense and intuition can help you analyze symptoms and make a decision. Never give up on the healing process and your higher power. Conventional medicine cannot treat viral infections, cure most chronic degenerative diseases, effectively manage most kinds of mental illness, cure most forms of allergy or autoimmune disease, manage psychosomatic illnesses, or cure most forms of cancer. People must actively search out possibilities for treatments and cures following up on every lead. Each person heals in his own way and must unlock the key to success. Treatment must be customized for each individual, but it is useful to know about therapeutic approaches that can give the system a boost in healing. Dietary modifications, specific supplements and herbal medicine, can be of help. Natural treatments usually take longer, but they are not suppressive drugs. (255)

Exodus 15:19-21. "When Pharaoh's horses, chariots and horsemen went into the sea, the Lord brought the waters of the sea back over them, but the Israelites walked through the sea on dry ground. Then Miriam the prophetess, Aaron's sister took a tambourine in her hand, and all the women followed her, with tambourines and dancing. Miriam sang to them: Sing to the Lord for he is highly exalted. The horse and its rider he has hurled into the sea." There are times when the Bible seems to be a book of stories and God seems to be so far away, and then something happens to bring us to the truth of the matter. (256)

One of the dearest treasures we can ever hope to find is the company of lifelong friends. My dear friend Caroline Elizabeth Stewart Cox and her husband Doug Cox were coming home to Virginia for Christmas visiting family and friends. I had known Beth since I was five years old when we moved across the street from her family. Through the years I had learned that I could always count on Beth and missed her and Doug when they moved to Johnson City, Tennessee. Beth did not have a mean bone in her body and could always make me feel comfortable in my own skin. True friends have a healing effect on the people that they are around and they make the world an easier place in which, to live. I had always heard the story growing up that Beth's family went back to Mary Queen of Scots, and since I had ancestry.com I thought I would do a little research and give it to her for Christmas. Beth's mother was a Vinson and I traced their family back to La Havre, Normandy, France, where her family and my biological family the Creasey's both held family seats before the Normandy wars. Beth's father was a Stewart and his line is traced back to Walter "Bailloh" Stewart the 3rd High Steward of Scotland. (257)

As I researched further back I found that this Scottish family descended from the Egyptian Princess Scota, the founder of the Dalriad dynasty. This princess was the daughter of the Pharaoh who was drowned in the Red Sea as Moses and his people fled Egypt. She married Gathelus, a son of Crecrops, King of the Athens. The pair and their followers fled Egypt and sailed to Spain to escape the plagues the Lord God Almighty had loosed upon this Pharaoh's reign. The couple fled onto Ireland and then went over to Scotland, bringing with them the coronation stone of Scone. (258)

The stone of Scone or The Stone of Destiny, is the stone upon which, the true kings of Scotland have been crowned. The stone is called, "the speaking stone," or the stone that would proclaim the chosen king. The stone is an oblong block of red sandstone with markings on it. There are many legends associated with the stone as some say it goes back to biblical times and is the stone Jacob used as a pillow at Bethel. Jewish legend says it is a pedestal of the ark in the Temple. Only the stone itself knows the mystery and secrets of the past and why it was held in such reverence by the Kings of old. It is a small world and we have all traveled great journeys to get to and live in America and to find the Holy Grail treasure to be friendship of a lifetime. Only God would know how to place a friend in our path to heal our hearts. (259)

Beth Cox ran into a friend from high school one day in Johnson City, who is working on becoming a licensed Yoga teacher at Mountain Yoga, Inc. Beth started into a beginners Yoga class and could feel a difference that it makes in her day. She is more relaxed and has time for her mind to switch off the day's workload. She has met knew friends in the community and this helps when her husband is away travelling on his job. The body stretches help her as the couple enjoy hiking on the weekends. Mountain Yoga offers restorative Yoga which takes it very easy to relieve stress and is very calm and quiet. Back care is designed to relieve back pain over time and strengthen the back in a safe manner. Beginners flow classes move a little faster from pose to pose. You will begin to get your heart rate up in this class. Power classes works on the more difficult poses and is more challenging. Yin Yoga is known as a quiet practice and the student will hold postures for long periods of time to get into a deep stretch. Strength and muscle building for your body. There is also a hot/warm class where the room is heated to 85-95 degrees and 75-85 degrees for warm classes. Yoga classes are intended to help people heal without medications. Mountain Yoga has a teacher training program that covers all aspects of Yoga, and how to prepare you to be a Yoga instructor. They specialize in functional anatomy of the body and how to apply that knowledge. This also includes meditation and mindfulness. (260)

Dr. Dharma Singh Khalsa has studied scientific programs that are a key to understanding Brain Longevity. Your brain is flesh and blood like the rest of your body. It will respond to the lifestyle measures you take to strengthen it. Mind/Body exercises are an ancient art of brain regeneration. Human beings and all matter in the universe are physically composed of electrons, protons, and neutrons. These are constantly moving within your cells as "dancing cells of light." So we humans possess a high degree of energy potential at the cellular level. Mind/Body exercises can shift large amounts of energy to your brain, nerves and endocrine systems. This will teach you to use energy more efficiently, balancing the energy of your brain and nervous and endocrine systems. You will function at a higher level without exhausting your mind and body. Mind/body exercises are one of the most powerful tools we possess for brain regeneration. Yogic exercises have been used by yogic masters for thousands of years. Kriya is a combination of movement, breathing, posture, a mantra, and a positioning of the fingers. Each Kriya is designed to increase blood flow, energy flow, to the brain, the nervous system, and to glands of the endocrine system. Blood flow has a powerful effect and immediate boost to cognitive function. It supplies large amounts of oxygen and glucose. This improves the long-term health of the brain enhancing neuronal metabolism. In the Indian Yogic tradition this is called prana and the energy releases and channels in the body, what is called Kundalini. (261)

The body's Kundalini energy is stimulated by Kundalini Yogic energy exercises. This is sometimes referred to a vital energy as it is "cosmic energy." All forms of yoga seek to unite body and mind. Kundalini, Yoga, Meditation, and a carefully balanced diet are the keys to success. The goal of Kundalini yoga is to channel and move energy from the nervous system and the meridian system. This also transports energy from the base of the brain. You function at such a heightened sensitivity that your brain can function at its optimum capacity, causing you to become totally aware. As a physician Dr. Khalsa states that these mind/body exercises are excitatory, neuro protective, memory-enhancing and anti-aging.

When alone properly this process offers a transcendent experience. All people have the ability, sleeping within them, to be totally intuitive, creative, and effective. These exercises remove neurological barriers. Remove the barrier and with time you take people to a state where nothing is lacking. Yoga is also an ancient yogic art form of chanting or mantra yoga. You say specific sounds while you are exercising and meditating. (262)

Naad Yoga employs only primal sounds such as "OM." These primal sounds invigorate specific endocrine glands and the brain through simple vibrations. Certain movements of the hands and fingers help the brain to pattern physical coordination. Positioning the hands and fingers has an effect upon cognitive function. According to yogic masters each area of the hand reflexes helps to control a particular area of the brain. Practitioners believe that it is possible to influence the brain by stretching the fingers, crossing them, or touching the fingertips to the thumb or to another part of the hand. This is what yogis call mudras. All of the elements of movement, breath, mantra, and mudra form the mind/body exercise Kriya. As you learn to perform this you will see the individual powers of each Kriya. (263)

Research into the effects of vibrational sound currants on cells has yielded results. The notes of D, C, E monitored technologically have results on decreasing the malignant reproductive rates of cancer cells. Sound current indicates considerable power. In the future sound or ultrasound may be used in combating diseases. Pet scans have also shown changes when mantras were chanted. Eastern medicine tells us that these are seventy-two energy meridians that flow throughout the body. These are also three central Kundalini energy channels that flow up the spine into the brain. Along these meridians and channels is believed to be a continual state of vibration. The meridians are reflex points and according to yogic philosophy, eighty-four of these reflex points are located in the upper palate of the mouth alone. The chanting of primal sound is believed to stimulate the reflex points in the mouth. The tongue strikes many of the reflex points during the Naad yoga. One of the benefits of repeating mantras is that they "silence the internal dialogue." This gives your mind a few moments of peace. (264)

Yogis practice a powerful exercise called "The Breath of Fire," This exercise is supposed to "Kindle your personal flame." Three minutes of the Breath of Fire will increase your physical and mental energy. The exercise stimulates the splanchnic nerves in the abdominal cavity. When these nerves are stimulated the release of epinephrine and norepinephrine. This will cause a mild perspiration on your forehead. Yogis believe this is psychic heat or topa. It takes practice to generate topa. The Breath of Fire requires the person to breathe through the nostrils rapidly, inhaling and exhaling. Breathe down from your diaphragm and keep the chest relaxed. You should focus your mental energy on your navel area. This exercise produces alpha rhythms in the brain. So the exercise simultaneously creates calmness and increased alertness. This also increases oxygen to the brain. Neurons in the brain are cleansed and rejuvenated. Instead of reaching for a cup of coffee for quick energy, many people use the Breath of Fire. (265)

There is another exercise for creating energy and the flexibility of the spine. Yogis measure the age of a person in terms of spinal flexibility. This helps to move energy throughout the body. Studies at the University of California show increased amounts of strength of Alpha and Theta waves. With this exercise Yogis chant a mantra, Ong Namo Guru Dev Na Mo, which means "I bow before my highest consciousness." It is believed that this links you to the master teachers who have taught these exercises throughout history. (266)

The Kirtan Kriya meditation for creativity celebrates the cycle of creation, birth, life, death, and rebirth. This involves chanting primal sounds that represent the stages of life, which are Sa which means birth, infinity or cosmos. Ta which means life or existence, Na which means death or completion, and Ma which means rebirth. Yogis believe chanting this mantra stimulates your pituitary. Using the finger positions are also part of this exercise. The Kirtan Kriya may increase your intuition, creativity, and mental energy. Anyone can benefit from mind/body exercises. (267)

Dr. Khalsa gives us the most powerful tool against stress in our lives, meditation. There are many forms of meditation such as watching mindless television. When people watch television their brain waves shift to the alpha state, which is a meditative state. Television has a hypnotic effect and many times we do not even concentrate on the content. Meditation evokes a relaxation response. If the body is in a relaxed state more often, we are less vulnerable to the stress response. Prayer is also a powerful form of meditation. Combining mind/body exercises and meditation has a physical effect and facilitates physical healing of the body. Prayer is sometimes looked upon as a healing science. It is a mystery that cannot be explained, but has a psychological effect that virtually always contributes to physical health. Mentally projecting prayer has a calming and an activating influence upon people that have been studied. Prayer has even been thought of as a form of extrasensory perception. It might be that a person who is prayed for somehow senses another person's concern. If this is so the person senses a caring attitude that is of psychological benefit. Many people believe that prayer connects them to a divine spirit, and this process is evoking the loving, healing energy of God. Dr. Khalsa feels he owes his patients his prayers as well as his scientific knowledge. True healers should personally care about their patients. The services of science should also provide the power of prayer. (268)

Christianity is founded on the worship of Jesus Christ of Nazareth as the son of God. The unique self-revelation of God to the human race. Almost all we know about Jesus comes from the four accounts of his life in the Gospels of the New Testament. Jesus was born just before the death of Herod the Great, King of Judea, in BCE. Jesus lived about 33years of life here on earth as far as we have knowledge from historical records. The Jewish people were subject to local princes appointed by the Roman emperor under the direct rule of Rome itself. The Sadducees were a priestly party that accepted Roman rule and the Pharisees who became dominant were less concerned with politics. The Pharisees concentrated on the study and application of the Old Testament Law. The Essenes were a group of Jews who did not accept Jewish society and set up isolated communities, such as Qumran. There were Jewish people who resented Roman rule and revolts would break out. The Jewish people longed for a "messiah," a savior from God that would save them. Jesus was born in Bethlehem in Judea, and brought up in Galilee. Galilee was regarded as an uncultured, half-pagan area. Jesus would have had a northern accent that would have been noticed. Jesus family was respectable, affluent and he was trained as a carpenter. (269)

Jesus birth took place in King David's town of Bethlehem in very down to earth circumstances according to the Christian Gospels. Angels were present and proclaimed him the promised savior. It was maintained that Jesus was not conceived by human intercourse, but by the power of God. In the three years of his ministry the Gospels have Jesus, preaching, teaching, and healing. He and his followers adopted a lifestyle of wandering and being independent. As a preacher Jesus drew large crowds who followed him everywhere. He was well known as a healer who had compassion for all people. The Gospels speak of his curing many different types of illnesses and deformity. Jesus healed by a simple word and a touch or sometimes by a word alone, because there was no elaborate ritual for him to follow. Jesus had a power which responded to physical need as he met it. He was also an exorcist trained to drive out demons by a word or command. Because of his healing power and teaching he was sought out by the crowds. (270)

Besides recorded miracles of healing, a number of incidents are recorded where Jesus displayed a supernatural control over nature. His power always responded to a need, such as the time he multiplied a little food to feed a large crowd. He also calmed a large storm on the lake by a command. These miracles made a huge impression on those around him. Jesus demanded that his disciples have a total dependence on God to supply all their needs. He spent time teaching these disciples privately to preach and heal. Jesus taught the disciples to see themselves as distinct from other people and to win people to be his disciples. Jesus message was a call for faith and loyalty to himself as the arbiter of people's destiny. He proclaimed forgiveness and salvation by his own life and suffering and death. He is the messenger and also the heart of the message. Jesus brought people to God and is the way to God. The worship of Jesus as the Son of man came after his resurrection. The disciples believed they had been walking with God. (271)

To be a Christian is to make the confession "Jesus Christ is Lord," this is part of a spiritual relationship and the believer is then baptized to be reborn with him. After the day of Pentecost a gift of the Holy Spirit and the birth of the Church was given. The gift of the Holy Spirit by anointing with oil is given to each person. So a Christian can be defined as a person who has received the gift of the Spirit. (272)

When you walk into her home your eyes fix upon an oil painting of a beautiful young woman and her three children. I felt safe as if I were home with all the love in the universe around me. It is the energy of Rev. Jeanne Greening a woman who has spent her life healing and caring for others. She has a knowledge base that is apparent from years of study and classes in the healing arts. Rev. Greening attended National Cathedral Boarding School and learned from the Priest at the National Cathedral as she would talk to them because they were so spiritual. She taught the Episcopal Priest in Sarasota, Florida Reiki and taught Reiki at the Anada Ashram Yoga Society of New York for a week. Jeanne Greening is an example of what God can do in the life of someone he bestows gifts upon to do his work. I had come for more than healing when I first met Rev. Greening. I had a calling into the ministry and Rev. Greening helped me to answer my need with the Alliance of Divine Love Ministry program with classes in her home-based healing and teaching business. A personal interview with Rev. Jeanne Greening:

I guess the first thing I can remember about healing was from growing up, I always had people telling me their problems whether it was in the drug store or the grocery store. When my Dad died and we got letters from everyone there was one special letter that I happen to get and read and it struck home. They said he had the ability to always read people. I began to realize that was exactly what I was doing with people who were in my life or on the periphery. I knew I had learned it as a child with things that had happened. It was an awakening. I knew it was something I really wanted to do to help people in their lives. (273)

The second thing that happened was I had a very ugly divorce and went to live at the Gulf Beach for three years. During that time I had my feet healed. After three operations, I was unable to go up and down on my toes. In ten minutes the healer had my toes bending and when I stood up I could go up and down on my toes like a ballet dancer. It changed my podiatrist's life just seeing me do that. He converted and started doing yoga, etc. It also changed my life and I knew from the healing that I was going to learn it as this was the best way to help people. It was medically impossible for me to go up and down on my toes and yet I could do it. (274)

During my stay at the beach for three years I read all the positive books out on the market. "I'm Ok Your Ok". "I Aint Much Baby but I'm all I've got". I used each book as a workbook and started changing my life and perception on things. A Lutheran minister taught me how to meditate, and I began to see life as I had always felt it was on all levels. One morning I was down on the beach and started writing all the names of the men and boys I had been attracted to during my life and suddenly realized they were all alike. I developed a healing technique from that to help people work out patterns. I also found many teachers who helped me and after taking numerous classes, and perfecting the technique, I started doing it professionally, which I did for 40 years and am still doing. I took every type of class that I could, such as Reiki I, II and the Mastership from three different individuals so I could teach it, Cranial sacral, touch for health, Omega, and many more as I took classes from everywhere I could find them. Among some of the classes numerology, astrology, Astara, White Eagle where I became a lone healer, outer and inner brother with the organization, theosophy and the Rosicrucian and many more. I taught classes in the different books by White Eagle. In 1989 I decided to take the Alliance of Divine Love ministerial course, which I loved, and decided to become a minister. Not only did I start to marry people but also taught the course. I started doing more of Pastoral counseling. I started traveling and going on the circuit to different cities in the United States teaching, giving workshops and classes in healing and teaching the ministerial course. I wanted to take and use everything that I had learned. Someone used to say you couldn't do that, but I have learned from experience that each thing we learn we integrate into our energy field and soon we have formed an energy with the Universe that is our own. That is what you use to work with the rest of your life. It doesn't have to have a specific name, it is what you have learned and put into practice. (275)

What have I learned from all this? It really isn't all I have learned, it is all that has been taught to me to find my truth within. One of the major things I have learned is to be a good listener. I hear things from each person that I am working with and I am also hearing what they aren't saying but feel and what they really mean. I have also learned that my life of learning was all meant for me to do this mission. I have never had people come to me where I haven't been going through a similar learning experience myself. The same as they are. It helps me to relate to them and to what they are experiencing. It also gives me the ability to offer more than one way to accomplish or work out problems. I use to think there was only one way. It has also helped me with pastoral counseling. It has given me the ability to know when I can help someone and when I can't. I will say up front if I will not be able to help them or if it is questionable. I have learned to be honest and have integrity. I have learned to cancel an appointment if I am having problems with my emotions. The client picks up on it and it throws the energy off for what they came to heal. (276)

I decided to take the Medicine Woman Course. I was excited because I had studied with an Apache Shaman earlier in my life and we learned how to make a medicine wheel and to do sweat lodges. I had an organic farm at the time and so we had workshops on it. The medicine wheel was so special to use as a spiritual place to go and just "Be". I would go out and sit on a stone that meant something to me. Each stone or rock that you place in a medicine wheel has a significant meaning. It was my "Church". When I took the Medicine Woman I learned more about the herbs that Native American's used for their medicine. I learned about the sacred bundles made up of sacred stones and artifacts which have been sacred and Spiritual. These bundles are in my home in my healing areas. (277)

Out of all of this learning and helping people, my truth has grown. The most beautiful part of the whole learning process has been the opening of my Spirituality. My life has steered me to always have faith that Spirit will be there for me at all times. One of the greatest lessons I have learned as a healer and at 79 I have finally learned the word discernment. Why I say this is the greatest lessons, is because I have learned finally something that has brought me contentment. One judges with their head and you Discern with your heart. Judgement is cold, logical, right or wrong. When you judge other people, you invest yourself in other people's energy. You become responsible for the actions of the other person. You put yourself in jeopardy because you cannot control the actions of others that you have taken responsibility for. (278)

Discernment is seeing how things are and letting the other person be who they are, then deciding how much interaction with them you desire to have. Do you wish to be a part of it? Or just walk away. When you choose to become a part of it, it becomes a part of you. Learning discernment is one of the most important Spiritual lessons we have to learn on this planet. (279)

The other contentment and happiness was cleaning my aura to the point that I had released my old patterns and attracted someone in my life that really loved and cared for me. I also have close friends that are the same energy. That is why we have to let go of all those old memories that keep surfacing. This is why so many people have colon problems as this is the area we hold on to emotions. (280)

We go through many tests throughout our lives until we make our transition. No one knows, even us, what is in our subconscious. It takes memories or as I call them buttons that are pushed, to see what we are holding on to or what thoughts and situations we need to let go of. (281)

The main thing is to love yourself, honor and respect who you are, and stop worrying what everyone else thinks. They are the judges – who want things as they think. Don't you want to be different? I do. I just want to be me. I desire to help people achieve peace of mind and teach them how to heal themselves. That is what I came in to do and I ask Spirit to help me every day. (282)

Dr. Eben Alexander graduated from the University Of North Carolina at Chapel Hill in 1976 with a major in chemistry and an M.D. from Duke University Medical School in 1980. His focus was neuroendocrinology at Massachusetts General Hospital and Harvard. He completed a fellowship in cerebrovascular neurosurgery in Newcastle-Upon Tyne in the United Kingdom. Dr. Alexander then spent fifteen years on the faculty of Harvard Medical School as an associate professor of surgery, with a specialization in neurosurgery. His research work involved the development of advanced technical procedures like stereotactic radiosurgery. He also helped in developing magnetic resonance image-guided neurosurgical procedures. He was devoted to science to help and to heal people. Dr. Alexander had a wife and two lovely children and knew he was a lucky man. (283)

On November 10, 2008 at the age of fifty-four years old he was struck down by a rare illness and thrown into a coma for seven days. His entire neocortex which is the outer surface of the brain was shut down. The brain is the machine that produces consciousness. Dr. Alexander went through a near death experience. He was alive but free of the limitations of his brain. Dr. Alexander and his family had moved to Lynchburg, Virginia and he worked at Focused Ultrasound Surgery Foundation in Charlottesville, VA. He thought he had the flu and then his body became paralyzed. Mrs. Alexander had him rushed to Lynchburg General Hospital which is one of the busiest emergency rooms in the state of Virginia. He had been on a trip to Israel and picked up a primitive form of Escherichia-Coli. Dr. Alexander went with his family to the Episcopal Church on occasion. His life in the scientific world of academic neurosurgery had made him question if God and the afterlife existed. (284)

In the coma Dr. Alexander moved through a vast darkness to what appeared to be a lighted Orb. He was aware of God the creator whom he called OM. The orb was a companion and an interpreter. The Om presence was warm and understood humans. Through the orb the Om told him that there are many universes and love lay at the center of all of them. Evil was necessary because without it there would be no free will. This caused growth to be possible and we all have a chance to be what God wants us to be. Dr. Alexander saw life throughout the universes with some whose intelligence was advanced far beyond that of humanity. There were countless higher dimensions that could only be experienced directly. Cause and effect also exist in these dimensions. Time and space is meshed with these other worlds. From these higher worlds one could access any time or place in our world. Insights happened directly and knowledge was stored without memorization. The information was clear and did not fade from the mind. Science and spirituality can exist as God is all knowledge and love. When a person is in a coma the body is there, but the essence is somewhere else. We are all part of the divine and nothing can take that away. We get closer to the genuine spiritual self by manifesting love and compassion. They are real and concrete making up the fabric of the spiritual realm. (285)

After seven days Dr. Alexander's eyes opened as if he were seeing the world for the first time. Physical life is characterized by defensiveness, whereas spiritual life is the opposite. This was a life changing experience for Dr. Alexander. He is still a doctor that searches for truth and most of all a healer. His near death experience has inspired him to make the world a better place. WWW.Eternea.org is a vehicle set up to advance research, education, and applied programs concerning spirituality transformative experiences by Dr. Alexander and his partner. (286)

Parallels exist between ancient healing practices, Christianity and modern medicine as students learn the healing art of Chaplaincy at Roanoke Carilion Clinic. Carilion Roanoke Memorial Hospital's Chaplains make rounds that cover the hospitals 703 beds and 60-bed neonatal intensive care unit. They are helped by one part-time and five flex-time chaplains and by students in Carilion's Clinical Pastoral Education program. Students are learning the art of practicing a ministry that requires being present with people and their stories. (287)

Carilion Clinic's Clinical Pastoral Education program runs two units a year for interns. The program is open to clergy and lay ministers. The chaplain's role isn't to preach or save souls, and Gideon Bibles are no longer allowed in hospital rooms. They are there for support and to listen to the needs of people that want to talk about their lives and hardest moments. Students are taught how to do this in a program. The students go through 100 classroom hours and 300 hours practicing in the hospital. The program is accredited by the Association for Clinical Pastoral Education. Brown and Nathaniel Bishop, President of Jefferson College of Health Sciences, wanted an accredited program in Southwest Virginia to train hospital Chaplains. There are currently three students, all of whom are from Liberty University of Lynchburg, VA, which is a private Christian College. The students learn how to go into a room and how to leave, and in between how to have a conversation, how to listen and how to talk. The students are taught pastoral conversations, crisis intervention, End of Life, family systems, and abnormal psychology.

When students enter the program they learn an understanding of Carilion's ministry program and to develop into this role. Who knew that modern medical facilities would now be training Ministers? (288)

Carilion Clinic has partnered with Virginia Tech to form Virginia Tech Carilion School of Medicine. This will enhance Carilion Clinics transformation to a clinic model. It will provide the Internal Medical Residency with exciting growth opportunities in the area of scholarly work. (289)

Clinical pastoral education is education to teach pastoral care to clergy and others. This is the primary method of training used for hospitals and hospice chaplains, and spiritual care givers in the United States, United Kingdom, Canada, Australia and New Zealand. The program is both a multicultural and interfaith experience. Pastoral care has a long tradition in Christianity and in some other faiths. In 1925, Richard Cabot, a physician and adjunct lecturer at the Harvard Divinity School, published an article suggesting that every candidate for ministry receive clinical training offered to medical students. This led to Rev. Anton Boison placing theological students at the Chicago Theological Seminary in supervised contact with patients in mental hospitals. In the United States, the Association for Clinical Pastoral Education is recognized as an accredited organization for CPE programs by the Department of Education. (290)

The American way of health care is both expensive and innovative. The cost of healthcare is growing far too fast for individuals and businesses. There are many debates concerning many areas of healthcare in medical practice, prescription drugs, and emergency room use. Our approach in how we pay for healthcare in the United States results in our spending much more than other industrialized countries, for no better results. In most of the developed world universal coverage is standard. In the United States most facilities are private and often for-profit. The overall practice of medicine is more entrepreneurial than elsewhere. Our physicians are more specialized and likely to be paid on a fee-for-service basis. They have financial interests in health care facilities and products. Business incentives dominate our system influencing the behavior of all facilities, for profit and not-for-profit. Our present health care system is flawed and needs work. (291)

Whatever the future brings in healthcare does not take responsibility off of the individual to choose a better lifestyle. Learn to grow some of his own food or buy more organic. We must learn preventive health measures, how to make sure our water is cleaner. We can no longer walk into a doctor's office and just expect him to fix us. Part of this process involves meditation techniques to clear out the negative influence that come into the mind. People need to seek and spend time with God no matter what religion they practice. The future of good healthcare lies in the intention of good body, mind and spiritual practices. (292)

Rev. Donald Eldridge is a Melchizedek priest and a Reiki master in his own right. He has written several books on Ascension, Quest for the Light, Spiritual gardening and Holistic gardening. Rev. Eldridge writes under the pen name of Don Elwood. He worked as an Aerospace Engineer all over the world where he would meet people of all walks of life interested in natural healing methods. Don had helped to put man on the moon and worked in close proximity with many technical experts. His book, "Knocking on the Gate", is a research guide of using white gold powder that the Pharaohs of Egypt used to bless the crops with and use for its magical powers to attain enlightenment and ascension. The Pharaohs of old Egypt consumed a magical white gold powder which gave them extraordinary physical, mental, psychic and spiritual abilities. Their spiritual centers were opened and their extra sensory perceptions would function at full capacity. They could read the minds of others and know what the future held. Alchemists have claimed for centuries that a philosopher's stone exists that had magical powers and could cure most diseases. (293)

I met Rev. Don Eldridge at the Roanoke Metaphysical Church and he told me about the practice of Reiki. I knew that I had to take this class and I took the first two classes from Rev. Eldridge. He said I needed to wait at least 6 months to take the third course as I would undergo a lot of changes in my body. He was correct and I did wait and then took the third class. Rev. Eldridge would call me when he had a new student and I would sit in to learn how to teach Reiki myself. Rev. Eldridge had learned to use Reiki III prayers with the prayers of "Mana" and would grow a more abundant garden. His plants were taller and produced more food. He also taught me to be careful when you say a prayer as to how it will affect other people. When you combine Reiki prayers and Manna and you ask God for rain you may start a flood. You need to always think about your words first and then pray for nice gentle rains for your garden. Say a pray of gratefulness after the rains start so you will not have an over- abundance of rain. Rev. Eldridge will tell you that if you conform to the laws of love you will change. A person must first focus on attunement with God and then comply with the spiritual laws in our daily life. We must also be patient for others to awaken and start the spiritual development process. (294)

On one hot summer day Rev. Eldridge called me and asked me to stop by his house and meet someone. He introduced me to a small four foot, 109 pound lady in her sixties. He said ask her some questions Diana and you will be amazed. I asked her to tell me a little about herself and I did ask her a few questions. I soon realized this small woman had a huge gift that she kept as a secret. Rita Mitchell had grown up in Richlands VA, attended the local Baptist Church and worked as a Certified Nursing Assistant at Mattie Williams Hospital. One day when she was around 15 years old her mother was out of town and she felt someone touch her shoulder and tell her he was her guardian angel. From here on Rita has had an unusual gift where she can connect to Heaven at will and answer any question you ask her. She dreams into the future with revelations about people that often come true. Rita works at the Christian Soldiers Food pantry which is a program that ministers to people as they come to receive free food from stores all over the Valley that donate over surplus of food and food which has just run out of date. This program helps many people in the valley as no questions are asked about your circumstances, only that you reside in the Roanoke Valley. Veterans are allowed to go first in line and a prayer is always said before the line starts going through. Rita tells me her gift is to bring joy and peace to others as she helps people out. I found Rita to be a wonderful resource when I am stuck in tracing my genealogy. Sometimes she will straight out give me the answer or she will give me a clue that helps me.

I am forever grateful for her friendship as she always has an ear to listen and never judge's people and I have learned that some secrets are best kept from plain sight. The Doctors are also stunned that Rita is alive and walking, she has multiple health problems yet she keeps on going and doesn't let her health hold her back. She is also evidence to me that God places people in your path when you need them. (295)

2 Corinthians 12:1-3. "I must go on boasting. Although there is nothing gained, I will go on to visions and revelations from the Lord. I know a man in Christ who fourteen years ago was caught up to the third heaven. Whether it was in the body or out of the body I do not know, but God knows what was caught up to paradise." (296)

The Life-stream Center in Roanoke is a 501(c)3 non-profit learning center for mind, body, and spirit. This is the 20th year of the center offering classes, workshops and programs that give people opportunities to practice well-being, inner personal work and take responsibility for their own health. Carolyn Bratton runs the center and teaches Feng Shui, energy work and Life Activations. The 22-Strand DNA Activation is very empowering spiritually and helps one have more light and be more on track with one's life purpose. The 22-strand DNA Activation enables a person to bring in and actually hold more light in the physical body. It empowers you to maximize your potential and bring forth unrealized talents and abilities. It gives you more energy and clarity, strengthening your immune system and assists in releasing unconscious patterns. It increases your ability to use more of your brain capacity and facilitates clearing of family and genetic Karmic patterns. The 22-strand DNA Activation gives you a wonderful gift of empowerment. Your DNA contains the blueprint for who you are as a Divine Being. It is God-given, holy, and sacred and defines the uniqueness of you personally. Ancient metaphysical teachings reveal that the original divine blueprint for humans consisted of a multidimensional 24 strand DNA. At present most humans only have about 3-5% of their DNA turned on, as the rest lies dormant. By activating our DNA we gain greater access to our full potential. Carolyn is a Reiki Master and has devoted her life to providing many kinds of services and teachers for healing and growth at the center. (297)

2 Corinthians: 10:4-5. "The weapons we fight with are not the weapons of the world. On the contrary, they have divine power to demolish strongholds. We demolish arguments and every pretension that sets itself up against the knowledge of God, and we take captive every thought to make it obedient to Christ." (298).

Spiritual development would be so much easier if we had all of the tools and knowledge available to us with nothing hidden. Throughout the ages the information to develop your innate gifts were withheld by the church and committee's decided what information we would be given. The Apocrypha were considered secret books of the bible once included in the Geneva Bible and the King James Version of 1611. These fourteen books were meant to teach lessons and wisdom of the Jewish sages. The books include First Book of Esdras, Second book of Esdras, Book of Tobit, Book of Judith, Additions to the Bok of Esther, Wisdom of Solomon, Ecclesiasticus or the Wisdom of Sirach, Book of Baruch, Story of Susanna, Song of three children, Story of Bel and the Dragon, Prayer of Manasseh, First Book of Maccabees, and the second book of Maccabees. These books are of great value to our history and have all but disappeared from almost all Bibles. British and American societies more than 100 years ago voted them out of publication. The first Book of Esdras written by the profit Ezra refers to the laws given to Moses. It appears as if Ezra is talking to or channeling an Angel. His instructions are that the tribes of Judah and Benjamin are not to marry alien or foreign people. The wives and children are to be cast off by the men who have broken these laws. In the book of Esdras he is having a series of dream visions. The Englishmen and Puritans did not want people to know such skills existed. Growing up in a Baptist Church we were taught that an Angel came in a dream to Mary and Joseph, not to ordinary people. Prophecy of the unknown was not accepted in our culture or the culture the Puritans wished to establish disapproving of these books. The Puritans discredited these books because they could not be found in Hebrew writings. (299)

The vast majority of Americans who represent the notable decline in being "religious" say they still believe in God, or the concept of a higher power, and consider themselves "spiritual not religious." Most people here have an initial introduction to a "spiritual path being Christian have become known as "New Age Christians," or "Awakening Christians." There are many titles that people identify themselves by. These people still believe in the basic tenets of Christianity such as love, inclusion, and forgiveness, but reject the constraining structure and claims of absolute truth found in the traditional Protestant and Catholic Dogmas. These people are part of a trend, across religions, toward a more self-contained spirituality and quest for internal peace with a connection to God. They are looking to trust a voice within, believing we are not really separate from God. Religion is a set of beliefs concerning the cause, nature, and purpose of the universe with a belief in God or Gods. Spiritual is of the spirit or soul. Religion doesn't exclude growth, but only allows it through a very narrow and defined structure that creates a wall between us and God. Spirituality infers that we are part of God. Our efforts are to be focused on our thoughts and actions, not on attending a certain church on Sunday and only a certain set of beliefs as absolute truth. (300)

Christianity sprang from the spiritual teachings of Jesus. The firsthand accounts of his life come from the recollections attributed to some of his disciples that make up the first four books of the Bible. Diana Butler Bass, a PhD in religious studies wrote in her book "Christianity after Religion," that the early believers in the teachings of Jesus understood spiritual practices that offered a meaningful way of life in this world not as a set of doctrines, an esoteric belief, or the promise of heaven. By practicing Jesus teachings followers discovered that their lives were made better on a practical spiritual path. Early Christianity was called "the Way." Members of the community were not held accountable for their opinions about God or Jesus. The community measured faithfulness by how well members practiced loving God and neighbor. For several hundred years different Jewish sects followed texts and beliefs. In the early 4th century, the Council of Nicaea convened to organize a comprehensive text and doctrine. The council selected and edited what would be the Bible, rejecting over 45 texts that were then in use. Anything that evoked mysticism as a belief in a direct relationship with the Soul and God was censored. The role of women in ministry was changed and they were no longer allowed to participate as deacons, teachers, or priestess. It was at the Nicaea assembly that Jesus was ordained as "The Son of God," through the virgin birth. The trinity was born connecting the Father, Son, and Holy Ghost as one. This established the worship of Jesus, not his teachings as the focus of the followers. This became the only way to practice Christianity as the Catholic Church was established. The Catholic Church developed as the supreme authority of religious practice and dominated the social structure. (301)

Worship was in the form of rituals. Salvation became the focus of Christianity and the only path to salvation through the hierarchy of the Church and its rulings. Only the priests and the hierarchy had actual access to God. The use of fear was overwhelming and this is against the teaching of Jesus. The church and the council of Nicaea, rejected reincarnation and the laws of karma. Practices such as yoga and meditation have become main stream. People have developed their own belief systems and a new path is emerging. Spirituality as an individual practice can be seen as taking responsibility for one's actions and thoughts. We are not at the mercy of "God's will." Religions need to align with assisting the individuals approach to spirituality and to help believers create greater connections to each other and to God. We are all part of God and not a tribe. Change comes one mind at a time. (302)

Psalm 104:33-35 "I will sing to the Lord all my life; I will sing praise to my God as long as I live. May my meditation be pleasing to him, as I rejoice in the Lord. But may sinners vanish from the earth and the wicked be no more. Praise the Lord, O my soul. Praise the Lord." (303)

For healing practitioners and those seeking physical, emotional, and mental wellness, Kabbalah can be a powerful employing energetic healing method. Mark Stavish is the Director of Studies for the Institute for Hermetic Studies in Wyoming Pennsylvania. He teaches the exercises, rituals, practices, and techniques to learn Kabbalah for Health & Wellness that can be easily learned and performed. The effectiveness is based on traditional symbols, key ideas and regular practices by students. The exercises build on one another to build an even and balanced development of healing skill and technique. Practicing specific techniques are designed to enhance spiritual awakening and healing potential. The very fact that you call upon God, the archangels, the invisible ones of Creation, they respond and are present with you. As we petition them we become aware of them. Kabbalah is to be studied as a path to illumination and as a result certain gifts are bestowed along the way. This is why daily practice is essential, such as a daily schedule of fifteen minutes a day working on visualization or meditation. The brain and the stomach like their food in small, digestible doses several times a day. Psychological and spiritual exercises also require time for their seeds to grow. Keeping a notebook of your experiences for self-review is important. It is also important to understand your dream life and the activation of symbols within your psyche. (304)

Energetic Healing is a traditional method of using physical and psychic energies of the body to assist in the healing process. The emotional and mental wellness are also important in the process. One must first create healthy changes in the mind with the practices of energetic healing using prayer, meditation, visualization, and ritual. Herbal products are also used in the process. It is the use of the mind that maintains health and wellness because mind based techniques can be used anytime and anywhere. Material medicines are important when needed and should be recognized for their value along with spiritual principles. There are seven principles of energetic healing:

1) The health of the body reflects our consciousness.
2) All comes from the one thing: "As above, so below."
3) All things exist as an adaptation or modification of the original seed, the One Thing.
4) We assist Nature.
5) Universal Justice, or karma, must be properly understood for healing to take place.
6) When faced with a life threatening condition, a compelling reason to live, being simply afraid to die, must be the motivator.

7) It is the duty of each in life to prepare in life for death, so that when it comes, we may transition more easily to the invisible worlds. (305)

Mark Stavish states that one of the most interesting aspects of the psychic body as it relates to the physical form is the concentration of energies around the heart and the radiation of energies from the hands and fingers. These two points of practical application have the greatest effect in spiritual healing for ourselves and others. He also points out that prayer is a word bridge between the inner and outer parts of self that unites the separated parts of awareness. We become aware of whatever we focus our mind on. When we focus on psychic or spiritual matters we become more aware of them. Meditation focuses the mind or consciousness on a single idea. This is composed of an image, symbol or a word. When we strengthen our mental muscles of concentration and visualization, we are able to move obstacles such as fleeting thoughts, random emotions and indecisiveness. This brings greater harmony between our interior and exterior experiences. Prayer is slightly different from meditation, yet it seeks to achieve the same goal. Prayer is effective in promoting the healing of animals, humans, and the growth of plants. Stretching out the hands in blessing over the person, place, or thing being prayed for increases the effectiveness of the prayer. (306)

Several years ago I opened a letter in the mail from Saint Matthew's Churches in Tulsa, OK. I began a relationship with a Bishop that does Pastoral Counseling through private letters to the individual. This Bishop and his wife have been doing this kitchen table ministry for over fifty years. This ministry is a non-profit organization (5013C). This Bishop has a gift of prophecy and knows how to lead you along the path of spiritual growth. He always channels a word of knowledge by the Holy Spirit to the individual. The path of spiritual growth is difficult at times and I truly believe that everyone needs a spiritual counselor that he or she can talk with in private as you go through this journey. This Bishop teaches you how to use Bible Scriptures in your present circumstances. Part of this process is the cleaning out of your mind from negative thoughts that you have been programmed by world influences. (307)

When people awaken to the gifts of the Spirit it can be overwhelming. Classes such as Reiki and the 22-strand DNA attunement instill further changes to your body. Suddenly you are different from other people that are around you in society. These people sense that you are different and may not be at the same place that you are on the path. They can cause havoc in your life and you sometimes need a person that you can trust to help you navigate your new life with gifts. The Old Bishop at Saint Matthew's Churches teaches you that God is always there in every circumstance and will never leave you or let the world hurt you. Many times from close friends I have heard, "Diana if you get these higher degree's you will never be able to find a job." The Old Bishop will tell you that God can open any door and move any mountain in your life. There came a point in my career where a message was sent to me from the Holy Spirit that I would need to work for myself so that I could be myself. The doors did open for me to do several thigs to make a living and finish my education. I started doing private home-health care and started a craft business while still working towards a ministry program. I also realized that God had found a wonderful vessel to work through with this Bishop at Saint Matthew's Churches. The blessings of God are not limited to salvation of the soul. Saint Mathew's Churches believes that God wants to bless you, his child spiritually, physically, and financially. It is God answering prayer, not us, that is making these wonderful things happen for people. This ministry operates through donations to the program and the Bishop also has books published that are sent out to people for free all over the United States. He has a seed tithing program that funds his work to help anyone in need. I have been truly blessed by this ministry. (308)

Romans 1: 1-6. "Paul, a servant of Christ Jesus, called to be an apostle and set apart for the gospel of God, the gospel he promised beforehand through his prophets in the Holy Scriptures regarding his Son, who as to his human nature was a descendant of David, and who through the Spirit of holiness was declared with power to be the Son of God by his resurrection from the dead: Jesus Christ our Lord. Through him and for his name's sake, we received grace and apostleship to call people from among all the Gentiles to the obedience that comes from faith. And you also are among those who are called to belong to belong to Jesus Christ." (309)

The Holy Spirit, Trinity in this Trinitarian passage the Spirit is said to have disclosed Christ's divine son-ship by raising Christ from the dead. The Spirit is always associated with Life and breath. The Holy Bible is a connection to God from the prophets of long ago. The Gift of Healing exists in different forms only given by the power of God. (310)

In conclusion I would like to look at the contribution of the Native American culture that has brought more to the gift of healing than credit has been given. Teosinte is a wild grass that is an ancestor of the cultivated corn that made it possible for the growth of cities and culture in ancient Mexico. The teosinte pollen was carried by the wind to other corn-like grasses which produced a hybrid that helped to ensure a stable food supply. The hunters began to rely less on game and wild plants and more on planting corn. Farming brought permanent villages with the knowledge to also plant squash, beans, and chili. Native Americans grew in skills and knowledge weaving strips of fiber to fish and to weave mats. They learned to weave baskets, make pottery and canoes. The Native Americans learned there was a purpose of every plant on earth to counteract evil. Even the weeds had a useful purpose that had to be studied and learned. They believe that the spirit of the plant would tell them what the plant was used for. The Native Americans discovered the properties of salicylic acid, caffeine, morphine, reserpine, and digitalis. Both salicylic acid and caffeine are used today. (311)

Salicylic acid is an essential ingredient in pain-relieving aspirin. Caffeine is a stimulant found in coffee, tea, Kola nuts and cocoa. Caffeine serves as a diuretic causing greater production of urine. Some pharmacologists believe that the Indians knowledge of herbal curatives and palliatives surpassed modern man's expertise with natural drugs. Native Americans respected the resources of the world and took only what they needed. Of all the plants in nature's domain tobacco was the most miraculous plant. When used in the Native American tradition tobacco was thought to have supernatural powers to heal or to hurt. Tobacco could bring good fortune or ill, to suppress hunger, induce hallucinations, ward off evil spirits, bring forth beneficial spirits, and ensure affection between a husband and wife. Tobacco leaves were infused with the force of the supernatural through rigidly prescribed rituals known as remaking. Tobacco leaves were held up to the sun and an incantation was said to ward off ones enemies. A similar ceremony was used to conjure up the forces of good. Tobacco was also boiled with red sumac and drank to heal head and chest complaints. (312)

Daniel E. Moreman is the Professor of Anthropology at the University of Michigan. He is recognized for his years of work in the field of Native American Ethnobotany. His book is intended to help people understand the use of plants that Native Americans used to treat disease. In the book of Native American Ethnobotany you will find 55 items categorized as Cancer Treatment, in the Catalog of Plants. Cancer is a more important disease in Modern Medicine than it was in Native America. The reason is that Native Americans did not suffer from cancer nearly as often as modern Americans. Cancer is a relatively recent disease that is somewhat dependent on carcinogens or substances that cause or accelerate cancer. These carcinogens are industrially manufactured like food colors, radioactive materials, and x-ray machines. Native Americans would share a bowel of tobacco with a dozen or more people. Europeans and Euro-Americans industrially manufactured products with significant carcinogens. This process accounts for the lack of cancer in Native Americans. (313)

Indians used Podophyllum peltatum or may-apple for a broad range of things such as cathartic, an insecticide and rheumatism. A resin from the roots is used in Western Medicine for venereal warts caused by a virus. It is also used for the basis for the production of Etuposide, a semisynthetic derivative of podophyllotoxin. This is a chemical found in the may-apple. Etoposide is widely used in the treatment of several forms of cancer. Another cross-cultural drug is taxol. Taxol is found in the leaves and the bark of several species of yew, of the genus taxus. Native Americans used three species of Taxus for anti-rheumatic, cold remedy, lung medicine and other ailments. Western Medicine had this plant screened at the National Cancer Institute in Washington, D.C. This Native American drug once used by Indians to treat cancer may be an important modern cancer drug. Plants do produce a broad range of chemicals that serve a variety of purposes that can be used for healing in people. Plants also produce herbicides to inhibit the growth of competing plants. Salicylic acid which is what aspirin is made of is a water soluble phytotoxin (plant poison) that washes off the leaves of willows and other plants to the ground, inhibiting the growth of competing plants. Juglone which is produced by black walnut trees does the same thing. (314)

Parallels exist between uses of plants by Native Americans and modern Western Medicine. There are 1649 species included in Native American Ethnobotany that were used for food by Native Americans. Plants are still used for our food supply in the Western World. Medicines have very strong powers in nature and this is why western physicians are only allowed to prescribe them. The Rose family is also an important source of plant medicine used medicinally by Native Americans for the treatment of dermatological, gastrointestinal and gynecological problems. It has also been used as a food. Honeysuckle is used for food and as a medicine. (315)

The following is an extensive list of plants and herbs used for healing cancer by Native American Tribes.

Abies, Pinaceae, Conifer was used by the Iroquois as a cancer treatment poultice of gum and dried beaver kidneys applied for cancer.

Aesules pavia (Red Buckeye) used by the Cherokee for cancer treatment poultice of pounded nuts used for tumors and infections.

Aralia mudicaulis (wild sarsaparilla) was used also by the Iroquois as a blood medicine purifier used for cancer treatment plan.

Arnoglossum atriplicifulium was used by the Cherokee as a cancer treatment poultice and to draw out blood or poisonous matter.

Artemisia alaskana, Alaska sagebrush used by Tanana, upper tribe as a cancer treatment decoction taken for cancers.

Athyrium filex-femina (common ladyfern) was used by the Hesquiat tribe for cancer treatment, eaten for internal ailments such as cancer of the womb.

Blechnum (Deer fern) was also used by the hesquiat tribe as a cancer treatment. The leaflets were chewed for internal cancer. This medicine was first learned about from watching the deer, rub their antler stubs on the plant when their antlers would break off.

Ceanothus Velutinus was also used by Thompsons Indians as a decoction for cancer and for venereal disease and all forms of gonorrhea.

Celastrus Scandens or American Bittersweet was used by the Chippewa as a cancer treatment by boiling the roots and using as an ointment.

Chamaesyce Maculata (Small spotted sandmat) used by the Cherokee for cancer treatment as a decoction prepared with herbs and taken for cancer.

Chimaphila umbellata is a plant used by the Cherokee and Iroquois as a decoction of roots or stems to purify bad blood or stomach cancer.

Cirsium Vulgare (Bull Thistle) is a plant that the Iroquios also used for cancer treatment.

Cornus alternefolia (Alternate Leaf Dogwood) one reported case mixed with something else to cure facial cancer.

Crepis, Asteraceae was used by the Meskwaki tribe as a cancer treatment and dermatological aid as a poultice of whole plant applied to open area is a carbuncle or cancer.

Crptantha, used by the Hopi for a cancer treatment and growth in the throat.

Cynoglossum virgin, anum (wild comfrey) used by Cherokee as a treatment for cancer.

Dryopteris campyloptera (Mountain woo fern) used by Hesquiat for cancer treatment of the womb.

Epilobium, onagraceae used by the Kawkiutl for cancer treatment. A poultice of seeds and oil applied to wound after cutting open the tumor.

Euphorbia, flowering spurge was used by the Cherokee as a cancer treatment decoction prepared with herbs.

Fritillaria atropurpurea (spotted mission bells) was used by the Lakota for cancer treatment. The plant was pulverized into a salve and applied to scrofulous swellings.

Gaillardia was also used by the Thompson Indians as a cancer treatment infusion of whole plant used for cancer.

Hackelia Virginiana was used by the Cherokee as a cancer treatment. The Bruised root with bear oil used as an ointment for cancer.

Hydrangea was used by the Cherokee for cancer treatment of tumors.

Hydrastis (Golden Seal) used by Cherokee in treatment for cancer.

Lachnanthes (Dandy Carolina Red root) was used by the Cherokee as an anti-hemorrhagic taken for spitting blood and for cancer treatment. This was used as a wash for cancer.

Larix occidentalis was used by the Okanagan as a cancer treatment. Small pieces of branches and tops were used for cancer. Plant tops were used to wash the area affected by cancer. The treatment was used after a western doctor diagnosed a breast cancer patient as being terminal.

Larrea Tridentata (Creosote Bush), was used by the Cahuilla for cancer treatment as an infusion of stems and leaves for cancer.

Maianthemum Race Mosum (Feather Solomon's Seal) was used as a cancer treatment decoction of rhizones taken in several doses over a period of several days for cancer.

Oplopanax, Araliaceae is another plant used by the Native Americans for cancer treatment.

Orobanche Fasciculata (clustered broomrape) was used by the Montana Indians for cancer treatment parasite (cancer root) sweet sage roots used for cancer.

Ostrya, Betulacere was used by the Iroquois cancer treatment decoction of bark was used for rectum cancer.

Qxalis corniculata (Creeping wood sorrel) was used by the Cherokee when cancer first started.

Pedicularis Canadensis (Canadian Loosewort) was used as a cancer treatment by the Meskwaki as a poultice of root applied to tumors.

Picea Engelmannii (Engelmann's Spruce) was used by the Thompson Indians for cancer treatment as a decoction of needles and gum taken for cancer. The decoction was taken with a spoon directly from the bark blisters and in concentrated form.

Polystichum Munitum (Western Sword Fern) was used by the Hesquiat for cancer treatment. Shoots were chewed for cancer of the womb.

Prunus, Emarginata (Bitter Cherry) used by the Kwakiutl for a cancer treatment. It was used as a wrap after treating tumors.

Pteridium, Dennstaedtiaceae, Fern was used by the Hesquiat as a cancer treatment. Young shoots were eaten as a medicine for troubles on the inside, such as cancer of the womb.

Pyrola Elliptica (Waxflower shinleaf) was used by the Nootka as a cancer treatment poultice of bruised plant applied to tumors.

Shepherdia Cauadensis (Russet Buffalo Berry) used as a cancer treatment decoction of branches and leaves taken in a 1-cupful dose for stomach cancer.

Taxus Breuifolia (Pacific yew) was a Tsimshian cancer treatment plant used for cancer. Internal medicine plant used for internal ailments.

Tradescantia Virginiana (Virginia Spiderwort) was used as a cancer treatment by the Cherokee as a poultice of root and rubbed on for insect bites.

Trifolium Pratense (Red Clover) used by Shinnecock as a cancer treatment. A teaspoon of powder mixed in boiling water and taken for cancer. An infusion of the heads taken for stomach cancer.

Trillium Erectum (Red Trillion) was used by the Cherokee as a cancer treatment poultice used for putrid ulcers, tumors and inflamed parts.

Ulmus Americana (American elm) was used by the Montana Indian as a cancer treatment. The inner bark was used as an emollient for tumors.

Xanthorhiza (Marsh, Yellow Root) used by the Cherokee as a cancer treatment of ashes "Burnt from Green switch" for cancer. This was taken as a blood tonic. (316)

Plant medicines were boiled or steamed and sometimes mixed with bear grease or other herbs, or water. They were used in a more natural state to cure illnesses. Sometimes leaves and twigs were placed on a fire and then the fumes were inhaled. The fresh leaves were often chewed and preparations were made into teas. A fire pit was made of large stones like a large oven. The Thompson Indians stored and dried Rose Hips to make tea. We are deeply indebted to the Native American tribes that crossed a continent to a new world through the glacial cold to study and learn the secrets of the New World. They are the true scientists who gained meaningful and useful knowledge of the world around us. The Native Americans also used plants and trees for ceremonial, magical items, cleaning agents, containers, fertilizers, fuels, incense, fragrance, insecticides, jewelry, lubricants, musical instruments, preservatives, smoking, snuff, soap, waterproofing, tools, toys, and weapons. There are lessons to be learned from these people about creating a good and healthy environment. The future study and use of plants has a great potential for the survival of all of us as we are all connected on this planet. (317)

Conclusion

The Christian Holy Bible is a useful guide of healing stories from the ancient prophets of long ago. Life has limits and we all need to have a relationship with God and know he loves and cares for us.

Exodus 15: 26 "He said, "If you listen carefully to the voice of the Lord your God and do what is right in his eyes, if you pay attention to his commands and keep all his decrees, I will not bring on you any of the diseases I brought on the Egyptians, for I am the Lord, who heals you." (318)

One of the seven names of God is Jehovah-Rapha which means "I am the Lord that heal-eth thee." Forgiveness and healing were offered universally wherever Christ preached.

The Prayer of Faith, James: 13-16. "Is any one of you in trouble? He should pray. Is anyone Happy? Let him sing songs of praise. Is anyone of you sick? He should call the elders of the church to pray over him and anoint him with oil in the name of the Lord. And the prayer offered in faith will make the sick person well; the Lord will raise him up. If he has sinned, he will be forgiven. Therefore confess your sins to each other and pray for each other so that you may be healed. The prayer of a righteous man is powerful and effective." (319)

The Holy Bible Scriptures give us a better understanding of the gift of healing through the prophets and a fuller understanding of who Jesus Christ was to become. Prayer is no longer taught in public schools and our young people have become lost to this connection to God. Yoga is interpreted as a form of exercise and not allowed in many churches for fear that it will lead to dancing. Many of the Spiritual leaders in the churches have awakened and are still not teaching the congregations to read the scriptures, pray, meditate and ask the Holy Spirit to interpret the meaning to the person. We can learn step by step to heal our lives and the world around us with the techniques discussed in this paper. My goal with the research in this paper is to open the mind that people do have control over their lives, a God who loves you, and the ability to search out ways to heal yourself and the communities where you live.

Prayer is the absolute key to seeing God's mighty hand move in our personal affairs. Throughout our history, God has exercised supreme power when people call upon him for help. Our hope for a future is in God alone. Prayer is a universal practice to ask God to expel darkness out of our lives and homes. I believe morally and spiritually something happens when I have positive prayerful thoughts. When God's people move into covenants of prayer an awakening to the culture can occur. This can impact families, whole cities and stir a nation. After we pray our spiritual eyes can be opened in meditation as we listen to the creative influence of God. Meditation is a method God can use to lay his heart over our heart. Our spiritual senses must be as developed as our physical senses. We must teach people how to see and listen to the Holy Spirit of God. Forgiveness can open doors to new beginnings as our thought process changes with the help of God. Dependence on God is essential for our very survival.

In this paper my research illustrates how to pray with "mana- mana-loa," one of the most powerful prayer techniques that pierces the veil of heaven into the light. Blessings can come into your life because this is a key to opening the doors of your mind to allow God to give you solutions to your problems and answer your questions. God does not mean for any of us to suffer or go without our basic needs being met. I personally pray with mana- mana-loa, every day of my life and feel that it works sometimes within seconds and other times when I am ready to accept the answer and learn the lesson before me.

I would also have an opportunity to test my research on myself as the pollen season was here and I had also picked up a cold virus. I knew to take Echinacea three times a day until the herb killed the virus in my body. A cold has always gone to my throat with a dry hacking cough. I was gagging and having spasms in my throat from coughing so much. My doctor had always told me to use a cough syrup with guaifenesin, but this was not working at this point and I coughed all night. I remembered that Hana Kroeger used a pendulum to ask questions about what herbs to use for different people. I googled natural herbs for dry hacking cough and found Licorice root to be one of them. My pendulum gave me a yes answer and I happened to have a bottle of this herb because I used it for one of my dogs. I took one capsule and within thirty minutes I stopped coughing and slept through the night. Natural herbs take longer to work, but I have found them to be a great relief in healing my own body.

My case studies also provided unknown research that can give us insights into further possibilities of future study, such as:

1) The case studies in this thesis uncovered important factual information. The genealogy of the Stewart family leads back to the Holy Bible Scriptures and the Book of Exodus. Pharaoh the king- of- Egypt had problems with Moses and the God of the Israelites. Pharaoh's daughter and her husband escaped to Europe and their descendants later came to America where they live today. A side of God comes through as he reveals that his problems with Pharaoh did not stop him from protecting Pharaoh's daughter and her descendants. We see a Divine Love from God and not a vengeful God.

2) The case study with Rev. Jeanne Greening brings through information that she was able to break through barriers and teach Reiki Therapy to Priests.

3) The case study of Rev. Donald Eldridge brings forth information of combining Reiki Prayers and Mana-Mana-Loa prayers can cause a flood to occur. When a prayer is made we must be careful to consider our wording and how this prayer will affect other people.

4) The case study of Rita Mitchell brings forth information of people with gifts that are hidden amongst us. This shows us that there is a need for further research that acknowledges the

spiritual gifts and teaching methods to help all people learn to find their own gifts and how to use them properly.

The truths contained in the research of this paper are meant to unite us. Within, we are all the same, and face the same spiritual and physical challenges. It is my intent that we all find healing for ourselves and this planet called Earth.

Bibliography

Introduction

1) "New International Version Disciple's Study Bible." Holman Bible Publishers, Nashville. Copyright 1988. 6. Gen. 1:29-30.
2) "New International Version Disciple's Study Bible." Holman Bible Publishers, Nashville. Copyright 1988. 76. Exodus 3: 7-9.
3) Gulbrandsen, Don. Edward S. Curtis Visions of the First Americans. Chartwell Books, Inc. Copyright 2006. 32.
4) Gulbrandsen, Don. Edward S. Curtis Visions of the First Americans. 35-38.
5) Gulbrandsen, Don. Edward S. Curtis Visions of the First Americans. 44-48.

Native American Healing

6) Gulbrandsen, Don. Edward S. Curtis Visions of the First Americans. 53-63.
7) Shimer, Porter. Healing Secrets of the Native Americans Herbs, Remedies and Practices that Restore the Body, Refresh the Mind and rebuild the Spirit. Black Dog & Leventhal Publishers, New York. Copyright 2004. 123-126.
8) Shimer, Porter. Healing Secrets of the Native Americans. 193-198.
9) Shimer, Porter. Healing Secrets of the Native Americans. 198.
10) "Hanna's Herb shop." www.HannasHerbshop.com. 2007-2013. Hanna's Herb Shop. All Rights Reserved

11) Kroeger, Hanna. Instant Herbal Locator. Copyright 1979. Hanna Kroeger. Pg. ii, IV, 96.

12) Kroeger, Hana. Instant Herbal Locator. 97-99.

13) Buchman, Dian D. Ph.D. Herbal Medicine. Copyright 1979. Wing books, Random House. VII, VIII, IX, X, XII, 3-7.

14) Buchman, Dian D. Ph.D. Herbal Medicine. 33, 69-71.

15) Buchman, Dian D. Ph.D. Herbal Medicine. 51-55.

16) "New International Version Disciple's Study Bible." 340, 649, 1173.

17) Shimer, Porter. Healing Secrets of the Native Americans. 196-198.

18) McGaa, Ed. Mother Earth Spirituality. Harper Collins Publisher. Copyright 1990. 44-46.

19) McGaa, Ed. Mother Earth Spirituality. 46-52.

20) McGaa, Ed. Mother Earth Spirituality. 52-63.

21) McGaa, Ed. Mother Earth Spirituality. 99-125.

22) McGaa, Ed. Mother Earth Spirituality. 125.

23) "New International Version Disciple's Study Bible." John 3:16-17. 1320.

24) Wheeler, Rachel. To Live upon Hope. Copyright 2008 by Cornell University. 108-109-107-136.

Examination of Religious Experience

25) "New International Version Disciple's Study Bible." John 3: 19-21. 1320.

26) Long, Max Freedom. Growing In the Light. Copyright 1955. DeVorses & Co. Publishers. 1-5.

27) Long, Max Freedom. Growing in the Light. 8-29.

28) Long, Max Freedom. Growing in the Light. 29-33.

29) Long, Max Freedom. Growing in the Light. 46-48.

30) Long, Max Freedom. Growing in the Light. 49-59.

31) Long, Max Freedom. Growing in the Light. 62.

32) Long, Max Freedom. Growing in the Light. 63.

33) Chaffee, John Ph. D. The Philosopher's Way. Copyright 2005. Pearson Prentice Hall. 256-260.

34) Chaffee, John Ph.D. The Philosopher's Way. Copyright 2005. 261.

35) Chaffee, John Ph.D. The Philosopher's Way. Copyright 2005. 22-25.

36) Byrne, Rhonda. The Secret. Copyright 2006. Beyond Words Publishing. 25-30.

37) Byrne, Rhonda. The Secret. 31-47.

38) Yukteswar, Swami Sri. The Holy Science. Copyright 1949. Self-Realization Fellowship. Los Angles, California. 56-59.

39) Yukteswar, Swami Sri. The Holy Science. 60-62.

40) "New International Version Disciple's Study Bible." Ecclesiastes. 1:7.790.

41) Ryrie, Charlie. The Healing Energies of Water. Copyright 1999. Journey Editions. 153 Milk St. Boston, Mass. 02109. 1-17.

42) "New International Version Disciple's Study Bible." 2 Kings 2:19-22. .432-433.

43) Ryrie, Charlie. The Healing Energies of Water. 18-21.

44) Ryrie, Charlie. The Healing Energies of Water. 26-33.

45) Ryrie, Charlie. The Healing Energies of Water. 37-41.

46) Ryrie, Charlie. The Healing Energies of Water. 45-57.

47) Ryrie, Charlie. The Healing Energies of Water. 61-74.

48) Ryrie, Charlie. The Healing Energies of Water. 76-77.

49) Savary, Louis M., Berne, Patriciah., Williams, Stepheon, K. Dreams and Spiritual Growth. Copyright 1984. Paulist Press 545 Island Road, Ramsey, NJ. 17446.8-13-16.

50) New International Version Disciple's Study Bible. 1170.

51) Savary, Berne, Williams. Dreams and Spiritual Growth. 118-121.

52) Teresa, Mother. Words to Love By. Copyright 1983. Ava Maria Press. Notre Dame, Indiana 46556. 1-6-7-18-24.

53) Lesser, Elizabeth. The New Spirituality. Copyright 1999. Random House. 245, 268, 269,277.

54) Lesser, Elizabeth. The New Spirituality. 279, 280.

55) Lesser, Elizabeth. The New Spirituality. 337

56) "New International Version Disciple's Study Bible." 1625.

57) Edgar Cayce's Association for Research and Enlightenment. www. EDGARCAYCE.org

58) Puryear, Herbert B. Ph.D. The Edgar Cayce primer. Copyright 1982. Published by
The Association for Research and Enlightenment, Inc. 3, 4, 18.

59) Puryear, Herbert B. Ph.D. The Edgar Cayce primer. 203,204.

60) Puryear, Herbert B. Ph.D. The Edgar Cayce primer. 205,206.

61) Puryear, Herbert B. Ph.D. The Edgar Cayce primer. 207.

62) "New International Disciple's Version Study Bible." 721. Psalm 107: 20-21.

63) Puryear, Herbert. Ph.D. The Edgar Cayce primer. 209.

64) Puryear, Herbert B. Ph.D. The Edgar Cayce primer. 165, 166, 167.

65) Puryear, Herbert B. Ph.D. The Edgar Cayce primer. 167,168, 169.

66) Puryear, Herbert B. Ph.D. The Edgar Cayce primer. 197.

67) "The Holy Bible Douay-Rheims Version," The Old Testament- 1st Published by English College at Douay. A.D. 1609, and The New Testament 1st Published by the English College at Rheims, A.D 1582. With annotations and references by Bishop Richard Challoner, 2008 Copyright. Baroniius LTD.Press LTD. Press. Michael Tweedale. Preface.

68) "The Holy Bible Douay-Rheims Version." Preface.

69) "The Holy Bible Douay- Rheims-Versions." Esther: Ch. 16-16. 553.

70) Snow, Lorenzo. Teachings of the Presidents of the Church. Published by The Church of Jesus Christ of Latter Day Saints. Salt Lake City Utah. Copyright 2012 by Intellectual Reserve, Inc. V, Intro., 2-3-7.

71) Snow, Lorenzo. Teachings of the Presidents of the Church. 15-17.

72) "New International Version Disciple's Study Bible." Mark 16:15-18. 1257.

73) "New International Version Disciple's Study Bible." John 3: 5-8. 1319-1320.

74) "New International Version Disciple's Study Bible." Acts: 38-39. 1365.

75) Snow, Lorenzo. Teachings of the Presidents of the Church. 19-20-30-32-38-39-47-52. 55-78-84-249-254-277.

76) "The Church of Jesus Christ of Latter-day-Saints." www.ids.org/

77) "New International Version Disciple's Study Bible." Gen. 9:12-16. 16.

78) Lewis, Roger. Color and the Edgar Cayce Readings. Copyright 1973. A.R.E. Press Virginia Beach, VA. 1-2.

79) Lewis, Roger. Color and the Edgar Cayce Readings. 8-10.

80) Lewis, Roger. Color and the Edgar Cayce Readings. 11-15-16-17-19.

81) Lewis Roger. Color and the Edgar Cayce Readings. . 28-43.

82) New International Version Disciple's Study Bible. 2 Chronicles 7: 12-16. 511-512.

83) Lake, Alexander. Your Prayers are always Answered. Simon & Schuster, New York. Copyright 1956.15.

84) Lake, Alexander. Your Prayers are always Answered. 20-21.

85) Lake, Alexander. Your Prayers are always Answered. 23-32-33.

86) Herzog, David. Mysteries of the Glory Unveiled. Destiny Image Publishing Inc. Copyright 2000.

87) Rawlings, Romy. Healing Gardens. Willow Creek Press Minoqua, WI. Copyright 1998. 6-9.

88) Rawlings, Romy. Healing Gardens. 9-10-11.

89) Rawlings, Romy. Healing Gardens. 11-12-13-16.

90) Rawlings, Romy. Healing Gardens. 36-39-40-41-42.

91) Rawlings, Romy. Healing Gardens. 120-121.

92) Rawlings, Romy. Healing Gardens. 96-97.

93) Rawlings, Romy. Healing Gardens. 125-126.

94) Rawlings, Romy. Healing Gardens. 126-127.

95) Rawlings, Romy. Healing Gardens. 128.

96) Rawlings, Romy. Healing Gardens. 129-130.

97) Rawlings, Romy. Healing Gardens. 130.

98) Rawlings, Romy. Healing Gardens. 152.

99) Rawlings, Romy. Healing Gardens. 152-153.

100) Rawlings, Romy. Healing Gardens. 158.

101) Readers Digest. Family Guide to Natural Medicine. The Readers Digest Assoc. Inc. Pleasantville, New York/Montreal. Copyright 1993. 118-119.

102) Readers Digest. Family Guide to Natural Medicine. 214-215-216.

103) Sun, Wei Yue. M.D. & Chen, William, Ph.D. Tai Chi Chu'uan, the Gentle Workout for Mind & Body. Sterling Publishing Co. Inc. New York. Copyright 1995. 4-5.

104) Sun, Wei Yue. M.D. & Chen, William, Ph.D. Tai Chi Chur'an, the Gentle Workout for Mind & Body. 6-7-8.

105) Vineyard, Missy. Learning the Alexander Technique. Marlowe & Company, New York. Copyright 2007. 1-2.

106) Vineyard, Missy. Learning the Alexander Technique. 3.

107) Vineyard, Missy. Learning the Alexander Technique. 5-11.

108) Vineyard, Missy. Learning the Alexander Technique. 57-58-97.

109) Vineyard, Missy. Learning the Alexander Technique. 150-152-154-157-159-288.

110) Gienger, Michael & Maier, Wolfgang. Healing stones for the vital organs. Healing Arts, Press, Rochester, Vermont. Copyright 2007. X-1x-2-3-5.

111) Gienger, Michael & Maier, Wolfgang. Healing stones for the vital organs. 9-10-19-21.

112) Gienger, Michael & Maier, Wolfgang. Healing stones for the vital organs. 33-34-44-55-56-66-68.

113) Gienger, Michael & Maier, Wolfgang. Healing stones for the vital organs. 77-78-84-92-93-125.

114) Gienger, Michael & Maier, Wolfgang. Healing stones for the vital organs. 16- 136-137-156.

Gemstones in Healing

115) "New International Version Disciple's Study Bible." Exodus Ch. 39: 1. 122.

116) "New International Version Disciple's Study Bible." Exodus Ch. 39: 8-14. 122.

117) Peschek-Bohmer, Dr. Flora A. Healing Crystals and Gemstones. Copyright 2002 W. Ludwig 1-4.

118) Buchuergag, Munich Germany. English Translation 2003 Konecky & Konecky. 5-6.

119) Peschek-Bohmer, D., Flora A. Healing Crystals and Gemstones. 7.

120) Peschek-Bohmer, Dr. Flora A. Healing Crystals and Gemstones. 7-8.

121) Peschek-Bohmer, Dr. Flora A. Healing Crystals and Gemstones. 11.

122) Peschek-Bohmer, Dr. Flora A. Healing Crystals and Gemstones. 18-19.

123) Peschek-Bohmer, Dr. Flora A. Healing Crystals and Gemstones. 21.

124) Peschek-Bohmer, Dr. Flora A. Healing Crystals and Gemstones. 27-45.

125) Peschek-Bohmer, Dr. Flora A. Healing Crystals and Gemstones. 47-48.

126) Peschek-Bohmer, Dr. Flora A. Healing Crystals and Gemstones. 49-50-51-53.

127) Peschek-Bohmer, Dr. Flora A. Healing Crystals and Gemstones. . 154-155.

128) Peschek-Bohmer, Dr. Flora A. Healing Crystals and Gemstones. 246-247-280-281-96—288-289.

129) Peschek-Bohmer, Dr. Flora A. Healing Crystals and Gemstones. 140-294-56.

130) Peschek-Bohmer, Dr. Flora A. Healing Crystals and Gemstones. 66-212-213.

131) Peschek-Bohmer, Dr. Flora A. Healing Crystals and Gemstones. 214-215-174.

132) Dermutt, Philip, Palmer, Lyn. Sacred Stones and Crystals. Published by CICO Books, 2011.www.CICOBooks.com. 6-7-8-15-16-17.

133) Dermutt, Philip, Palmer, Lyn. Sacred Stones and Crystals. 18-22-25-38.

134) Dermutt, Philip, Palmer, Lyn. Sacred Stones and Crystals. 51-52-63-84.

135) New International Version Disciple's Study Bible. Deut. 11: 26-29. 228.

136) Dermutt, Philip, Palmer, Lyn. Sacred Stones and Crystals. 86-87.

137) Dermutt, Philip, Palmer, Lyn. Sacred Stones and Crystals. 88-89.

138) Dermutt, Philip, Palmer, Lyn. Sacred Stones and Crystals. 90-91-100.

139) Khalsa, Hari Singh Bird." Transformational Properties." www.HariSingh.

140) "New International Version Disciple's Bible." Matthew 5: 13-16. Pg. 1176.

141) "New International Version Disciple's Bible." Matthew 5: 17. 1176.

142) "New International Version Disciple's Bible." Matthew 6: 22-23. 1180.

143) Muahl, Lars. The Law of Light. Copyright 2010, 2014. Watkins Media LTD. London. 12-13-14.

144) Muahl, Lars. The Law of Light. 14.

145) "New International Version Disciple's Bible." John 8: 31. 1332.

146) Muahl, Lars. The Law of Light. 8-16-18-19-23.

147) Muahl, Lars. The Law of Light. 23.

148) Muahl, Lars. The Law of Light. 24-25.

149) Muahl, Lars. The Law of Light. 27-28.

150) Muahl, Lars. The Law of Light. 31-34-35.

151) Muahl, Lars. The Law of Light. 37-39-40.

152) Prophet, Elizabeth Clare. The Lost Years of Jesus. Summit University Press. Copyright 1984. 9-11-12.

153) Prophet, Elizabeth, Clare. The Lost Years of Jesus. 13-15-16-17.

154) Prophet, Elizabeth Clare. The Lost Years of Jesus. 19.

155) Prophet, Elizabeth Clare. The Lost Years of Jesus. 20-22-23.

156) "New International Version Disciple's Study Bible." John 1: 32-34. 1317.

157) Prophet, Elizabeth Clare. The Lost Years of Jesus. 111-112-217.

158) "New International Version Disciple's Study Bible." Matthew 28: 18-20. 1224.

159) Parsley, Rod. God's Miracle Anointing. Results Publishing, Columbus, Ohio Copyright 1999. 19-2123-26-27.

160) "New International Version Disciple's Study Bible." Mark 16:15-18. 1257.

161) Parsley, Rod. God's Miracle Anointing. 27.

162) "New International Version Disciple's Study Bible." Luke 4: 18-19. 1271.

163) Sumrall, Lester R. The Gifts and Ministries of the Holy Spirit. Whitaker House, New Kensington Pa.13-14-18-19.

164) "New International Version Disciple's Study Bible." 1 Cor.12:1-11. 1462-1463.

165) Sumrall, Lester R. The Gifts and Ministries of the Holy Spirit. 19-20-23.

166) "New International Version Disciple's Study Bible." Gen. 1: 1-3. 4.

167) Sumrall, Lester R. The Gifts and Ministries of the Holy Spirit. 19-20-23.

168) Foster, Richard J. Prayer Finding the Heart's True Home. Harpers San Francisco. Copyright 1992.159-160-163-145-146-147-148.

169) Foster, Richard J. Prayer Finding the Heart's True Home. 203-204-208-209.

170) Donahue, Bill & Robinson, Russ. Building a Church of Small Groups. Zondervan, Grand Rapids Michigan. Copyright 2001. 21-24-26-27.

171) Donahue, Bill & Robinson, Russ. Building a Church of Small Groups. 32-33-38-40-45.

172) Donahue, Bill & Robinson, Russ. Building a Church of Small Groups. 81-86.

173) Quest, Penelope & Roberts, Katy. The Reiki Manual. Jeremy P. Tarcher, Penguin, New York Copyright 2011. 29-30.

174) Quest, Penelope & Roberts, Katy. The Reiki Manual. 5-10-11.

175) Quest, Penelope & Roberts, Katy. The Reiki Manual. 12-15-16.

176) Quest, Penelope & Roberts, Katy. The Reiki Manual. 21-23-25.

177) Quest, Penelope & Roberts, Katy. The Reiki Manual. 39-41-42-43-45-46-47-48-83.

178) Quest, Penelope & Roberts, Katy. The Reiki Manual. 295-296-297-298.

179) Usui, Mikao & Petter, Frank Arjana. The original Reiki Handbook of Dr. Mikao Usui. Lotus Press-Shangri-La seventh English edition 2011. 7-8-9-16-16-17.

180) Usui, Mikao & Petter, Frank Arjana. The original Reiki Handbook of Dr. Mikao Usui. . 22-23.

181) Schuller, Robert A. Getting through what you're going through. Copyright 1986. Published in Nashville, Tennessee, By Thomas Nelson, Inc. 1-27-32.

182) Schuller, Robert A. Getting through what you're going through. 30.

183) Schuller, Robert A. Getting through what you're going through. 52-54.

184) Schuller, Robert A. Getting through what you're going through. 69-70, 94-96, 118.

185) Schuller, Robert A. Getting through what you're going through. 126,165-166-172.

186) Schuller, Robert A. Getting through what you're going through. 179-180-183, 188-189.

187) Hanwerk, Brian. "Great Surprise" – Native Americans Have West Eurasian Origins. National Geographic.

188) Nerburn, Kent. The Wisdom of the Native Americans. MJF Books, New York. Copyright 1999.195- 196-1-2-3.

189) Nerburn, Kent. The Wisdom of the Native Americans. 14-15.

190) Nerburn, Kent. The Wisdom of the Native Americans. 25-29-31-34.

191) Nerburn, Kent. The Wisdom of the Native Americans. 34-36-37-40.

192) Nerburn, Kent. The Wisdom of the Native Americans. 69.

193) Nerburn, Kent. The Wisdom of the Native Americans. 70-71-74-77-78.

194) Nerbern, Kent. The Wisdom of the Native Americans. . 86-87-88.

195) Nerbern, Kent. The Wisdom of the Native Americans. 89-90-93-94-101.

196) Hewitt, William H. Hypnosis for Beginners. Llewellyn Publications St Paul, Minn. Copyright 1997. Xii-xII-3-5.

197) Hewitt, William H. Hypnosis for Beginners. 6-7-151-154-217.

198) "New International Disciples Study Bible." Matthew 11: 11-16. 1188.

199) "New International Disciples Study Bible." Matthew 17-11-13. 1200.

200) Hewitt, William H. Hypnosis for Beginners. 79-80-88-92-94.

201) Swerdlow, Stewart. The Healer's Handbook: A Journey into Hyperspace. Sky Books, New York. Copyright 1999. 35.

202) Swerdlow, Stewart. The Healer's Handbook: A Journey into Hyperspace. 36.

203) Graham, Billy. Angels God's Secret Agents. Doubleday & Company, Inc. Garden City, New York. Copyright 1975. 13.

204) "New International Disciples Study Bible." Colossians 1:16. 1527.

205) Graham, Billy. Angels God's Secret Agents. 13-14.

206) Graham, Billy. Angels God's Secret Agents. 17-18.

207) Graham, Billy. Angels God's Secret Agents. 19.

208) Graham, Billy. Angels God's Secret Agents. 20-21.

209) Graham, Billy. Angels God's Secret Agents. 22-23.

210) "New International Disciples Study Bible." Daniel: 10: 13-14. 1057.

211) Thompson, Ruth, Williams, L.A. & Taylor, Renae. The Book of Angels. Sterling Publishing, New York. Copyright 2006. 10-11-22.

212) Thompson, Ruth, Williams, L.A. & Taylor, Renae. The Book of Angels. 23-30-31-36.

213) "New International Disciples Study Bible." Daniel: 9: 21-23. 1056.

214) Garlow, James L. Partners in Ministry. Beacon Hill Press of Kansas City, Kansa City, Missouri. Copyright 1981. 12-23-25-31.

215) Garlow, James L. Partners in Ministry. 35-40.

216) "New International Disciples Study Bible." Ephesians 4: 11-12. 1509.

217) Taylor, Terry Lynn. Messengers of Light. H.J. Kramer Inc. Tiburon, California. Copyright 1990. 2-3-4-5.

218) Taylor, Terry Lynn. Messengers of Light. 6-7-8.

219) Taylor, Terry Lynn. Messengers of Light. 28-33-34.

220) Taylor, Terry Lynn. Messengers of Light. 46-47-50.

221) Taylor, Terry Lynn. Messengers of Light. 51-61.

222) Vanzant, Iyanla. Tapping the Power Within. Copyright 2008. xvi-xvii-xviii-xix-xxi.

223) Vanzant, Iyanla. Tapping the Power Within. Xxii.

224) Vanzant, Lyanla. Tapping the Power Within. 9.

225) Vanzant, Lyanla. Tapping the Power Within. 10-12-13-15.

226) Vanzant, Lyanla. Tapping the Power Within. 16.

227) Vanzant, Lyanla. Tappng the Power Within. 17

228) Vanzant, Lyanla. Tapping the Power Within. 285.

229) Mc Burney, Louis M.D. Counseling Christian Workers. General Editor Gary Collins, Ph.D. Copyright 1983 International bible Society. 24-25-26.

230) Mc Burney, Louis M.D. Counseling Christian Workers. 27-29.

231) Mc Burney, Louis M.D. Counseling Christian Workers. 31-32.

232) Mc Burney, Louis M.D. Counseling Christian Workers. 41-42.

233) Mc Burney, Louis M.D. Counseling Christian Workers. 43-44-46-47.

234) Mc Burney, Louis M.D. Counseling Christian Workers. 48-49-50-51-61-62

235) Mc Burney, Louis M.D. Counseling Christian Workers. 64-65.

236) Mc Burney, Louis M.D. Counseling Christian Workers. . 233-234-236.

237) Mc Burney, Louis M.D. Counseling Christian Workers. 239-243-244-245-254-255-257-258-259.

238) Webber, Robert E. Ancient Future Time. Baker Books, Grand Rapids, Michigan. Copyright 1984.20-23-35.

239) Izzo, John PhD. The Five Secrets you must discover before you die. MJF Books, New York. Copyright 2008. 10-11-13-14-15.

240) Izzo, John PhD. The Five Secrets you must know before you die. 13-14-15-16-17.

241) Izzo, John PhD. The Five Secrets you must know before you die. 39-43-4764-75.

242) Izzo, John PhD. The Five Secrets you must know before you die. 85-90-91.

243) Izzo, John PhD. The Five Secrets you must know before you die. 103.

Further Research and Case Studies

244) Grosso, Stephen. Experiencing Lourdes. Published by Servant Publications. Copyright 1996. 11-12,13-23.

245) Grosso, Stephen. Experiencing Lourdes. Pg. 24-25.

246) Newton, John. "Health Beyond Belief." www.healthbeyondbelief.com.

247) Newton, John. "Health Beyond Belief." www.healthbeyondbelief.com.

248) Weil, Andrew M.D. Spontaneous Healing. Published by Ballentine Books. Copyright 1995. Intro., 3-4-5-7.

249) Weil, Andrew M. D. Spontaneous Healing. 13-14-15-154-155-156.

250) Weil, Andrew M.D. Spontaneous Healing. 156-170.

251) Weil, Andrew M.D. Spontaneous Healing. 171-174-176.

252) Weil, Andrew M.D. Spontaneous Healing. 195-197.

253) Weil, Andrew M.D. Spontaneous Healing. 198-200.

254) Weil, Andrew M.D. Spontaneous Healing. 204-207-208.

255) Weil, Andrew M.D. Spontaneous Healing. 221-226-251.

256) "New International Version Disciple's Study Bible." Exodus 15:19-21. 92.

257) Ancestry.Com www.Ancestry.com

258) Lee, Henry. New York. R.L. Polk and Co. Inc. Fort Wayne, Ind. Copyright 1920. "History of the Stewart or Stuart Family." www.Archive.org.

259) Historic UK. www.historic.uk.

260) St Clair, Diana. Cox, Beth Stewart. Interview. Mountain Yoga, Inc. Johnson City Tenn. 12-2015.

261) Khalsa, Dharma Singh & Stauth Cameron. Brain Longevity. Warner Books. Copyright 1999. Intro.-363-364-365.

262) Khalsa, Dharma Singh & Stauth, Cameron. Brain Longevity. 370-371.

263) Khalsa, Dharma Singh & Stauth, Cameron. Brain Longevity. 372.

264) Khalsa, Dharma Singh & Stauth, Cameron. Brain Longevity. 373-374.

265) Khalsa, Dharma Singh & Stauth, Cameron. Brain Longevity. 377-378-379.

266) Khalsa, Dharma Singh & Stauth, Cameron. Brain Longevity. 384-385.

267) Khalsa, Dharma Singh & Stauth, Cameron. Brain Longevity. 53-54-70-71.

268) Khalsa, Dharma Singh & Stauth, Cameron. Brain Longevity. 318-319.

269) Partridge, Christopher. Introduction to World Religions. Fortress Press Minneapolis. Copyright 2005 Lion Hudson. 317.

270) Partridge, Christopher. Introduction to World Religions. 318-319.

271) Partridge, Christopher. Introduction to World Religions. 319-320-323.

272) Partridge, Christopher. Introduction to World Religions. 332.

273) St Clair, Diana. Interview with Rev. Jeanne Greening.

274) St Clair, Diana. Interview with Rev. Jeanne Greening.

275) St Clair, Diana. Interview with Rev. Jeanne Greening.

276) St Clair, Diana. Interview with Rev. Jeanne Greening.

277) St Clair, Diana. Interview with Rev. Jeanne Greening.

278) St Clair, Diana. Interview with Rev. Jeanne Greening.

279) St Clair, Diana. Interview with Rev. Jeanne Greening.

280) St Clair, Diana. Interview with Rev. Jeanne Greening.

281) St Clair, Diana. Interview with Rev. Jeanne Greening.

282) St Clair, Diana. Interview with Rev. Jeanne Greening.

283) St Clair, Diana. Interview with Rev. Jeanne Greening.

284) Alexander, Eben. M.D. Proof of Heaven. Simon & Schuster Paper Backs. New York, New York. Copyright 2012. 7-8.

285) Alexander, Eben. M.D. Proof of Heaven. 10-11-2148-49-73-75-76.

286) Alexander, Eben. M.D. Proof of Heaven. 85-117.

287) Roanoke.com. The Roanoke Times 3-2-2016. Article by Luanne Rife. Luanne.Rife@Roanoke.com.

288) Roanoke.com. The Roanoke Times 3-2-2016. Article by Luanne / rife. Luanne.Rife@Roanoke.com.

289) www.CarilionClinic.org/Internal Medicine. Carilion Clinic. Copyright 2015.

290) en.WikiPedia.org. Clinical Pastoral Education. 10-25-2015.

291) Relman, Arnold M.D. A second opinion, Rescuing America's Healthcare. Copyright @2007. The Century Foundation. XI-XII.

292) Relman, Arnold M.D. A second opinion, Rescuing America's Healthcare. Copyright @2007. The Century Foundation. Pg. 1-2.

293) Elwood, Don. Knocking at the Gate, The white gold adventure. The Foundation for the Betterment of Mankind. Copyrighted 11-1-1996. 1-2-3.

294) St Clair, Diana. Interview with Rev. Don Eldridge 2-15-2016.

295) St Clair, Diana. Interview with Rita Mitchell 2-29-2016.

296) "New International Disciple's Version Study Bible." 2 Corinthians 12: 1-3. 1485.

297) St Clair, Diana. Interview with Carolyn Bratton. 3-4-2016.

298) "New International Disciple's Version Study Bible." 2 Corinthians 10: 4-5. 1483.

299) Goodspeed, Edgar J. The Apocrypha an American Translation. Copyright 1983 by Edgar J. Goodspeed. Copyright 1959 Random House, Inc. V-VIII.

300) Whitson, Ray. New Age Christians. Awareness Exploring Spirituality. Issue 1/2016. 26.

301) Whitson, Ray. New Age Christians. 27.

302) Whitson, Ray. New Age Christians. 27.

303) "New International Disciple's Version Study Bible." Psalm: 104: 33-35. 717.

304) Stavish Mark. Kabbalah for Health & Wellness. Llewellyn Publications, Woodbury, MN. Copyright 2007. 1-2-3-4-5.

305) Stavish, Mark. Kabbalah for Health & Wellness. 9-10.

306) Stavish, Mark. Kabbalah for Health & Wellness. 32.33.

307) St Clair Diana. Saint Mathews Churches. P.O. Box 21838, Tulsa OK. 74121.

308) St Clair, Diana. Saint Mathews Churches. P.O .Box 21838, Tulsa OK. 74121.

309) "The New International Disciple's Version Study Bible." Romans 1: 1-6. 1416.

310) "The New International Disciple's Version Study Bible." 1416.

311) Maxwell, James A. Readers Digest. America's Fascinating Indian Heritage. Copyright 1978 Readers Digest Association, Inc. 44-89.

312) Maxwell, James A. Readers Digest. America's Fascinating Indian Heritage. 90.

313) Moerman, Daniele. Native American Ethnobotany. Timber Press Portland, London. Copyright 1998.13.

314) Moerman, Daniele. Native American Ethnobotany. 13-14.

315) Moerman, Daniele. Native American Ethnobotany. 15.

316) Moerman, Daniele. Native American Ethnobotany. 33-51-81-92-93-115-125-146-146-153-158-165-176-184-186-190-203-212-230-240-241-255-270-270-294-296-297-332-364-369-373-373-380-398-426-441-452-457-528-551-565-567-568-276-602.

317) Moerman, Daniele. Native American Ethnobotany. 11-12.

Conclusion

318) "New International Disciple's Version Study Bible." Exodus 15:26. 92-93.

319) "New International Disciple's Version Study Bible." James 5: 13-16. 1595-1596.

About the Author

Dr. Rev. Diana B. St. Clair has earned several degrees, including a doctor of philosophy in religious studies from Metropolitan University and a master of divinity and bachelor of divinity from Metropolitan Theological Seminary. She has been an ordained minister of The Alliance of Divine Love Inc. since May 6, 2012, and is a skilled spiritual counselor and spiritual healer. Diana currently lives in Roanoke, Virginia.

www.ingramcontent.com/pod-product-compliance
Lightning Source LLC
Chambersburg PA
CBHW030436290526
45786CB00001B/312